D0398662

FOWL WEATHER

Also by Bob Tarte

Enslaved by Ducks

FOWL
WEATHER

by BOB TARTE

ALGONQUIN BOOKS OF CHAPEL HILL

2007

Published by
ALGONQUIN BOOKS OF CHAPEL HILL
Post Office Box 2225
Chapel Hill, North Carolina 27515-2225

a division of
Workman Publishing
225 Varick Street
New York, New York 10014

While the people, places, and events described in the following pages are real,
location and human names have been changed for the sake of privacy.

Library of Congress Cataloging-in-Publication Data
Tarte, Bob.
Fowl weather / by Bob Tarte.
p. cm.
ISBN-13: 978-1-56512-502-5 (hardcover)
ISBN-10: 1-56512-502-9 (hardcover)
1. Pets—Michigan—Lowell—Anecdotes.   2. Animals—Michigan—
Lowell—Anecdotes.   3. Human-animal relationships—Michigan—
Lowell—Anecdotes   4. Tarte, Bob.   I. Title.
SF416.T38 2007
636.088'70977455—dc22   2006027491

10 9 8 7 6 5 4 3 2 1
First Edition

To My Mom

Contents

· ·

Cast of Characters

Listed more or less in order of appearance and by type.

. . . .

NONHUMAN

Indoor Birds

Ollie: the Mussolini of *Brotogeris* pocket parrots
Stanley Sue: endearing African grey Timneh parrot
Howard: ring-necked dove who's anything but peaceful
Dusty: knot-tying Congo African grey parrot
Louie: proud "male" cockatiel who surprised us with an egg
Bella: gentle but ear-biting African grey Timneh parrot

Indoor Mammals

Agnes: take-charge outdoor cat
Bertie: ultimately tailless Netherland Dwarf bunny
Walter: lumbering Checkered Giant rabbit
Rudy: cuddly escape-artist dwarf bunny
Moobie: insists her cat water bowl be held for her
Penny: upstairs hidey cat
Frieda: tonnage masquerading as a New Zealand rabbit

Outdoor Birds

Liza and *Hailey:* African goose sisters
Victor: Muscovy duck who prefers chomping watermelon
    to Bob
Louie/Lulu: spoiled white Pekin duck
Hamilton: menacing alpha-male Muscovy duck
Ramone: the world's shyest Muscovy duck
Richie: ladies' man white Pekin duck
Buffy: Buff Orpington hen, possibly a philosopher
Matthew: considers topknot hairdos an affront to geese
Angel and *Patty:* presumed goose brother and sister

HUMAN

Bob Tarte: long-suffering author
Linda Tarte: long-suffering author's put-upon wife
Bob's mom: Bob's mom
Joan Smith: Bob's sister who's enslaved by ferrets
Bette Ann Worley (Bett): Bob's organizational-genius sister
Eileen Kucek: grade school classmate turned grade A nuisance
Judy Teany: well-meaning neighbor to Bob's mom
Mrs. Martoni; or is it "Martini"?
Henry Murphy: master gardener who tramples plants
Marge Chedrick: tireless wildlife rehabber
Kate: owner of spoiled house duck Louie/Lulu
Dr. Hedley: zoo vet genius
Bo: co-owner of the Weigh and Pay restaurant
Roswitha: Bob and Linda's neighbor on the river
Dr. Fuller: avian vet extraordinaire

INHUMAN

Noises in the night: only Bob seems to hear them
Ed: a sock monkey
Hose demon: sinister force that snags and kinks garden hoses
Telephone: brings one dollop of unpleasantness after another
Bill Holm: two-dimensional buddy to Bob
Mom's purse: frequently hides in the bread drawer
Bobo the Roller Clown: precipitator of coincidences

FOWL WEATHER

CHAPTER 1

· ·

Alien Abduction

Linda sprang up from her chair to reheat her food in the microwave yet again. "Ollie, if you don't let me eat, I'm going to brain you." She was talking to a little green parrot slightly larger than a parakeet. "I'm not shaking the pill bottle. We don't fight with the pill bottle at dinner. We eat our peas."

His squawking distracted me just long enough for my parrot Stanley Sue to twist the spoon from my hand, spilling mashed potatoes; the spoon clattered to the linoleum and sent her flying across the room in fright. The passage of Stanley Sue attracted the ire of Howard the dove, who considered the dining room airspace exclusively his own. From his perch on top of the refrigerator, he took off in pursuit of Stanley Sue, just as she chose the worst possible spot to make her landing, clinging like a thistle to the side of large Congo African grey parrot Dusty's cage.

"Dusty, no!"

I had no chance of reaching Stanley Sue before Dusty could bite her feet through the bars, so I snatched a place mat and hurled it toward the greys. Although the missile hit the parakeet cage instead, it succeeded in launching Stanley Sue a second time. Dusty banged to the floor of his cage, Ollie sailed haplessly toward the window, and a panicky Howard shot into the living room, where black cat Agnes lay observing the melee from the back of the couch.

"Get Howard!" Linda hollered, but he wasn't in danger. Lighting on the coat rack out of reach of the bored cat, he flicked his wings and hooted his indignity at the inconvenience of it all. By the time I had extracted Howard's toes from Linda's scarf, Stanley Sue had waddled across the floor and climbed to the top of her cage, where she clucked in anticipation of the next spoonful of food as if nothing unusual had happened.

"Agnes!" Dusty called in a perfect yet somehow unflattering imitation of my voice. "Come here, Agnes." But he didn't fool the cat.

As I stepped back into the dining room cupping Howard in my hands, my big toe failed to clear the two-foot-high plywood board that theoretically bunny-proofed the rest of the house, knocking it to the floor with a familiar *thwack*. Linda bent down to maneuver it back into position, but not before tiny, donkey-colored Bertie charged the breach and disappeared into the living room. I plopped Howard into his cage, then joined Linda in the rabbit hunt.

"Oh, no, you didn't go there?" she groaned. "My back can't take this." But he had. Energized by his escape, Bertie had managed to scrabble over the TV tray that I had angled between a stereo speaker and the wall to prevent him from hiding behind the entertainment center—exactly where he had wedged himself.

Taking advantage of our absence, Agnes bounded over the board and into the dining room for a closer look at the birds. Scolding chirps advertised her presence. "I'm watching you," I informed her.

Kneeling in front of the almighty television, I flung open a cabinet door of the entertainment center, surprising Bertie just long enough for me to snatch him up with one hand and extend him toward Linda, who reached the dining room just as the board tipped over again in protest. Catching Linda's admonishing glare, Agnes fled down the stairs to the basement. I slammed the door shut behind her.

"Can we eat in peace now?" Linda asked the room as she replaced the board for what she hoped would be the last time that evening.

"I doubt it," I muttered darkly.

THE WEIRD SOUNDS outside the window didn't penetrate the haze of my bad mood at first. Stanley Sue's bell was still clattering around inside my head. Three times she had rattled her bell since dinner, demanding a peanut. Three times, when I had lifted her cage cover, she had refused to take it. Finally, after I had cajoled her with baby talk, she had deigned to pluck the nut from my fingers, only to hurl it to the floor of her cage.

Immersed in gloom, I shut off the bathroom faucet, pouting because I hadn't wanted to watch a rerun of *The Beverly Hillbillies* featuring Jethro's sister, Jethrine. I had wanted to watch *Monster House*, a decorating show where people lose control of their homes without the involvement of a parrot. Grousing to myself about the shocked faces I'd missed seeing, I flung a wet washcloth toward the bathtub, then froze and cocked my head at the window and a noise like bubbling water.

I moved closer to the wall, careful to keep my skinny shadow from falling on the shade and frightening the visitor with the silhouette of a giant stick insect. As the warbling intensified, I decided that two animals were making the sounds. They were either conspiring against me in hushed tones right outside the house or, having just watched *Monster House*, whooping it up beyond the backyard fence down in the hollow.

I've heard this before, I thought. *But not in our yard.* I associated the sounds with the tropics, which didn't make a lot of sense, considering that I rarely got much nearer to the equator than northern Indiana.

"Linda," I whispered, poking my head around the door frame. "Come listen to this. Tell me what it is."

Lying flat on the living room floor in her usual spot, Linda closed an old issue of *Good Old Days* magazine, kicked off her afghan, and clambered to her feet. The unreliable disk between the fourth and fifth vertebrae in her lower back had gone out again as a result of the rabbit chase. I was reluctant to disturb her, but this struck me as a miraculous event.

I popped back into the bathroom, squeezed my eyes closed, and concentrated. I'd heard the vocalizations before on an episode of *The Crocodile Hunter* perhaps — or on the CD of rain-forest sounds I listened to during my pathetic attempts at meditation. But by the time Linda had clomped to my side at the window, the animals had clammed up. This was typical. I couldn't even count the number of times an incessant singer like a red-eyed vireo had shut its beak the instant she had stepped outdoors to hear it with me.

"What is it?"

I raised a finger to my lips. "Monkeys, it sounds like."

She flashed me an exasperated look.

"Or baboons," I told her. "I haven't quite gotten it yet. Listen. They'll do it again."

We stood quietly as air hissed through the furnace duct at the base of the sink. The bathtub drain gurgled right on cue.

"That?" she asked. I shook my head vehemently, frowning and wiggling my hand toward the window. "Something outdoors? An animal?" she quizzed me, as if we were playing charades. "It's probably just a couple of raccoons."

"Raccoons?" I followed her into the living room. "In February? They're hibernating."

"So are all the Michigan monkeys."

I threw a heavy jacket over my powder-blue pajama shirt, then stuffed my bare feet and green plaid pajama pants cuffs into a pair of boots. Rummaging through the back of the pet supplies closet, I fished out a flashlight that, quite unexpectedly, lit when my thumb clicked the switch. "I'd better take a peek at the ducks," I announced. "If those are raccoons, I want to make sure everybody's safe." As I pulled a stocking cap over my ears, I told her, "I know what raccoons sound like, and those things aren't raccoons."

I didn't worry excessively about our backyard birds. Barring a grizzly bear attack, they were secure in their pens—and I hadn't tangled with a grizzly since the Ice Age of 1967. Thinking back, I decided it had probably been a snarling Sister Rachel who had chased me underneath a desk in my Catholic Central High School English class. In those days, I'd paid scant attention to animals. But after I'd married Linda, ten years ago, we'd slowly started accumulating critters, and I had grown fond of even the most illtempered ones.

Much of the accumulating was inadvertent. Our first duck cropped up when my brother-in-law Jack rescued her from the parking lot of an auto-parts warehouse whose employees were peppering her with stones. We had bought another duck to keep her company and within a scant few years had also taken in orphaned geese, turkeys, and hens. Similar chaos had unfolded inside the house. We had naively begun with a belligerent pet bunny, added a canary, a dove, and a tyrannical parrot, and soon found ourselves providing a home for the winged and unwanted— including the abandoned baby songbirds that Linda raised and released each summer.

At first, the joys and jolts of caring for thirty-odd oddball animals had worn me down to a nubbin. Gradually, however, the relentless grind of countless cleanup chores, endless home veterinary tasks, and limitless feedings had become as easy as falling off a log and sustaining contusions from head to toe. My unusual life had ceased to strike me as extraordinary any longer. I longed for the unexpected, and that was always a mistake.

I DIDN'T SERIOUSLY expect to discover a troupe of primates cavorting on the back deck. That just didn't make sense. But I did hold out hope that a supernatural animal might be paying us an interdimensional visit. I'd been reading John A. Keel's *Strange Creatures from Time and Space* and Loren Coleman's *Mysterious America,* about anomalous critters that show up where they don't belong. Phantom kangaroos bounded across Chicago suburbs, panthers roamed Michigan's Oakland County, and birds the size of ponies buzzed Ohio Valley farms. The breathless possibility that the miraculous could leak into even a life as dull as mine was all there in matter-of-fact black and white. So if a saddle-soap salesman in Saskatoon could surprise a Sasquatch, I surmised, why couldn't I astonish an ape in our apple tree?

I walked out the front door of a house on the edge of slumber and entered a world in turmoil. One moment I'd been sinking into the nightly lull after tucking in a dozen indoor animals; the next moment I was immersed in swirling snow. The storm had moved in without so much as a polite rap on the door to inform us it was coming. Five hours ago, when I had changed the water in the duck wading pools, I hadn't seen so much as a feather in the air. But six inches of snow had piled up in the dark, like compounded interest on a credit card.

Leaving the glow of the house behind, I trudged toward the silhouette of our barn. Raising the flashlight beam from the ground encased me in a blinding capsule of confetti. Next to a fenced-in area where Linda grew sunflowers in the summer, I hurried a little. That part of the yard always felt creepy after dark, as if space aliens regularly picked me up, wiped my memory clean, then plopped me down among the seed hulls. I coughed to announce my presence to any entities within earshot.

The barn door was securely shut. Nothing could have gotten inside, but I gave the interior a check with my flashlight, throwing shadows of roosting hens around the walls and annoying our Muscovy duck Victor, who was instantly at my side panting and hissing with menace. "You're okay, hon," I told him. I swept past the amber eye of a chicken, slammed the door behind me, and headed for the pen behind the house. As far as I could tell, the snowfall was fluffy and unbroken by the tracks of a giant hairy hominid. The ducks muttered as I checked the latches of their pens. Our goose Liza croaked an inquisitive honk, urging her sister Hailey to second the question, but I moved on before they decided to erupt.

As I followed my footprints back to the front yard, I realized, to my amazement, that I had actually enjoyed my walk—somewhat, more or less, at least. I hated winter and any other season that made me lace myself up in thigh-high boots. But the disorienting aspects of the storm had won me over. The snow had camouflaged the landmarks of our property by adding rounded, flowing corners to the shrubs, mailbox, and porch steps. The sidewalk, gravel shoulder, and asphalt road had completely vanished. Ten feet from my own front door, I was in terra incognita. I stared at the streaming snow-flakes, doing my best to hallucinate that they were static and I was shooting upward, but the house and Linda's car shot upward with me, and that ruined the illusion. I gave up and retreated indoors.

"Did you see it?" Linda asked as I stomped my boots on the doormat that read THE TARTES. Stripping off my coat in the living room, I felt chilly for the first time. It took me a moment to recall what she was asking me about.

"No," I said. "Nothing. Not even a raccoon."

BACK HOME FROM work the next day, I walked into the kitchen to find Stanley Sue settled comfortably on the countertop. From the fresh set of chew marks decorating our wooden bread box, I could see what she'd been doing. For months she had made the tops of Bertie's and Walter's rabbit cages her base of operation for launching attacks on the already decimated windowsill and floor molding. And if the bunnies were foolish enough to rouse from their daylight-hours naps, she might snap ineffectually at them through the wire mesh while strutting above their heads.

For reasons known only to Stanley Sue, one afternoon she'd abandoned her obsession with rabbits and woodwork, marched across the linoleum, and applied herself to the kitchen instead. She attached herself by the beak, opening and slamming shut any cupboard doors within reach, then beveling the corners to suit her artistic sensibilities. Climbing a ladder of drawer pulls, she gnawed her way up to the countertop, adorning the Formica edge with a signature chip before sculpting the front of the silver-ware drawer. We tolerated all this destruction because it unfolded slowly over time. But Stanley finally went too far when she tested her athletic abilities by picking up Linda's cow-shaped ceramic spoon rest and giving it a discus toss.

We'd already limited her out-of-cage hours to circumvent problems with the other birds. We rarely let Howard loose at the same time as Stanley Sue, because the defenseless dove would foolishly pick a fight with our winged whittler. We couldn't trust Elliot the canary and our parakeets to keep clear of her as they buzzed between the rooms like colorful bumblebees. And the incessantly squawking Ollie proved too tempting a target for any of us. More than once, I had lunged at him myself. Remarkably, our two African grey parrots barely acknowledged each other's existence, though Stanley Sue had enjoyed ambushing her previous owner's macaw. That would have been a bad mistake with Dusty, who came out twice a day to play with Linda and menace me.

Once we'd made the decision to keep Stanley Sue out of the kitchen, barring her way seemed ridiculously easy at first. She was inexplicably afraid of intimacy with many common household objects, including cardboard wrapping-paper tubes. We placed one of these across the floor in the space between the refrigerator and the dishwasher where the dining room became the kitchen. It made a most effective gate. Whenever Linda inadvertently squashed a tube underfoot on her way to the microwave with a heat pack for her back, she would simply replace the tube with another from the top of the refrigerator. A cluster huddled there, awaiting duty for thumping to drive the bunnies back into their cages when their morning or evening liberation came to an end.

Although Stanley Sue could fly, it apparently never dawned on her that she could effortlessly sail above the cylindrical sentinel. The tube's terrible power extended from floor to ceiling in an impenetrable curtain. Her timidity lasted just over a week. One day my e-mailing session upstairs was interrupted by the clunk of a drinking glass downstairs. I found Stanley Sue at the sink in an animated mood. The cardboard tube lay at a confused angle across the floor, the upended glass had darkened the rug with spots of water, and all was right with Stanley Sue's world again. She had finally mustered the courage to shove the tube aside.

A barricade of three tubes seemed promising. But its deterrent effect petered out after only an hour. Shooing Stanley Sue back to Bertie's cage top, I placed our stuffed sock monkey Ed on the kitchen counter. At first sight of his face, her pupils dilated in distress and her feathers flattened against her body. She elongated her neck and stared at Ed with deep suspicion from across the room. The doll, which my Grandmother Ordowski had made for me decades ago, was now reborn as a scarecrow. To reinforce Ed's menacing potential, I would occasionally lift him a few inches above the countertop and flop him back in forth in a madcap monkey dance. From Stanley Sue's cocked head and taut posture, it appeared that she was genuinely relieved to have resumed her post at Bertie's cage.

She had even invented a new project for herself. By poking her beak between the cage bars at just the right spot, she could grab the bunny's food dish and dump it upside down. It was a black afternoon when I headed to the kitchen for coffee and encountered Stanley Sue not merely sitting on the counter but further elevated on top of a gallon jug of spring water, as if to underscore her newfound primacy over the stuffed primate. Ed slumped ineffectually against the bread box.

"You're not doing your job," I informed him.

"I chased her off there fifteen minutes ago," Linda told me as she rolled in the vacuum cleaner to tidy up the dining room for the ninetieth time that day. "She just goes right back up there again. We'll either have to keep her in her cage or get something with flashing lights to keep her off my counter."

"What do you mean, 'something with flashing lights'?"

A HORRIFIC HOWL close to the house jolted me awake—a long, descending banshee call resembling a siren. Clear, unquavering, and downright scary, the sound had the same round-toned *whoop* quality that I had heard on the night of the furious snow. It wasn't the wail of a dog or a coyote. It was primate-like rather than canine. An ascending howl followed, briefer but just as window rattling. I reached out a reassuring arm to Linda that was actually intended to reassure me. But her place in the bed was empty. I remembered that before we had turned in, she had told me that her back was bothering her and she might move upstairs so as not to bother me. In her absence I hugged my pillow.

Although I had wanted another chance to hear the mystery animal, this was too much of a good thing and far too close besides. It might, after all, be how Bigfoot announced his presence before peeling the wall off a house. In full light of day or by the flickering light of *The Beverly Hillbillies*, the howl would have intrigued me rather than compacting me under the covers. But this wasn't a mere counterpoint to a host of familiar noises. It was the classic cry of a monster in the dark that creature-feature movies had warned me about since childhood. Only a bit player slated for first-reel extinction would get up and investigate.

I lay quietly as the clock ticked off my fears, hoping to hear telltale thumps from above, indicating that Linda had gotten out of bed and was on her way downstairs. She would be worried about the safety of the ducks rather than a mythical being. Checking on the animals was exactly what I needed to do, even if it involved nothing more physically compromising than glancing out at the backyard pen. If I was fortunate, I might merely witness an unearthly apparition that would doom me to spend the rest of my days on talk shows, trying to convince jaded studio audiences that hairy humanoids were real. I might not get off that easily,

though. I might witness a scene so unimaginable—such as a peanut-shaped spaceship piloted by an African grey parrot—as to
crack my poor brain open like an egg.

Marshaling my courage, I swung my legs over the side of the
bed and sat for a while. Then I sat for a while longer. Having pretty
much mastered sitting, I forced myself to my feet. Turning nervousness into momentum, I marched through the dark into the
living room, then into a dining room flooded with moonlight.
Our birds and rabbits snoozed peacefully in their cages without
a care. Through the window, the ducks and geese at the bottom
of the hill appeared unfazed as well. The pen doors were safely
closed. The wire walls and roof remained intact, and the wooden
uprights hadn't been splintered like so many matchsticks by a
raging behemoth.

The outdoors looked ominous in the glow of the nearly full
moon. The woods were a confusion of inky shapes reaching up
and thrown back down to the ground in sinister shadows capable
of concealing a particularly skinny intruder—such as my evil
twin. Each ditch and depression in the softly glowing snow hosted
dark areas that a mouse-size being could have made into a hiding place. The spectral quality of the scene and my giddy state of
mind created an inverted sense of seeing that pushed the familiar
further away rather than bringing it closer, as if I were staring at
an X-ray of our property. I found myself actually hoping for a bit
of a scare. Even so, I wasn't able to psych myself into projecting a
mystery animal onto the landscape. A deer in the right spot might
have helped. I would even have welcomed a skunk.

Aware of my presence, Stanley Sue flapped her wings inside her
covered cage. In another moment she would ring her bell, annoyed
that my worried lurking was disrupting her sleep; then Howard
would awake and start to coo, Dusty would whistle and imitate

the ringing of the phone, and the curtain would crash down on my brush with nonordinary reality. Taking one last dispirited look, I shuffled back toward the bedroom, only to collide with a colossal white shape in the hall. It turned out to be Moobie, the overweight cat that was straining our feed bills and floorboards until we could find her a home.

"WHAT SOUNDS?" LINDA asked the next morning as we sat on the edge of the bed drinking cups of acid-free coffee. "Did that raccoon come by again?"

In the full light of day it was difficult to convey the mystery and fear I had felt while cringing under the covers in the wee hours. My description of the unsettling howl piqued her interest only slightly.

"Are you sure it wasn't an owl?"

I knew the voices of the common Michigan owls—barred, great horned, and screech—and they didn't in the least resemble this piercing clarinet wail from hell. "I think it was a howler monkey," I told her. "Or maybe some sort of gibbon."

"Funny you're the only one who seems to hear these things."

"That's because you don't fascinate the space people the way I do."

"It was probably an owl. Owls make all sorts of sounds."

I protested this ridiculous suggestion with dignified silence.

After breakfast I hopped onto the Internet and began downloading sound files of owls, along with those of other birds that might have ventured out into the Michigan night no matter the time of year, from goatsucker to nightjar to long-eared owl. I listened to hoots, groans, croaks, whinnies, barks, gasps, and whistles, along with a *whip-poor-will*, a *chee-chee-chee*, and even a *pee-ant*. But nothing with wings filled the bill.

If a Bigfoot-size creature had paid us a visit, it would have plowed a hard-to-miss path through the snow. A multitentacled extraterrestrial might have left sucker prints behind for a sucker like me to find. I felt almost intrepid as I suited up for a tracking expedition, donning a pair of barn boots fitted with ice cleats in case the terrain got rough, and pulling rubber work gloves over cotton gloves to keep my hands dry should I need to rummage in the wet for clues. As a finishing touch, I slung my binoculars over my shoulder, in case, I suppose, I wanted to spy on suspicious squirrels on the bank of the Grand River.

I never made it as far as the river. The soft ground cover of a few days earlier was truly a thing of the past. Thawing and re-freezing had created a crunchy surface that collapsed and threw me off balance with each lurching step. The cleats were useless under these conditions, though they saved me from falling once I'd crawled over the backyard fence and rapidly descended the hill on a sheet of ice courtesy of nine wild turkeys and my wife. The turkeys' daily visits for scratch feed scattered by Linda had packed down the snow and polished it into a toboggan run.

Turkey prints were only the beginning. As I trudged through the hollow I discovered a complex freeway system of animal routes. I crisscrossed deer, squirrel, rabbit, house-cat, and possum paths along with prints from critters I couldn't identify. Several tracks looked promisingly weird until I got on top of them and found familiar hoofprints at the bottom. Faced with so many prints to investigate and no obvious primate or cephalopod shapes, I called it a day after less than twenty minutes. The amount of traffic was mind-numbing. The animals were clearly the property owners. Linda and I were just squatters huddled inside a box.

Back indoors, I kept replaying the howl through my head until the idea that I had heard it before paid off. I rooted through my CDs and found a collection of Malagasy music called *A World Out of Time, Volume 2.* Linda was cleaning birdcages in the dining room when I triumphantly slid the disc into the boom box and hit the play button. Overlapping primate whoops burst forth over a drumbeat.

"What is that?" she asked as she filled Howard's seed dish.

"Lemurs," I announced with a note of triumph in my voice. "Indri lemurs. Native to Madagascar and found nowhere else on the planet."

"That's a sound Dusty would love to copy. We'll have to start playing it for him."

"That's more or less what I heard in the yard both times," I said. "Not *exactly* what I heard, but closer than anything else I've found."

"You could make that sound, couldn't you, Dusty?" Her parrot was not only adept at dead-on mimicry of our voices but also impersonated electronic appliances, hand claps, creaking doors, and ice cubes falling into a drinking glass. "Maybe you just heard Dusty," she said.

"Dusty? How could it have been Dusty? He hasn't even heard the lemur calls until this very minute. I haven't played this CD in years."

"But he could have made a sound like that. It could have been Dusty."

I retreated upstairs.

Shifting my short attention span to our gnawed kitchen woodwork, I recalled reading about high-end robotic toys that moved and emitted sounds in response to motion or noise. They seemed tailor-made for discouraging Stanley Sue from venturing into the room. I found the budget version at a store just down the road. The blue mechanical bird with transparent red crest, wings, and tail feathers resembled a cross between a baby blue jay and a tuna can. The two pairs of eyes hinted at the dual nature of what proved to be a troublesome toy. Red plastic domes the size of quarters bulged from either side of the head where a bird's eyes ought to be. But a black rectangle up front, just above the yellow beak, contained two more eyes. These were red LEDs that blinked and changed shape from hearts to X's, depending upon the robot's mood.

Waving a small magnetic corncob near the beak was equivalent to feeding the bird, and the automaton expressed its gratitude by chirping "Merrily We Roll Along" or another annoying ditty, accompanied by head swivels, wing flaps, beak snaps, and enthusiastic bowing. A sharp noise near the toy caused a happy twitter, as did waving a hand across the light-sensitive eyes, which I hoped could detect a close encounter with Stanley Sue.

More than anything else, though, the mechanical bird craved pressure on its crest. Pressing the plastic plume whenever I entered the kitchen kept the toy nattering joyously in response to the piercing chirps, squawks, and whistles from our parrots and parakeets. Failing to press the plume or forgetting to proffer the magnetic corn plunged the bipolar robot into a silent depression so unshakable that no crescendo of noise in the room could lift its spirit.

This insistence on attention proved to be the toy's downfall. For nearly two weeks, Stanley Sue stayed in the dining room, well away from the mechanical bird with its repertoire of random-interval song-and-dance routines. My heart soared with hope that her behavior had finally changed. But the robot bird's behavior had shifted, too. The sadists who had programmed its microchip had decided that every few days it would be fun to have the toy cycle through a sullen phase that required intensive plume pressing and magnetic feeding. Otherwise the mechanical bird merely issued a brief grumble in response to stimuli. Frankly, I wasn't having it. It was one thing to coddle a flesh-and-blood pet; it was quite another to include a plastic bird in my daily schedule of chores and visits. For a while, I solved the sulking problem by turning the toy upside down, then removing and replacing its batteries. This reset it to a state of chirpy ecstasy. But I grew sick of the battery changing, and Stanley Sue soon decided that an intermittently active bird was no threat whatsoever. She retook her prized countertop and perched on top of the water jug.

"If you want to stay up there, you can't be near the bread box," I informed her.

She took exception to the restriction. When I moved the water jug toward the center of the countertop, out of reach of things wooden, she startled me by springing off it and flying back to her cage. She didn't fly short distances gracefully. Her wingbeats were as loud as those of the robotic bird, and she bobbled slightly off balance when she landed.

I looked at her. You could almost hear the snap of a spark as our gazes locked. I drifted toward her, pulled across the room by the irresistible force that bound the two of us together. *Oh, that alien,* I thought. *That alien has got me again.* My two eyes focused on her one eye. I came closer. I smiled at her, and the black pupil changed size ever so minutely, pulsing in and out as it floated in a thick white yolk lit with a hint of gold.

Her eye was welcoming, but that's because I knew she welcomed me. In point of fact, I'd noted the same glint in the eye of a parrot that wanted nothing better than to chomp my hand. You couldn't see the affection in her face. Her upper beak curved backward in a frown from the wickedly pointed tip, then, at the last moment,

flowed upward in a smile. That mouth could mean anything. She
was aggressive toward our other birds, having once sent Howard
to the vet in terrible shape. Another time, she caught our canary
in midair and threw him to the floor like a ceramic spoon rest.
But she was tolerant toward my wife and the essence of gentleness
with me. Leaning over the cage top, she lowered her head beneath
her feet and raised it again, never taking her eye off me, in what I
had learned was her silent approximation of a chuckle.

"Stanley," I told her. "Stanley Sue."

She opened and closed her beak, making a quiet clucking that
was probably her attempt to mock my speech. Unlike Dusty, she
didn't talk, but she spoke volumes nonetheless. I leaned down,
touching my nose to her beak. I laughed, and she clucked. Dem-
onstrating her extreme satisfaction, she began to preen the feathers
on her chest, ignoring me as I finally walked away. Before leaving
the kitchen, I picked up the mechanical bird and placed it on top
of the refrigerator, where it could keep the cardboard wrapping-
paper tubes company.

THAT NIGHT, I ASSUMED my post at the bathroom window,
hoping to hear the primates whooping it up again. It wasn't a pleasant vigil. Linda had replaced the heating grate next to the sink,
because it had started to rust. But she'd had trouble fitting the new
grate in place until a stroke of inspiration had convinced her to rip
out the metal vanes that limited the heat flow. A shower became
a visit to the sauna. While the water faucets glowed red-hot, and
toothbrushes melted into sticky puddles, a cup of steaming tea
anywhere else in the house froze solid in a matter of seconds.

I slept lightly most of the week, keeping one ear cocked for
teeth-jarring cries. One night, a disturbance out in the duck pen
woke Dusty, and he responded with a descending whistle, which

I tried to pin on a geographically challenged lemur. But the harmonic complexity was missing. Dusty hadn't made my mysterious nocturnal noises, if there had been any noises after all. I started to convince myself that I had dreamed the entire thing.

I sat up in bed an hour or so later to find a grey-skinned extraterrestrial skulking near the bed and bent on the usual kidnapping. I played along with the abduction, but once we reached the front door, I grabbed the little fellow by the scruff of the neck, ushered him off the porch into the hard-packed snow, and turned to close the door. His baseball-size eyes bore a wounded look.

"Nothing personal," I said as I watched him pad away. "You're welcome back when you can tell me what all of this means."

CHAPTER 2

....

Vanished

I didn't waste my days pondering whether paranormal creatures inhabited our woods; I was too busy battling the hose demon. Linda had snapped the handle off the push broom while using the brush end to bludgeon the ice in the girl ducks' wading pool. That gave me the brainstorm—which should have come six years earlier—of emptying the pools in the pens before we went to bed, so that they wouldn't freeze overnight. But our ice was like a disgruntled rat. Rousted out of one hole, it took up quarters somewhere else. As I yanked the handle of the duck-pen door, the door deflected several inches at the top but refused to budge at the bottom. Freeing it meant spraying the ground with hot water, then sloshing away the water with our mended broom so that it didn't freeze again within minutes.

Leaving snow prints across the basement floor, I grabbed the loose end of the hose that was attached to the laundry sink and began walking it down toward the clamoring ducks and geese. It stretched taut prematurely, a victim of the hose demon. I snapped the hose like a whip. An inverted U sped across the yard, then another and another, as I continued thrashing my arm without effect. Groaning, I threw down the hose and cut a fresh path through the snow back to the basement.

The coupling between the two fifty-foot-long hoses had somehow managed to snag on a chip in the concrete floor no larger than a Susan B. Anthony dollar and no deeper than a mosquito's wing. Dislodging the connectors, I trudged back downhill, yanked the hose toward the agitated waterfowl, and was caught short a mere yard from my goal. This time, the narrow lip of the coupling hugged the edge of the open basement door, an obstacle so circumspect and unobtrusive I never could have purposely snared it there if I'd tried a hundred times. Flailing the hose vertically and horizontally, then whirling it around and around in jump-rope fashion failed to convince the dozen or so molecules of the coupling that held hands with a few atoms of the door edge to abide by normal physical laws. Instead I was forced to troop uphill again into an arctic blast of air and liberate the hose by hand.

Linda met me just inside the basement door. "Who are you talking to?"

"What do you mean?" I asked. But I knew what she meant. I had been shouting, "Let go! Let go! Let go!"

"You look out of breath."

"It's that stupid hose. It keeps getting stuck."

"It catches on anything," she told me. "Does it ever stick on the door for you?"

I grimaced and headed back toward the duck pen. Linda had carefully shopped for an all-weather ultraflexible hose that wouldn't twist, tangle, or crease no matter how we abused it. Technology proved no match for the sorcery of the hose demon, which transformed our pricey "Kink-Not" model into the "Kink-Now." After turning on the laundry tub spigot full blast, I slumped back

outside to meet the tiniest trickle of hot water. A fold had mysteri-
ously formed in the sophisticated petrochemical hose exterior and
its woven miracle-fiber interior near the basement entrance, and
no amount of untwisting, untangling, or uncreasing via thrashing, flailing, or whirling would release the water flow. Once more
I scaled the hill and dragged myself toward the house as our goose
Hailey honked curses in my direction.

After I had melted the ice in front of both duck-pen doors, filled
the pools, replenished the food, and herded the ducks and geese
to their respective homes, I decided it was time to do something
about the doors. They had begun to stick to the ground at the
slightest provocation. The solution was trimming an inch off their
bottoms for the second time in a couple of years. Either the land
was rising, and we would soon have a mountain in our backyard,
or the doors were sinking and would be swallowed by the earth's
crust in a matter of months.

I was lying on my stomach, making the last awkward cut with a
reciprocating saw, when Linda appeared on the back deck, calling
me with a worried voice. "Joan's on the phone," she told me. "It
must be something serious. She said, 'I need to talk to my brother
right now.' She never calls you that."

I rushed past her into the house.

My mom sat on the gold chair near the picture window,
leaning forward. Her upper lip was white. I had never seen anyone with a white upper lip before. "Don't stand up, Bette," warned
Maureen, an administrative nurse who lived down the block from
my parents. "You look like you might faint."

"What am I going to do?" my mother asked.

Maureen explained to me and my sister Joan that my father had
probably died from a heart attack. "With older people, the aorta

wall can be very thin. When your dad fell, the aorta probably burst." He and my mom had been shoveling snow off the second-story porch of their house, and he had slipped on the landing on his way back inside. I wanted to ask why they would be out doing something like that at their ages—my dad, Bob, was eighty-four and my mom, Bette, was eighty-one—but it was a pointless kind of question, and I knew the answer anyway. Both of them had always enjoyed good health, except for my mother's occasional memory glitches, and they were proud of their independence. Just a few years earlier, my parents had ridden elephants across a river in Thailand to a place my father had called "the village of the long-necked women" with the authority of having heard the tour guide so describe it.

My father had made it as far as the bed before dying. His untidy posture, with legs hanging over the side, told me he was no longer of this world. A glance at the closet revealed two straight rows of polished shoes lurking in the gloom and belts hanging from an organizer on the door. Below the belts was a collection of ties. In my early years, my dad had barely set foot outside without wearing a tie, even while edging the lawn or washing the car. But he was genial rather than rigid, keeping things in their places and marking the calendar weeks ahead with tasks like "Clean Electric Razor" as a way of reinforcing his faith in the orderliness of the world. A friend of mine had once compared him to Beaver Cleaver's dad. That only worked if you subtracted the sanctimoniousness that made Ward a bit of a pill and replaced it with my father's good nature. I leaned down and hugged him. Air trapped in his lungs wheezed as I pressed against him, startling me for the briefest flash into supposing he might yawn, rub his eyes, and ultimately chuckle at my mom's mistaken conclusion about his condition.

For years I had worried about this day, waking up at night and

obsessing about losing one of my parents, while mice stirred between the walls and tree limbs creaked in the wind. Now that
the dreaded event had arrived and my father had departed, I had
turned into a monstrous soap bubble, hardly even there—an
elongated, thin-skinned, air-filled film. Barely holding my shape, I
floated toward the hairline cracks in the bedroom ceiling, dodged
a wooden alligator that my grandpa had made me as a child, and
steered toward the window on the landing to watch icicles melting. Photographs from the South Dakota Badlands and Monument
Valley lined the walls on both sides of the stairs, and I drifted
down a treacherous mountain pass.

I surfaced in the middle of a conversation between Maureen and
my sister that made me realize that my father's fall had plunged
us into a thicket of procedure. "The funeral home won't take him
until you make a police report, so you have to call the police first,"
she told us. "Then call the funeral home. They'll send an ambulance for him and work with the coroner's office on the death
certificate."

"Death certificate," said Joan.

"You'll need several copies," said the nurse. "You send one to his
insurance carrier, if he had life insurance. The bank will need a
copy, and so will your family lawyer. For the will."

"Dying is a complicated business," I remarked to nobody in
particular, just to experience the reassurance of my voice vibrating
in my head cavities. Death was beginning to seem distressingly
bureaucratic as Maureen reeled off suggestions for composing the
obituary, contacting the newspaper, and mailing notices to far-
flung friends. Rather than confronting the immensity of death, we
had run smack into a level of detail somewhere between applying
for a driver's license and buying a home. My father would have
approved. He would have been in his element with all the plan-

ning, while I was completely out of my depth. I was happy for the presence of my sister, who had already headed for the phone while I fought feeling overwhelmed by both minutiae and immensity. Only the middle ground of not-much-happening suited me. In my inability to act, I was approaching my mother's frozen state. But she wasn't merely in shock. She was diminished. My father had done everything for her, and with his life force gone, half of her own had vanished.

"The police are on their way," said Joan from a rocking chair in the dining room. Over her head hung a pair of wall-mounted, die-cast ashtrays from the Keeler Brass Company, where my dad had once worked as an engineer. One was shaped like a New England fisherman's head; the other commemorated the Bicentennial. "Do you want me to call the funeral home?"

"If you want to," said my mom. The rocking chair creaked as Joan leaned forward to flip through a notebook of phone numbers. So many of my parents' friends had died over the last few years that my dad had paper-clipped a business card from VanderLaan & Sons Funeral Home to one of the notebook pages to streamline checking visitation hours.

As I took my mother's hand, her quiet panic flowed down my arm and into my stomach, sucking the blood from my legs. I sat beside her, on the hassock. Watching Joan work the telephone calmed me down, as did knowing that my organizational-genius sister Bette Ann would soon be driving in from Fort Wayne. I suddenly felt a little less at sea as I decided that the protocols surrounding death were more of a salvation than a burden. Though losing my father was a unique and enormous event to me, millions of people had traveled this same path before. The funeral-home visitation, church service, reception, grave-site ritual, and all the other obligations were like motel stays in the course of a marathon road trip. Their sense of ordinariness helped fill the terrifying vacuum.

"I can't believe how suddenly he went," my mom told me.

"At least he didn't go through a long illness," I replied after a moment. It was all I could manage to say. "He would have hated to have had a stroke."

"He's in heaven with the Lord," said Linda, with more uplifting sentiment than I could have mustered. Then she switched gears to the practical. "Mom, would you like a cup of tea?"

She nodded.

I looked out the window to see Maureen standing on a porch across the street. As she spoke to someone on the other side of the door, someone half hidden in gloom, like my father's shoes, she turned her body toward my parents' house and gestured.

The simplicity of a cup of tea appealed to me. "I'll have one, too," I said.

I NEEDED TO GET my mind off my dad. That evening I tried working on my music-review column for *The Beat* magazine. A day earlier, I had started an introduction, grousing about the terrible winter weather and the forty-inch-high snowpack in our back-yard. These complaints suddenly seemed like small beans, but I couldn't come up with anything better. My brain refused to budge from my parents' living room and my mother's white upper lip. I reached for the *National Audubon Society Field Guide to North American Weather,* thinking I might find a snowfall fact to quote, but the book had vanished. Just that morning while listening to the BBC before breakfast, I had plopped it onto the cheap plastic parson's table next to my shortwave radio. Now it was just plain gone.

I became obsessed with finding it. Perhaps because I was powerless to do anything about the loss of my father, I wanted the small victory of holding the book in my hands again. The two stacks of CDs on the tabletop couldn't have concealed the thick, compact field guide even if they had conspired to do so, but I shuffled through them anyway. On the floor beside my chair sat a small pile of books. I examined each book carefully, assuring myself that the field guide hadn't disguised itself as a history of Congolese music or a Swedish murder mystery. I widened my search to a heap of papers on my desk, a mound of mail on the file cabinet, and other detritus scattered about the room. I checked the bookshelves, too—then the air conditioner, windowsills, and the stairs. Just to be on the safe side, I checked the parson's table again. The field guide had to be there, but it wasn't.

In the unlikely event that I had spirited the book downstairs, I decided to ask Linda if she had seen it. I didn't reach this decision lightly. She was always asking me where her things had gone, and I would answer, "I don't have any dealings with your Chap Stick" or "Your snow pants are entirely your own affair." Her eyeglasses got misplaced the most often. She literally had a basketful of them. Her prescription glasses were for walking-around seeing and driving. Then she had drugstore magnifying eyeglasses for watching television and stronger pairs of magnifiers for reading.

"Why can't you just use your prescription glasses?" I once asked her. "They're blended bifocals, aren't they?"

"The angle is wrong when I'm lying on the floor," she replied. "The blended part of the bifocal is too low."

Since her drugstore glasses were made of easily scratched plastic, she usually kept more than one pair of each magnification in the basket, where they could all rub up against one another and compound the scratching problem—if they made it into the basket at all. One fateful evening, I received the scare of my life upon walking into the living room to find Linda on her faux-sheepskin rug reading Thomas Hardy while wearing two pairs of eyeglasses at the same time, one pair on top of the other. "I can't find the 3.5-power glasses, so I'm using two pairs of 1.75s," she explained.

"Make sure and do that the next time people are over," I told her. "Or in a restaurant. I'd love to see the reaction in a restaurant."

Linda hadn't seen the missing field guide. We had field guides for trees, mushrooms, birds, birds' nests, fossils, insects, butterflies, the night sky, and Michigan wildflowers. What we needed was a field guide for locating the *National Audubon Society Field Guide to North American Weather.*

I RETURNED FROM the funeral home in a bad mood. That was understandable. A good mood just wasn't part of the funeral-home experience. But the visitation hadn't turned out to be the wrenching experience I had anticipated, because I hadn't had much of an opportunity to wrench. Despite our official status as the bereaved family, we'd been expected to play the part of good hosts. That meant my mom, my two sisters, and I ended up consoling visitors instead of the other way around, and I had no idea who most of the visitors were.

"Such a shock," said a man leaning against the most unusual walker I had ever seen. Snatching my hand, he clasped it briefly against one of the tubular metal wings that projected from either side; then he rolled toward my mother on large wheels. Behind him, his wife towed her portable oxygen canister. "We're so sorry," she told me with a quivering mouth. I touched her lightly on the shoulder and said it was okay.

Strangers continued filing in as "South Rampart Street Parade" tootled from hidden ceiling speakers in tribute to my father's love of big band music. Supported by my unflappable sister Bette Ann—Bett excelled in social situations—and Joan, who concealed whatever awkwardness she might have felt, I fulfilled my duties blandly enough to avoid monopolizing any guest. For the most part, I kept my composure by keeping my distance from the softly lit figure of my father in the casket and acting as gatekeeper to the room. Just when I thought I would emerge unscathed from my close encounters with humanity, a woman I hadn't seen in decades hailed me. Thin as a straw and with straw-colored hair to match, she was an old classmate of mine from Blessed Sacrament Elementary School, Eileen Kucek.

After telling me how sorry she was to hear about my dad, she said, "Have you heard anything from Marcie Jaglowski?"

"Uh, no," I told her. I knew the name but couldn't connect it to a face. "Should I?"

"From Miss Edkins's eighth-grade class," she reminded me. "Her nephew Albert died in a machine-shop accident last month. The company said it was negligence. His wife swears he wasn't drinking. She said Albert never drank on a work night."

"I guess not."

"They lived in New Mexico. Albert and his family moved out there because of his tree-pollen allergy, but he never got used to living in the desert."

"I guess it's the place to go for allergies."

"Well, I'm glad your dad wasn't sick for a long time," she said, echoing my pointless remark to my mom from a few days earlier. "Helen Roslaniec's father died from long-term stomach problems. I think Helen was in your homeroom at Catholic Central. I saw Mark Morowski at the funeral—Helen's cousin. His father died from tummy troubles, too."

"You've really kept up on things."

"Karen Shangraw told me about Helen. Actually, she's Karen Albers now. Her mother is in a nursing home with Parkinson's."

"Boy, with so much going on, it was nice of you to come tonight," I told her. "Be sure and talk to my mom while you're here. And wasn't my sister Joan in class with your brother?" Judas-like, I pointed at Joan across the room.

Resisting my efforts to sweep her toward other family members, Eileen continued her litany of former classmates I hadn't seen in over thirty years. My eyes flickered toward the corridor. I hoped a mourner who needed cheering up might still wander in. But it was late, just fifteen minutes before visitation would end, and I was trapped. "You heard about Frank Hammersmith, didn't you? He and his four children burst into flames at a skateboard auction," she told me — or something along those lines.

Back in our bedroom, I fumed that I'd been ambushed by a person who visited funeral homes as a hobby. It made me even angrier to realize that I lacked the opportunity to take up the pastime myself. Our animals didn't allow it. Feeding, cleaning, and following complex out-of-cage schedules kept Linda and me busy throughout the day, and to make matters worse, the big white cat that didn't even belong to us had taken up residence next to my pillow.

"Linda," I wailed. "What's Moobie doing up here?"

"Moonbeam," she corrected me. "You can't expect her to stay in the basement all the time."

"She preferred the basement at Ben and Ann's house."

"She was afraid Jamie might pull her tail."

"How does she know I won't?"

Linda had already started making phone calls in search of a home for the possible furry trigger for granddaughter Jamie's asthma, but so far she had struck out. Linda's son Ben had been on the verge of taking Moobie to the humane society when Linda decided she could live temporarily with us. "They might put her to sleep at the shelter," his wife, Ann, had suggested. "She's too nice of a cat for that."

And she was also too old to find a new owner easily. Most folks wanted a kitten, or at least a cat that hadn't received its AARP card yet. Aging pets were definitely a concern. Linda and I already faced a potential wave of pet extinctions, and after the loss of my father, this prospect seemed more immediate than ever. The furred and feathered friends that had charmed and annoyed us over the years had gotten long in tooth and beak, including Howard, Ollie the pocket parrot, rabbits Bertie and Walter, cat Penny, and assorted parakeets. Stanley Sue and Dusty were both around thirteen years old, but African grey parrots can live to be fifty or more, so I didn't worry about them. I did worry about taking on a geriatric cat that might keel over at any moment, if a cat could keel over from a perennially prone position. And despite her resemblance to an unusually immobile pillow, Moobie had still created a rift in the existing social order.

Penny hissed from the stairs as I ushered Moobie off the bed, which had been Penny's territory, after all. A visit to our bedroom in colder months often revealed a lump under the covers, courtesy of our reclusive grey cat. Though Moobie was happy to share space, Penny couldn't abide another feline. I had to wash the interloper's scent off my hands before heading upstairs to Penny's usual domain, or she wouldn't so much as glance at me. Sometimes washing my hands wasn't enough. I needed to change my clothes as well. If Moobie's aroma still offended, I was expected to also shave my head and roll around in catnip for a while.

Penny had reacted exactly the same way when we had taken Agnes into the house. A few years earlier, we had found the skinny black cat eating seed that had spilled from our sunflower feeder after an unfeeling husk had presumably dropped her off. Once

Agnes convinced us that we should let her stay by feigning total disregard for anything with feathers, Penny retreated upstairs to make the guest bedroom her fortress. It had taken months for Penny to come back downstairs and attempt her first burrow under the bedcovers.

When the weather was warm, Agnes didn't even stay in the house during daylight hours. Her athletic love of the wild outdoors made her especially disdainful of Moobie. From what I could determine, she considered Moobie's shuffling, easygoing manner an insult to catdom and its ideals of aloofness and fussiness.

Agnes growled at Moobie from the couch as I herded the great white wonder into the dining room. "She can sleep in there," I told Linda. Once our birds were covered for the night, Agnes completely ignored them, while Moobie wouldn't pay attention to a bird unless it stole her space on my side of the bed. Even then, she would simply glare at it until it flew away out of sheer boredom.

Around five-thirty the next morning, I was awakened by the oddest noise. It wasn't a bloodcurdling howl or the burble of an unknown primate this time. It resembled a cross between a thumping and a scraping, a kind of drum solo using padded mallets. Hauling myself out of bed, I realized that the source of the disturbance was Moobie raking the bedroom door from the other side with her clawless front paws. Wondering what was up, I followed her sleepily into the bathroom. She hopped onto the toilet — fortunately, the lid was down — then from the toilet to the sink, from which vantage point she fixed me with her best bird-intimidating stare, until I realized that she wanted the water turned on. Too bleary to resist, I accommodated her. She continued giving me the evil eye while I tried various velocities of water flow. Finally, when I had reduced the output to a rapid drip, she stuck her head under the faucet and proceeded to drink.

"You've got a bowl of water on the floor," I informed her as I trudged back to bed. "Don't bother me again." I made the mistake of leaving the door open. A few minutes later she was up on the bed raining her soggy paws against my head, pummeling me with the unspoken command "Pet me, pet me," and purring the whole time. I finally gave up, got up, hauled myself into the living room, and read *The Far Side Gallery 5*, fretting about what I might have missed in galleries one through four.

THANKS TO MISSED SLEEP, I wasn't at my best as my sisters and I played archaeologists, rooting through my dad's vast collection of papers in search of bank records, insurance policies, brokerage reports, and, in my case, insight into his relaxed but tightly buttoned persona. Bett chose a set of metal boxes from the bedroom closet. Joan opted for the backroom file cabinet, while I sat down at his desk in the sunroom. Excavating the uppermost stratum of the bottom drawer revealed a bundle of tiny diagrams that I hadn't seen since Miss Edkins's eighth-grade class. It took me a moment to reacquaint my brain with page after miniature page of his freeway-interchange designs. I remembered him drawing while engaged in what he termed "Just paying bills." This semi-mysterious evening-long activity was primarily an excuse for smoking a pipe and listening to the radio more or less undisturbed.

Some of the freeway drawings bore names like "Lansing" or "Phoenix" and were paper-clipped to yellowed newspaper articles announcing the latest advance of the superhighway system across the country. But the majority of his interchanges were pure fantasy, though it was imagination expressed as straightforward on-ramp, off-ramp variations on the classic cloverleaf theme. A fascinating few designs consisted of impossibly complex spaghetti tangles, though. At first I thought of these as my father's mechanical-drawing equivalent to the discursive modern jazz of the late 1950s. There was a certain similarity between his carefully rendered squiggles and the geometric shapes on the covers of his Eisenhower-era jazz albums.

But a subsequent discovery unearthed from the Precambrian layer of the drawer made me reconsider them as a kind of substitute for poetry instead. Inside a dark brown folder dated 1933, I found an essay he had submitted to the University of Michigan admissions office. "I have always wanted to be a writer," he confessed in a two-page autobiography, "but due to the uncertainty of making a living in this field, I have decided to pursue engineering." This bombshell of a revelation added to the enigma of my father. Left forever unanswered was why he had never confided this early passion to me in the form of support or caution while I bumped along a curlicued writing path of my own. As I was about to share this with my sisters, my disgruntlement withered—I pulled out a recent envelope that unexpectedly reduced me to tears.

Joan came running into the room. "What is it? What happened?" she asked.

"Linda's artwork," I blubbered. Over the last few years, Linda had drawn her own Christmas cards. In contrast to the stately beauty of the religious-themed cards themselves, she had decorated the envelopes of my parents' card with whimsical doodles of Christmas trees, snowmen, Santa, and elves. These must have charmed my father, because he had cut them out and saved them.

"Do you want me to take over the desk for you?" asked Bett, who was sorting through old deeds, licenses, certificates, and canceled checks on the dining room table. One of the checks from 1960 that she had shown me read, "Bob's Mole Removal," on the comment line. Another from 1957 stated: "Muffin's Spaying."

"No, no," I told her. "Finding the pictures just surprised me. He sure liked Linda, didn't he?" And from the checks he'd saved, he apparently held a special place in his heart for dermatologists and veterinarians, too.

Grabbing a file folder titled "Warranties" and moving to the couch, I took a break from quarrying the drawers as my mother came into the living room. Five days had passed since my father's death, and she still wore a look of disbelief. "Joan and I are going to take turns driving you to church from now on," I told her.

"Oh, you don't have to do that," she said. "I can walk to church." And she could, in the same sense that I could walk to Nova Scotia, but it wasn't practical. "Do you want a can of pop?" she asked before melting back into the kitchen chores. She had asked me the same question twice already that afternoon, but I wrote it off to her distracted state of mind. She wasn't a woman who was shaken easily. When I was a tyke, she had opened the lid of a pressure cooker at the wrong moment and doused herself with scalding water, ending up in the hospital. Throughout the ordeal, she had kept her composure. But I didn't trust her calm this time.

Unlike my mom, I could be unraveled by less life-shattering events. That same morning just before breakfast, while checking my e-mail, I had happened to glance at the parson's table. In plain sight at the bottom of a stack of CDs was the missing *National Audubon Society Field Guide to North American Weather* that should have been there all along, but somehow wasn't. I simply stared at it, wondering if I was in the middle of a dream and annoyed that the dream didn't involve dancing elves or talking furniture.

"Did you find this somewhere and put it upstairs?" I asked Linda, carefully positioning the book beside my breakfast plate. I kept an eye on it while I fed the parrots bits of fried egg, as if the field guide might scoot off on its own.

"I didn't touch it," she told me, and I absolutely believed her. Linda was incapable of telling a lie. A thug could show up at the front door waving a gun and ask her point-blank, "Is that stupid husband of yours home, so I can put a bullet through his head?" If she knew for a fact that I was, she would suffer a crisis of conscience over having to deceive my prospective murderer.

I found myself obsessing about the field guide as I sat on my parents' couch. This wasn't by a long shot the first time the book imp had performed his dislocation trick. A few months earlier, a short stack of books on my desk had suddenly sprouted a short-wave-radio reference guide that hadn't been in the stack hours earlier. Linda had complained about similar events, though she tended to blame the book imp for problems that clearly weren't part of his job description, such as misplaced eyeglasses or missing coffee mugs—"Someone is coming into our house and stealing them," she'd insist. His favorite stunt wasn't as dazzling as snatching a book out of thin air, then replacing it later. He was most fond of obscuring the spine of a particular volume in my bookcase while someone I wanted to lend it to tapped a foot downstairs. As soon as my friend had pulled out of our driveway with a spray of loose gravel and without the book, the clouds that had obscured its location would lift, and a beam of sunlight would fall precisely upon the title.

I was wondering whether or not the hose demon shared shop-talk with the book imp when Bette Ann exploded in laughter, drawing Joan, my mom, and me into the dining room. Spread across the table was a complex chart consisting of what turned out to be thirty sheets of graph paper carefully taped together and folded in accordion fashion.

"He always liked to track his stocks," said my mother.

"These aren't stocks," Bett said. "This is a graph of Big Ten basketball games dating back to the 1968 season." My dad had used three colored pencils plus black to draw the chart, with black indicating most of the teams and blue representing the University of Michigan. Green and orange designated, respectively, archrivals Michigan State University and Ohio State University. Lighter shadings of each color juxtaposed the previous year's performance of these three teams, while squares, circles, triangles, and diamonds indicated . . . well, we couldn't figure out exactly what they meant.

"I'll bet a U of M graduate would love to get his hands on this," said Bett, who had been the only member of the family to share my dad's interest in college sports. The sound of my dad hooting and laughing at successful plays had reverberated through the house for decades and startled several of my friends. "Do you mind if I keep this?" she asked.

"He'd want you to have it," said Joan.

"Not that I know what I'll do with it."

When I sat back down on the living room couch, I realized that the pen I had borrowed from Bett was missing. After a search of the floor came up empty, I removed one of the couch cushions to receive another jolt. Staring me in the face was the copy of the *National Audubon Society Field Guide to North American Weather* that I had given Bett's husband, Dave, for Christmas. Apparently he had brought it with him from Fort Wayne to thumb through in between funeral-home visits and had forgotten where he'd put it.

So the book imp had restored the same book title to me twice within five hours. As borderline paranormal performances went, this was a solid tour de force.

IN VARIOUS SECTIONS of my dad's desk I excavated songs he had written in high school complete with his own musical notation system, memos from his job as a civilian engineer for the Department of the Navy during World War II, a hand-drawn floor plan of the bathroom, a list of personnel in Bob Crosby's Bobcats, a complete set of Keeler Brass Company pay stubs from the 1960s, letters from his sister Aba, a journal of dizzy spells including dates and descriptions, ancient instructions for my mom on how to start his Studebaker, a heavily underlined Shell Oil Company ad torn from an issue of *Time* magazine, and the names of friends and family members who had seen his slides of Egypt, Thailand, Morocco, and Mexico. I hated the thought that the only written record of his life was this nonnarrative diary.

"How did it go?" Linda asked as I slumped through the front door of our house holding a few of my father's big band CDs, his slide rule, and a cassette tape on which he had introduced his favorite Duke Ellington Orchestra soloists.

"Moobie, get out of the way."

She had planted herself directly in my path and, because I was far less intimidating than Agnes, she refused to move. I had to walk around her—and considering her size, it was quite a walk—to deposit the small heap of my father's things on the carpet in front of the entertainment center. She followed me into the bedroom for a nap. As I slept, she lay beside me, pressed against my leg. She didn't once bat my head with her feet and demand that I pet her, though upon awakening I was ordered to accompany her to the bathroom sink and adjust the trickle of water just so.

"Pest," I said in a low voice so that Linda wouldn't hear. And that reminded me.

"I still can't get over it," I told Linda after describing the second appearance of the book.

"Remember when I was reading *The Outline of History*?" Linda asked. "I couldn't sleep one night, so I took it upstairs and set it

on the floor in Penny's room. The next night it was gone. I looked
everywhere. Remember, I asked if you had seen it? Later it was
right in the middle of the floor again. Are you sure you didn't put
it there?"

I shook my head. "The book imp," I told her.

"How does he know where everything in the house is?"

"What do you mean?"

"He has to know where everything is in order to put it back
again in the right place."

I thought about that for a while and drew the usual blank. As
far as I was concerned, his choice of books, eyeglasses, and coffee mugs was the least impressive aspect of his craft. The essen-
tial mystery was where things went when they were taken from
us—those things that were so well accounted for but then one
day simply vanished. Where was my *National Audubon Society
Field Guide to North American Weather* before it reappeared on my
parson's table? And where had my dad gone? I kept looking at
his things next to the entertainment center, but I couldn't find a
clue.

CHAPTER 3

....

Ask an Expert

A bsurdity loves company. That's an elusive yet immutable law of nature, like gravity or the seventh-inning stretch. A few months after my father's death, the solemnity of his passing surrendered to an unprecedented barrage of silliness. As if to mock his levelheadedness, people who should have known better cropped up to offer pointless comments, proffer worthless advice, or just generally torment me.

My mom was in her front yard watering the impatiens when her longtime across-the-street neighbor Judy Teany strolled up the driveway to tell her, "Don and I really hate it that you have to eat dinner alone."

Thinking that an invitation for a meal was in the air, Mom answered, "It's just not the same without Bob. Sometimes I think God took the wrong person."

Mrs. Teany clucked sympathetically. "Whenever Don and I sit down for dinner and look over and see your kitchen light and know you're by yourself, we feel terrible. So we've been having dinner in the basement."

My mom reported this story to me over the phone.

"She said *what*?" I sputtered. I couldn't believe I had heard the conversation correctly. But she repeated it, leaving me to wonder why her good friend Mrs. Teany was delivering lines out of a bad TV sitcom. A couple of weeks earlier, my mom had reported talking to a friend in West Virginia who had been planning on visiting that summer with her husband. According to my mom, once Mrs. Dorst had heard the news about my dad, she told her, "Gee, Bette, I don't think we'll be keeping in touch anymore. Now that Bob's not around, Gene won't have anyone to talk to."

"Was that for me?" asked Linda as I stood next to the phone, trying to figure out my mom's friends. It never dawned on me that there could be a different explanation for these remarks. But that explanation wouldn't become apparent for another few months.

"It was my mom with an incredible story."

"I thought it might have been someone responding to my ad."

"Ad?" I immediately blanked out the conversation with my mom.

For ordinary folks, the first batch of crocuses poking their heads above the cold ground signified the arrival of spring. For Linda, as soon as overnight temperatures struggled above freezing and the first few migratory birds straggled into our yard, it was time to start placing a barrage of classified ads in the local weekly newspaper for gardeners, barn cleaners, duck-pen gravel changers, rubbish haulers, and animal-enclosure builders—things she couldn't do herself because of chronic back problems and I wouldn't do out of chronic laziness. Linda's ads addressed more esoteric topics, too. She sought people willing to drive her to her Grandville chiropractor, asked gardeners to share their "rare and beautiful perennials," offered to pay for a dependable spot for finding morel mushrooms, and rather hopelessly solicited pet sitters for boisterous animals with complex morning, noon, and night-time schedules.

If I didn't get stuck fielding endless phone calls from people who had misread the ads, I wound up having to meet a number of highly questionable respondents. When Linda advertised that she was available to do odd jobs for the elderly and housebound, teenage girls would call to apply for the nonexistent helper position. When Linda asked for volunteers to write letters on animal rights topics, a reader might phone to find out if we wanted a duck. And a person who sounded reasonable over the phone more often than not exhibited an ominous twitch or disturbing character trait in the flesh. One fellow who called about yanking three sick shrubs out of our front garden obviously didn't have the strength to yank a fleck of lint off a sweater. He wheezed like a cracked boiler as he staggered around the yard to appraise the work, and merely talking while standing up seemed to tax his lung power. Linda finally told him we were just taking names at that moment, but if we didn't call him for this job, we would probably use him for something else. I had an envelope that needed licking, but he left before I could suggest it.

I brightened slightly at the thought of the ads. "Was one of them about Moobie?"

"I've been running that one for three weeks. But I do have good news."

"You found a home for her?"

"I found a master gardener," she beamed. "He's stopping by on Saturday to test our soil and tell me which plants would do best in which gardens." A perplexed expression passed over her face, resembling the one that had just left mine. "There was something really odd about his telephone. I had to keep saying 'over' when I was done talking, and we couldn't both talk at the same time. And

I can't call him back. If I want to get hold of him, I have to leave a message with the Just Around the Corner Bait Shop and Ammo Shack."

"That isn't a good sign at all."

"He knows a lot about plants and soils. He's a certified master gardener. But I didn't understand something he said something about having strokes."

"He's had a stroke?"

"Not 'a stroke.' He said he has some strokes every day." She thought for a moment. "I think the word he used was 'numerous' strokes. He said he has numerous strokes every day. He might have even said hundreds."

"Please don't let him come here," I begged. "Call the bait shop, and get us off the hook."

OUR CHARCOAL GREY bunny Bertie lay stock-still in his cage.

"Bertie?" I said. "Bertie?" Sometimes when he slept flat on his side facing the wall, I couldn't see him breathing. Because of his advanced age, this had started to unnerve me.

"Bertie," I called again, but he didn't move. I bent down into a crouch. "Bertie, are you all right?" The instant I started to unlatch his cage door, he was up on all fours staring at me sideways, alert and ready to bolt from Bob the predator.

"It's okay," I told him. "Sorry. Go back to bed."

As I straightened with a groan, activity at the hummingbird feeder outside the window caught my eye. But hummingbirds weren't humming around it. Our hummingbird feeder had turned into a yellow jacket feeder. Leaving Bertie to wend his way back to the Land of Nod, I slogged downstairs and through the basement door to watch wasps flying back and forth between their food source and a nest in the ground next to our house.

In an overhang beneath our dining room was a small pile of
decaying wood left over from my feeble attempts to harvest logs
a full ten years earlier. Armed with a terrifyingly loud and, in my
hands, dangerous twelve-inch chain saw, I had left no deadfall in
our woods intact—unless the trees involved were larger than sap-
lings, lay more than a few steps from the backyard fence, or their
sawn products might challenge the loose musculature of my arms,
shoulders, back, or demi-chest. The glorified sticks that eventually
formed a pathetic hump against the house didn't even make good
kindling for our woodstove. They went up as quickly as matches
and burned about as long. Scraps of plywood abandoned in the
barn by the former owners of the house worked much better.
Once we began accumulating pet birds, I had my excuse to stop
accumulating twigs. Wood smoke interfered with avian breathing
passages as surely as exercise interfered with my lifestyle. So I left
what remained of the pile to rot and form a habitat for ants. But
without informing the ants, the yellow jackets had moved in.

I took down the feeder to rinse it off. One of the wasps buzzed
around my head, grew bored with the uninspired scenery, and
returned to the burrow. A few more streamed out, but they were
more concerned with foraging than with sightseeing at Mount
Bobmore. Gingerly I edged toward the woodpile and nudged one
of the sticks with my boot. A couple of dozen yellow jackets shot
out to investigate. I jumped back, brandishing the hummingbird
feeder in self-defense. Although I hadn't laid bare much of their
lair, I could see that a significant hive hid just below the surface. This was bad news, considering that the water spigot we
used for duck-pen chores in temperate weather—and to water
Linda's countless vegetable, flower, herb, and woodchuck-buffet
gardens—was right above their nest.

Under normal circumstances, Linda would place a classified

ad, and within a week a swarm of cranks would phone asking if we had honey for sale. But there was no time to lose. Linda had to find a crank right away. A display ad in the local paper depicted a cartoon termite and wasp with maniacal grins chasing a person half their size. "Pest Problems? Ask an Expert," urged the headline. Linda dialed the number in the ad instead.

"I'm in the process of ripping down a guy's wall right now," grunted Mark the pest-control expert from his cell phone. "I won't be able to get over there for a while."

"One thing," said Linda. "Can you move the nest without hurting the bees?"

"Beg your pardon?"

"I don't want the yellow jackets killed. I just want them moved, if possible."

"We don't do that, ma'am. I wouldn't know how to do it. It's far too dangerous."

"How about if you came in the morning when they weren't moving around much because of the cold?" Linda asked. "Couldn't you just scoop them up while they were sleepy and move them out into our field?"

"Cold has no effect on yellow jackets," he said.

"How come they're so subdued in the morning when it's cold?"

"Cold has no effect," he repeated. "It's the dew The morning dew gets their wings wet, and they can't fly around as well."

"He said *what*?" I asked Linda when she recounted the conversation. "He actually said it was the dew?"

"Well, anyway, he's coming tomorrow sometime, he thought. He was kind of vague about everything—except about the cold having no effect on them. It might not even be tomorrow. But he said we're on his list."

Later that evening, temperatures had fallen enough that I figured the well known "dew effect" would make the yellow jackets comparatively inactive. It seemed like the perfect opportunity to indulge in the classic mistake of prodding a wasp net with a broomstick. I decided that I could easily get back inside the basement before the sluggish squatters drew a collective bead on me, and I needed to see how difficult it might be to dislodge them.

I made sure that our cat Agnes was safely indoors. After switching on the floodlight, I crept outdoors stealthily enough to guarantee that any yellow jacket sentinels playing cards close to the surface wouldn't hear my footfalls. Then, with a sudden but by no means certain movement, I thrust a broomstick under several of the sticks, pushed my end down in lever fashion, dislodged the crumbling wood, and confronted a formidable buzzing hoard.

I ducked into the basement in time to hear the *tick, tick, tick* of hundreds of angry yellow jacket bodies pounding on the metal door and insisting I come outside and fight like a man. I heard the same sound, only louder, as I hurried up the basement stairs into the dining room. The yellow jackets had massed against the picture window. The scene resembled a horrifying take on a nature documentary with a close-up view inside a honeycomb, but these weren't amiable bees preparing little packets of ambrosia for their keeper. These were miniature cogs in a coordinated killing machine bent on stinging me into oblivion. I started worrying whether a mere pane of glass could withstand their fury. Surely by acting altogether they could lift the entire window out of its frame, fly it to a soft landing on the grass, and launch themselves at me unimpeded. As my nerves sagged against the yellow jackets' steady hammering, Stanley Sue startled me by clicking on the bars of her cage with her beak, then erupting into a full-fledged squawk.

"What's the matter, Stanley?" Linda called from the living room. "I'm taking care of her," I called back, hurriedly plying the parrot with a peanut, which, for once, she graciously accepted.

Desperate to hide the evidence of my folly, I raced down to the basement and snapped off the floodlights. The resulting silhouette of writhing wasps was muted against the outdoor gloom, and from the living room the ominous buzzing sounded like our refrigerator motor.

"You weren't planning on going outside for any reason, were you?" I asked Linda casually.

"Why, do you need something?"

"Oh, no, no," I told her. "It's much too dark and unseasonably cold to be outdoors. But when did you say that pest-control guy was coming?"

"He's calling us tomorrow. But don't forget that tomorrow the lady is coming to see about taking Moonbeam."

In the flurry of wings and my fear of stings, the good news about Moobie had slipped my mind. "That's great," I told her. Linda shot me a questioning glance when I added, "Make sure she uses the front door, okay?"

THE HOLE IN THE ground baffled me. The yellow jacket nest had been there the previous night. Now it was completely gone. A few disoriented wasps crawled disconsolately around the rim of what had once been their burrow, but only a gaping crater remained. They hadn't abandoned their nest. The nest had abandoned them. I couldn't find a trace of the grey papery material to prove it had ever existed, and neither could the wasps.

Linda and I determined that some animal must have stolen the nest after my broomstick excavation had unearthed its northern hemisphere. To figure out which animal might have been

responsible—and to quell potential blather about the return of the
mystery primate—my wife phoned Grand Rapids wildlife expert
Amy Martoni, whom she inevitably referred to as Mrs. Martini.

"Mrs. Martini said that it was probably raccoons," Linda said as
we stared at the hollowed-out burrow. One wasp wandered down
to the bottom, then returned to the top to confer with another
family member, presumably about their hive-owner's insurance.
"The thick coat protects them from getting stung, though they
might get a few stings on their noses. But she said raccoons would
have eaten the yellow jackets."

"What did you call her when you talked to her?"

Linda paused a beat. "Mrs. Martoni. What else would I call
her? She said it could have been a skunk, but raccoons were more
likely to have dragged the whole thing off."

Raccoons made sense to me. They had eaten three of our ducks
in the past, which proved their carnivorous tendency. And any
animal that didn't mind dining on garbage would probably consider wasps a delicacy. "Did you phone the pest-control guy and
tell him not to come? Tell him that the yellow jackets drowned in
dew overnight."

"He wasn't there, but I left a message. And Shelley will be here
any minute to see about taking Moonbeam."

"Speaking of pests."

Our great white cat wasn't overjoyed to meet her prospective owner. As soon as the young woman breezed in towing her
towheaded three-year-old daughter, Moobie made tracks for the
bedroom.

"Oh, what a pretty cat," said Shelley as Moobie's tail disappeared
through the doorway. "I've always dreamed of having a white cat."
The heavyset Shelley had a baby face that made her the little girl's
twin. But Emily bore a serious expression beyond her years, while

Shelley's smile was cherubic. Mom seemed like a good match for Moobie.

"She's got one green eye and one blue eye," I pointed out.

"Kitty!" cried Emily.

Our house wasn't exactly child-friendly. That realization hit me like a hornet sting as the girl scampered into the dining room, where Stanley Sue and Dusty waited with open beaks for small, chubby fingers to poke through their cage bars. But Emily put the African grey parrots on the defensive. Stanley Sue jumped off her perch with a worried flutter of wings, sending Dusty and all the caged birds flailing in a similar fashion, except imperturbable Howard, who cocked his head for a better view of the action. The breeze from the combined feather power blew sheets of newspaper that Linda had cut to fit various cage trays from the top of the refrigerator. Fortunately, Emily headed directly for the rabbits rather than the hookbills. She tried reaching the snoozing Bertie through the wire grid, but her hand wouldn't fit. When I brought out the bunny for her to pet, she whimpered and hid behind her mother's legs.

"What a sweet little girl," said Linda. "Do you like animals, honey?" Emily tightened her arms around Shelley's denim-clad thigh.

"Most of the time," said Shelley. "Well, we don't really know. She can identify 'cat,' 'dog,' 'cow,' and 'bear' in her favorite picture book."

"Kitty," complained Emily with a scowl when Agnes made a rare appearance in the bird room, requesting an immediate exit outdoors. Dusty gave me the evil eye as the aluminum door slammed shut, as if to say, "Is there no limit to what I'm expected to put up with in this house?"

"Let's go look at Moobie."

Linda's suggestion took root immediately with Emily, who had determined from their fleeting encounter that Moobie was utterly innocuous, even compared to a grapefruit-size bunny. As the girl ran back into the living room I remembered the glass figurines on the coffee table, a bowl of candy, and other temptations. But she bypassed these and tore upstairs to a minefield of CDs, books, outdated computer peripherals, a folk harp, and other detritus strewn everywhere that was easily stepped on and more easily tripped over. I had forgotten about Penny until a hiss from the grey cat in the guest bedroom sent Emily wailing and retreating downstairs.

"Penny," I said, sprinting up to the second floor to comfort the cat, who growled at me.

"Oh, dear," lamented Linda as Emily's howling hit high gear.

Moobie's frame of mind wasn't much better. Back downstairs, I found her in our bedroom closet, hiding behind an old suitcase that held single socks pining forlornly for their mates. When I picked up Moobie, she twisted her body in a fashion that no other animal could ever duplicate. Her front legs jerked stiffly to the right as her back legs jerked stiffly to the left, then vice versa as her head waggled back and forth. The spasms proved remarkably effective. She slid from my grasp just as I reached the living room. For a large land mammal, she was remarkably adept at avoiding Emily's lunge. Within seconds, she had discovered a new hiding place deeper inside the closet.

"Don't chase the kitty," Shelley told her.

"Oh, dear," Linda repeated.

"I think she'd be fine with us," said Shelley. "We live in a small trailer."

"With lots of closets?" I asked hopefully.

"We're just writing down names at the moment," said Linda. I found myself nodding in agreement.

"I probably shouldn't take her today, anyway."

I shook my head. "She seems a little upset. So does Emily." The child had started crying again.

"I want to see the kitty!"

"We'll get back to you," promised Linda.

THE BUMBLEBEE ROLLED into our driveway. Linda started calling it that right away. Henry, the master gardener, drove a dented yellow car of uncertain foreign origin and age with a black stripe across the sides and an orange rubber ball impaled on each of two antennae. One aerial served a nonfunctioning AM/FM radio. The other put Henry in touch with the world via a two-meter ham rig that allowed him to make completely free though highly inconvenient phone calls.

"I'm on my way over. Over," he'd told Linda from the supermarket parking lot minutes before his arrival. "I had to buy a camera first. Over."

I hid inside the house, peeping through the curtains, as Linda conducted Henry around the yard. She moved expansively from flower bed to flower bed, her red braids flapping as she gestured toward the plants while Martin followed unsteadily, as if walking were a hobby that he had just taken up. When he stepped into the middle of the largest front-yard bed and pointed at a patch of greenery, Linda waved her arms until he lifted his left tennis shoe and retreated to the lawn. Bending down, she tried propping up a squashed Oriental poppy.

Henry lagged behind, making entries in a spiral notebook that he'd extracted from a bulging envelope. Each time he finished recording an observation, he meticulously clipped the pen to his shirt pocket, then wiggled the pad until he managed to wedge it back inside the envelope. His slowness may have exasperated Linda, but it gave me an opportunity to pick the best vantage point for witnessing the same maddening procedures repeated in different sections of the yard. Linda would stiffen as he delivered a judgment on her floral aesthetics and walked into a grouping to demonstrate his point. Next would come the trampled flower, the attempted resuscitation by Linda, and the master gardener's notations regarding the plants that had so far survived his visit.

Eager to see the expert at close quarters, I caught up with them in the backyard as Henry shook his head at the triangular bed just outside the basement door. "We've got problems, here," he muttered. "The plants are too crowded again. You'll have to give the roots more room. You've read Thomas Merton on the virtue of solitude? The soil doesn't seem to have sufficient aeration, either. See that whitish color? That might be a case of excessive alkalinity, and different mulch could help. I'll need to do a chemical analysis."

"Watch where you step," pleaded an agitated Linda. "That's a Jacob's ladder behind your foot."

An arm's length from the unsteady Henry, I surmised a possible reason for his lurching movements as an aroma of alcoholic spirits washed over me. A small man in his sixties, slightly stooped, he had the classic drinker's nose with a latticework of veins, along with the telltale droopy eyes. "That's one ladder you don't want to step on," I suggested.

"Saint John of the Cross composed a poem about Jacob's ladder," he told her as he wrested his notebook loose from the envelope. "It was either him or Hildegard von Bingen, but you'll want to read Saint John of the Cross. I'll bring him along next time." He scribbled a memo to himself.

"I'd like to meet him."

"Henry, this is my husband, Bob."

His head snapped in my direction and he bounced in surprise, as if I had materialized at his side that instant. "A pleasure," he told me. "The Catholic mystics embraced the concept of evolution as God's consciousness at work in nature. You can see it in a garden. Before I leave today, I'll take a soil sample of each flower bed and test them for you."

"If you could just pull out some of the hostas for me and divide them, you could start working right now. There's plenty to do here," Linda said.

"It's all about science." He turned to me. "Science and religion make perfect partners." He slurred the final s. I shot a wide-eyed look at Linda, but she ignored me.

"I wrote down some ideas on how I'd like to see the beds arranged, if you want to come inside," she told him. "Would you like iced tea or a glass of water?"

"Caffeine is bad for my health."

Sitting at the dining room table, he shuffled through Linda's copious notes listing her goals for the various gardens, her design ideas, and plants she wanted to try. He set the pages aside and pulled out a sheaf of his own from his manila envelope, which showed signs of starting to tear along one side. "You're a writer," he informed me. "I've been working on a brochure to get my business started. Mostly, I do volunteer work at men's shelters."

He gave me a business card, which read, "Henry Murphy, Certified Master Gardener, Big Ideas for Every Space. The Purpose of Man on Earth Is to Glorify the Most High. Substance Abuse Counseling. Tax Preparation and Accounting Services. Leave a Message at the Just Around the Corner Bait Shop and Ammo Shack. Tell Them Henry Sent You."

"That's a lot to take in all at once," I said.

"Wait until you see my brochure."

Linda grabbed the first page of her notes, while Henry offered me a copy of the most confusing promotional sheet I had ever seen.

"Here are the things I would like done with each bed," Linda said. "The plants that need thinning, the perennials I'd like to add, and suggestions for improving the soil quality." Henry took the sheet from her and laid it on the table.

"So, what do you think so far?" he asked me.

His promotional sheet mixed claims of various areas of expertise—from gardening to business administration—with quotes from Thomas Aquinas and Pierre Teilhard de Chardin. "Well, you might want to add something about your qualifications and the benefits you can provide your customers. And you would probably want to limit this particular piece to the subject of gardening. I'd downplay the philosophy."

"Just a second," he told Linda, when he saw she was about to speak. "I have to write this down while it's still fresh in my mind."

"Do you have time to do anything today?" she asked.

"I'll take soil samples on my way out, and I may photograph some of your beds. If you don't mind, I'd like to walk around down by your swamp to see if there's a good place for planting a few cranberry bushes. I've always wanted to grow them. I won't charge you for that, of course," he chuckled.

"Why don't you take Linda's notes home with you and study them, so that you can start right in next time you come," I suggested.

"That's a good idea. And if you think of any more ideas for my brochure—either of you," he added, so that Linda wouldn't feel left out, "let me know. But you've given me plenty to work on."

As Linda was seeing Henry out the door, Mark, the pest-control expert, called. She waved good-bye to the master gardener, then ducked back into the house to explain why the yellow jacket nest was no longer a problem.

"He said *what*?" I asked Linda after she had hung up.

"He said that raccoons don't eat meat. I told him that we knew they did, because we lost several ducks to raccoons. He said some other animal must have been responsible, so I told him what Mrs. Martini had said about raccoons eating yellow jackets."

"Did he know who Mrs. Martini was?"

"Martoni," she corrected me. "I don't know, but he was adamant that raccoons were vegetarians."

I thought that this phone call put an end to the expertise for the day. Nearly an hour later, however, Linda hollered upstairs that I should take a look out the window. At first I thought I was supposed to see the cinder block–size woodchuck that had been hanging around the bird feeder. Then I noticed a section of brambles quivering on the edge of the swamp. The tremors reached a climax as an out-of-breath Henry burst through.

"Is everything okay?" Linda asked when she met him in the front yard.

"Just finishing my work," said Henry, smiling despite the mosquito bites that peppered his face and arms. His shoes and cuffs were caked with mud, which he tried to shake off before stepping into his bumblebee car. "You wouldn't believe the place I found for planting my cranberries."

H E WOULDN'T HAVE found any space on my mother's street. Cars lined the block, and I considered driving back home, parking in our swamp, and walking back to my mom's. I was afraid there'd been another medical emergency until I noticed a cluster of yellow balloons tethered to a GARAGE SALE sign in front of the Teany house. A chubby man and an adolescent boy examined a pair of greenish dressers, while a frowning woman jiggled the headboard of the matching bed. A cat lay curled up beneath a wicker chair that had seen better days a couple of decades ago. Joan was just pulling out of Mom's driveway, but she stopped when she saw me on the sidewalk.

"Are they gutting their house over there?" I asked her. "It looks like everything they own is on the lawn."

Joan rolled her eyes and changed the subject. "She's not doing well," she told me in a low voice, though Mom was indoors with the windows shut. "I asked her if she wanted to go to the sale with me, but she told me, 'It's too gloomy a day to do anything.'" Normally my mom would have been in the Teanys' yard chatting happily with the neighbors about current events and people's illnesses. But she had lost her motivation to do much of anything.

"Did you tell her it was her chance to see some really ugly bedroom furniture?"

"It's not even what you'd call cloudy out."

Joan waited for an elderly man in a station wagon to creep past the sale, trying to decide whether or not to stop, then headed back to work. I went inside, wishing that Linda were there to coax a chuckle from my mom with the story of our master gardener. My low-energy delivery didn't leaven her weighty mood, though the saga of our yellow jackets reminded her of the time that my father had jumped off the stepladder while swatting a bee.

"Why is it the good always seem to die young?" she asked.

"Well, he was eighty-four," I pointed out, "but I know that doesn't make it any easier."

I helped her pay the bills at the dining room table while we shared a tea bag and commented on the chocolate chip cookies the family in back of her had sent over. "Yours are much better," I pointed out. "Yours actually have chocolate chips in them."

"Someday I'll feel like baking again."

I returned home in the throes of her slump. I couldn't recall a single instance over the decades when she had ever acted glum before. Glumness simply wasn't in her repertoire, and she had never coddled anyone else who indulged in it. As a melancholy teen, I'd often been admonished, "Don't be such a droop." In my college years, when I had complained about depression, she had offered the remarkable observation "It's all in your head." Emotional problems needed to pack up and relocate to the torso in order to merit consideration. So her development of head trouble worried us. Joan ate lunch with her almost every weekday. I usually stopped by three afternoons a week, and Bette Ann drove in from Fort Wayne for weekends as often as possible and phoned her every evening. But we knew that even if we could spend twenty-four hours a day with her, our presence was still no substitute for the loss of my dad.

I brooded about this as I retreated to bed for a nap. Moobie snuggled beside me without demanding to be petted. She had an instinct for knowing when people were upset. Unlike Penny, who would cringe beside my file cabinet at the first sign of a bad mood, or Stanley Sue, who would squawk indignantly if one of us started to cry, Moobie was a sponge for negative emotions. She absorbed people's pain and transmuted it into purring. As I drifted off, I thought about how some people waited their entire lives for a cat as nice as her. And while I had dismissed her disinterest in our birds at first, it truly was extraordinary. I decided to let Linda talk me into keeping her.

The phone rang twenty minutes later. My mom's unexpectedly cheerful voice reported the good news of finding a green rubber band on the floor of the kitchen.

"That's really something," I stammered. Raising myself on one elbow, I struggled to wake up. "You can never have too many rubber bands."

"I found a red one on my dresser last night. And a paper clip, too."

"I guess you're all set for quite a while now. Two rubber bands and a paper clip."

"They weren't there before," she said. "They were just like the ones that Dad used."

It dawned on me what she was saying. Whenever my dad had practiced his weekly bill-paying ritual — originally at the bedroom card table and in later years at his desk in the sunroom — containers of rubber bands and paper clips had lay open and ready for use. I associated these with him to such an extent that if he had been a tribal leader in an indigenous culture, I imagined, his totem would have been a paper-fastening product.

"I had just cleaned earlier, and the rubber bands and paper clips weren't there," she continued. "Don't you think he's leaving these behind to let me know he's watching from heaven?"

"That sounds exactly like what he would do," I said, even though I didn't think it was. Despite my flirtations with the hose demon, the book imp, the anomalous lemur, and their highly relative relatives, I was conservative when it came to interaction with the dead. And if my father did have the ability to communicate from beyond the grave, would he do his talking through bits of rubber and metal? His ghostly, cardigan sweater–clad outline in the darkened upstairs hallway was the route a traditionalist like my dad would have taken. But I was happy that my mom had chosen an optimistic explanation rather than simply deciding she had overlooked the rubber bands and paper clips earlier, or had seen them and forgotten. I leaned toward the forgetfulness hypothesis, because her memory had been misfiring lately.

A month earlier, my friend Bill Holm and his wife, Carol, had bought a sprawling house in an exurban development, enriching a farmer and his previously unexploited woodlot. To flaunt their undeserved prosperity, Bill and Carol had held an open house and invited my mom.

"I'll bet cleaning this house is a lot more work than cleaning up your apartment," my mom had told Bill as we hung around the kitchen peninsula, close to the appetizers.

"Well, we haven't lived in an apartment in several years," Bill reminded her. He made a Jackie Gleason "wow" face after he sipped his drink. "You and your husband had been to our house in Heritage Hill a couple of times."

"That's right," said my mom as she gratefully accepted the gin and tonic he offered her. "Ooh!" She wrinkled her nose. "That's strong. Just the way I like it." After taking another swallow, she observed, "I'll bet cleaning this house is a lot more work than cleaning up your apartment."

"You can say that again," Bill unhelpfully replied.

At the time, I chalked up her repetition to the strain of facing a social situation without my dad. But this hadn't been an isolated incident.

"I think I found another rubber band on the bathroom floor last night," she said, snapping me back into the present.

"It's nice to know that Dad is saying hello in his own way."

"Speaking of saying hello, I got a nice phone call yesterday from that friend of yours from school," she told me.

I sat up in bed. An annoyed Moobie jumped down to the floor. "What friend from school?"

"That girl who was at the funeral home. I have her name written down somewhere."

"Not Eileen? It can't be Eileen Kucek."

"That's who it was," she replied. "She called to say she enjoyed meeting me, and she wished we could have talked longer. I told her to come over some night and watch a television program with me, and she said she would."

I could hear my mom's wall clock ticking in the background. "That's nice of her," I said with some reluctance. "And that was all she called about?"

"She did say she wanted to get in touch with you. I hope you don't mind. I gave her your telephone number."

A wave of dread shot through me. "Why did she want to talk to me?"

"What was it?" my mom mused.

"Something about one of our classmates? She keeps in touch with a lot of people."

She hesitated. "No, I don't think that was it."

"Something about another funeral?" I could just imagine her wanting to carpool to the cemetery. But that didn't ring a bell with my mom.

"I remember," she told me as a truck roared past our house, rattling the bedroom windows. "She wanted to give you a duck. She said it needed expert care."

CHAPTER 4

· ·

A Duck Out of Water

The lack of a sound rather than a sound woke me up. I must have been sleeping as shallow as a canary when the car shot past our house with a hum of tires on asphalt. Then, as if an invisible hand had hit the pause button, the humming suddenly stopped, snapping my thin thread to the land of oblivion. An instant after surfacing to my normal state of semicrabbiness, I heard the squeal of brakes, the sharp crack of something breaking, and then another squeal. I lay in bed, heart thumping, hoping that I had misheard and misinterpreted.

"I think someone just ran off the road," Linda told the darkened room as she threw off the sheet and pulled back the window shade. "I'd better call 911."

"Wait until I have a look."

I didn't want to have a look. A spate of driver's education films during my high school years had taught me that car wrecks tended to squash heads and lop off limbs in a disconcerting fashion, and the patch of Highway 21 in front of our house was a vortex for nasty accidents. Three times in the past ten years medical helicopters had flown in to rush unconscious victims to hospitals. Most of these accidents could be blamed on itchy motorists passing slowpokes who puttered along our winding, hilly, two-lane road at a mere sixty-five miles per hour.

Other vehicular mishaps were testaments to human ingenuity. One man had ditched a burning tanker truck loaded with diesel fuel near our mailbox, a drunken teen had rolled his car in front of our barn and hightailed it into the brush before the police arrived, a young mother had managed to slide her SUV into the lone tree stump at the end of our driveway one winter morning, and a groggy driver had left the road and landed in the woods near the spot where I now found myself once again directing a flickering flashlight beam.

"I didn't find anything," I told Linda as I came back in.

Neither did the sheriff's car, whose spotlight had caught me gawking on the grass as he crept up and down a half-mile stretch of shoulder before departing with a roar of fuel-injected impatience.

"But something happened. I heard the brakes squeal, a cracking noise, then another squeal," I reminded myself.

"The brakes squealed, there was a crack, then another squeal," Linda concurred.

"You know, it was exactly one year ago today when we had that fatal accident."

"It was?"

"No, but I thought I'd try to blame this on a ghost."

Linda went back to bed. Too nerved up from the nonexistent accident to sleep, I plopped down on the living room floor on Linda's faux sheepskin and promptly began to fret about my dad, worry about my mom, and fear that Linda might burst out of the bedroom and trample me in the dark.

My dad was foremost on my mind. The more I thought about him, the more he seemed to evaporate. I couldn't even fix a clear mental picture of his face. I recalled how years ago he had briefly grown a mustache. It had taken me a few visits home to notice, then another few visits to realize that he had shaved it off again. I couldn't even remember now when the mustache event had taken place, leading me to wonder if I'd dreamed the whole thing, or if the mustache imp had hidden his facial hair from me.

Certainly I should have been more attentive to him. After I had returned from graduate school in San Francisco, we had sat down one evening and listened to an LP of a Benny Goodman concert at Carnegie Hall. But the only music that I had cared about at the time projected chaos, rage, and gloom, so the carefully orchestrated big band performance had slipped right through my synapses. In recent years, as free-floating anxiety had replaced existential anger, I had come to appreciate the jumpiness of my dad's music. I had occasionally thought of repeating the listening session and now regretted never having bothered to actually do it.

Hardly a day went by since my father's death that I didn't want to phone him with yet another question about some subject that had never germinated with me. He had been my resource for questions about any aspect of home repair that didn't involve plumbing, plastering, electrical work, roofing, drywalling, or sawing more than a couple of boards, but he could always recommend the correct service professional to hire. He could wallpaper, if you gave him a week to do a room. He was a demon with a screwdriver, too, regaling me as a boy with his skill prying open a paint can or jimmying loose a stuck storm window, and few could match his sidewalk-edging diligence. As a teen, I briefly tried to shovel the walk with a level of thoroughness that left nothing for him to touch up when he came home from work, but every attempt was futile. He always found enough stray flakes to shove around until Mom called him in for dinner.

I hated to admit it, but for every memory of my father from my youth, I had at least ten of my mother. The reason probably had to do with my own low-key personality, which had absorbed my dad's talent for remaining in the background but couldn't reproduce his glow. While he had been a quiet source of strength and stability to my more easily irritated mother, his generous nature had decided to skip my set of genes. And the sourness that occasionally visited my mom was a permanent boarder with me.

I remembered him once coming into my bedroom to comfort me during a thunderstorm even though my mom had suggested — in a manner consistent with her upbringing in a large German-American family — "Just let him howl." The few moments spent tucking me in had delayed my parents' departure to their monthly cribbage-club dinner by an amount too insignificant to clock, but that brief encounter had stayed with me for a lifetime. My mom, of course, had been kind to me, too. I had fond recollections of her pulling me in a red wagon to the A&P grocery store down the street — probably hoping to exchange me for a half-pint of whipping cream.

Now it was my mom who needed comforting. Nothing brought her joy anymore. The presence of friends and family, the absence of friends and family, brilliant sun-drenched days, miserable storms, TV shows, Sunday Mass, and pestilence only served to remind her that her husband was every bit as gone from her life as he had been at the moment of his death. I tried mentioning that a grief support group sounded as if it might be fun. My comment got the reception it deserved.

I thought deeply about these things — if *thought* is the right term for wheel spinning that accomplished nothing except keeping me awake—until Moobie wandered up and charitably licked my hand. She collapsed in a heap, allowing me to pet her until she was purring like an overweight dynamo and my mental battery began to discharge. A car shot by. The hum of its tires gradually faded as the car clung politely to the asphalt.

I FELT WOOZY from yet another night of not getting enough sleep. I was glad that it was a Saturday, and Moobie had allowed us to slumber until seven A.M. "No she didn't," Linda said as we drank our coffee. "She jumped up on the bed at least five times this morning. I had to swish her off with my feet."

The geese erupted in happy honks when I let them loose in the yard, and their bugling helped dispel the low-hanging clouds that persisted from the previous night. Rarely was I stuck in a gloomy mood that a few minutes with Liza and Hailey couldn't brighten. After filling their dishes with food, I stepped over the backyard fence and trudged down the hill toward the seasonal pond, setting out little piles of scratch feed for the visiting wood ducks, who flew off with nervous whistles. We had started feeding the wild ducks when Linda was rounding up our brood one spring day and noticed two skittish extra mallards. The next few afternoons, she left food on the lawn for them. But after watching them pace back and forth like mechanical shooting-gallery ducks just beyond the backyard fence, Linda decided that they probably preferred dining at a farther remove from us.

To our surprise, Mr. and Mrs. Mallard began sharing their evening meal with a male wood duck. In the ten years that we had lived in our house, we had only briefly glimpsed these spectacular birds, whose crested iridescent green heads with bold white stripes looked as if they had been meticulously hand-painted to suit the tastes of a Chinese mandarin. Before we knew it, up to fourteen male and female woodies crowded our hillside buffet. To reduce squabbling among the patrons, we distributed the scratch feed in numerous small servings. But even this didn't prevent a pugnacious male from staking out the center of the restaurant and doing his utmost to chase away all comers except his mate. Wisely, the macho wood duck avoided showing up in the afternoon, when his actions wouldn't have impressed the wild turkeys that had also discovered alfresco eating.

Slapping a mosquito that was supping on my forehead, I climbed back into our yard just in time to see a man bending over Linda's sunflower patch.

"Hope you don't mind me just dropping in," master gardener Henry called with far more enthusiasm than the early hour warranted. "As ye sow, so shall ye reap, so here I am," he quipped.

Liza and Hailey bolted across the yard toward the unfamiliar voice, necks outstretched, wings flapping, and raising an unholy cacophony. By the time their complaints had died down, I'd eliminated the shouting distance between Henry and me. I didn't get close enough, however, to determine if hops and yeast played a role in his morning regimen.

"I had a little trouble with the soil tests," he told me.

"What's wrong with the lab?"

"Oh, I'm doing them myself. But the soil sat in my sinks all day without settling enough for me to do the tests. It makes me think there might be something odd about your soil."

"You've got special sinks for soil testing?"

"No," he said quickly, "just the ones in the kitchen and bathroom. If I get another customer, I'll have to use the bathtub."

I nodded as if this were the kind of conversation I had with people all the time and edged back toward the house for breakfast, wishing I could give my dad a call to hear his dry chuckle as I told him about this guy. But the day's annoyances had just begun, and I needed all the nourishment I could get. A couple of hours later, I was outdoors again greeting my old classmate Eileen, her friend Kate, and Kate's spoiled house duck, Louie, then standing aside as Eileen barged past me toward the house, leaving Kate, spoiled house duck Louie, and me on the front lawn.

"So where are all the little ones?" Eileen asked as I hurried to catch up with her.

Although she had never been in our house before, Eileen simply followed her ears to locate the dining room, where the pets lived. Dusty called out a hearty "Hello" when he heard the front door slam shut and added a howled "Woo!" Ollie had already been squawking his usual high-pitched chirp. Howard complained about the noise with a steady round of cooing.

"That's Bertie over there," I told her, trailing behind.

"Peewee!" she exclaimed.

"He is little, isn't he?" I stammered, taken aback by her exuberance. While Eileen unfastened the cage door to pet the bunny that had been sleeping peacefully, I mentioned to Linda that a woman named Kate was standing in front of our house looking sad and clutching a duck. I continued the introductions by pointing to the Checker Giant rabbit one cage over from Bertie. "This big fellow is Walter."

"Peewee!" Eileen cried again, flaring her nostrils and baring her teeth in a way that made me wonder if the bun on the back of her head was wound too tightly.

"And this is my good friend Stanley Sue," I ventured.

"What a little peewee!" she shouted.

Eileen met the rest of the birds, excitedly *peewee*ing each of them in turn. While these short outbursts were a welcome change from extended ramblings about old grade school classmates, I didn't know how to process them. "It's good to see you again, Eileen," I finally told her in my best bland funeral-home delivery. I almost asked her what was new, until I realized that I'd be throwing opening the door to a vast storeroom of information tethered to my distant past.

"Did you ever get a chance to visit my mom?" I asked. "To watch a television program with her? Remember that?" When she treated me to a blank and somewhat chickenesque stare, I said, "There are several more peewees outdoors, if you'd like to see them."

"Kate brought her duck."

"You told her that we were only meeting Louie today, didn't you? We talked about that on the phone. We weren't planning on keeping Louie." The question answered itself when I looked out the window just in time to see Linda guiding a thirty-something woman cradling a large white duck into our backyard pen. As soon as Kate set down the duck and tried to walk away, it ran quacking toward her through the pen door.

I led Eileen down the porch steps and stood back as she ecstatically greeted our ducks and geese. "I guess Louie would rather be back home," I told Kate.

"Louie's a Lulu," Linda informed me.

"The neighbors won't let me keep him," Kate said.

"How do you know?"

"She quacks like a girl," Linda said.

"They complained to the landlord. We live in an apartment, and Louie has gotten too loud for the bathroom."

"It's the girls that are loud," Linda explained.

"I'll say."

"Eileen told me how nice your ducks have it, and this is better than I ever imagined."

"Eileen hasn't seen them before, but thanks," I said.

"I won't worry about him so much knowing he's here."

"You can visit her whenever you want," Linda said. "You don't even have to ask."

"No point in that," I added with what I hoped was an edge to my voice.

With Linda's help, Kate succeeded in shutting the unhappy Lulu inside the pen. Never having witnessed a duck tantrum before, our two female geese and six female ducks gave the newcomer a wide berth as she churned her legs and struggled in vain against the first fence she had ever encountered in her life, wondering why she couldn't just walk through that which she could see through. Male ducks Stewart and Trevor in the adjacent pen enjoyed the spectacle and chattered happily about the arrival of a bodacious waterfowl babe. When Lulu unleashed the most plaintive series of quacks ever to simultaneously pierce my heart and eardrums, Kate turned without a word and headed back toward her car.

"I guess it was too much for her," Eileen observed with a rueful smile.

While I was still debating whether or not to go after Kate and see if she was okay, Linda reacted at once. "Everything's going to be fine," she promised, stooping down to console the distraught white duck. But Lulu regarded Linda as an impediment, not a comforter. She darted to the front of the pen, where Linda wasn't blocking her view of the weedy vista where her owner had last been seen. Spurned, Linda murmured a few more phrases of encouragement before disappearing through the backyard gate in search of Kate.

Just to divert my attention from Lulu's pleas, I found myself asking Eileen, "So how is it that you know someone who keeps a pet duck in her bathroom?"

"I met your sisters at your dad's funeral, and one of them told me about your ducks." She winced and stepped away from the squawking commotion. "I had lunch with Mary Vielbig the following Wednesday—Mary from your freshman German class at CC. I told her about running into you at the funeral home just like that, and I asked her if she knew anyone who had pet ducks, but she's too upset about her divorce to even think about anything else. 'Ask me about lawyers,' she told me. But she thought her brother-in-law might know somebody, and she gave me his phone number. He's the manager at a Home Depot, and he told Mary that farmers go in there all the time. But it was really funny, because it turns out that the guy who lives across the street from him is related to Kate, and that's how I happened to meet her, just sort of by accident."

"You could almost call it a coincidence," I replied, though I had ended up concentrating on Lulu's misery after all and hearing my father's voice in my head saying, *Now that's what I call a duck out of water.*

Eileen's arcane web of interpersonal connections baffled me as much as her sudden interest in us. Most people had innocuous hobbies like stamp collecting or window peeping. Hers was pitching a tent in the past. A flick of her head indicated that Linda had rounded the corner of the house with Kate, who was carrying an awkward bundle in her arms. I feared it was another duck, until she began unwrapping it.

"These are Louie's things," she told me with a heavy finality. She passed me a padded blanket. "This is the bed he sleeps on in the corner of the bathroom next to the register, and this is his stuffed bear, Peabody." I handed blanket and bear to Linda, since I needed both hands free to receive a thirty-inch-tall mirror with a yellow pine frame. "He loves to look at himself, especially in the morning when he first wakes up." At the sound of Kate's voice,

Lulu ratcheted up the intensity of her quacks. She darted from one side of the wooden door to the other, trying to figure out how to get to her.

The cloth items smelled of fabric softener, and the mirror was spotless except for my sweaty fingerprints. I was on the verge of telling Kate that if we put Lulu's possessions inside the pen, they would be soaked with wading-pool water and streaked with mud within the hour. But giving us custody of her house duck was as serious to her as it was incidental to the mysterious Eileen. I kept my mouth shut long enough for Linda to ask, "How did you ever end up with such a darling duck?"

"My daughter Geri and I were touring a farm in Indiana where you can bottle feed baby pigs and goats. There were ducks and chickens wandering all over. As we were leaving, she found an egg sitting all by itself in the grass near the parking lot. She ended up taking it home, and it was her idea to try to hatch it."

"Did you know it was a duck egg?" Eileen asked. "I wouldn't know a duck egg if you broke one on my head."

I made a quick scan of the yard to see if one was handy.

"We had no idea. I certainly didn't expect it to hatch, but I borrowed an incubator from Geri's school, because she was so into the whole thing, and before we knew it or were in any way prepared to be duck parents, Louie hatched."

"Aw," said Linda. "She sure thinks a lot of you."

"I think he wants his mirror. That usually calms him down."

"I think she wants you," Linda said.

Kate's body language told me that she was an animal person. It wasn't just that she crouched down to duck level to talk to Lulu and introduce herself to the curious geese. You could see that she had handed herself over to the birds. Her pupils dilated, she smiled, and everything about her manner expressed openness. I saw nothing of this in Eileen, who clearly loved drama more than people or animals.

I opened the pen door just wide enough for Kate to dart inside. Even though Lulu had been frantic for a reunion, Kate had to chase her through a flurry of complaining geese and ducks, who were sure that she was after them. But Lulu relaxed as soon as Kate picked her up and started stroking her orange beak. I leaned the mirror up against one of the posts while Linda arranged the blanket and the bear around the mirror. The items struck me as a sad tableau of a classic "odd duck" story.

"Geri has been quite adult about all of this, and she's only ten," said Kate. "She was the one who told me, 'Mom, Louie shouldn't have to live his whole life in the bathtub.' I think I'm having a harder time with this than she is. Eileen told me what wonderful people both of you were. She said she's known Bob for years and years."

"With one or two small gaps," I pointed out.

THAT SAME EVENING, a different sort of duck problem reared its head when Victor bit me on the leg. He had been shadowing me ever since I'd shooed the ducks and hens into the barn and made my rounds doling out fresh food and water. I had positioned the push broom between us, fending him off in the same manner in which a lion tamer wields a chair. But Victor sidled up behind me while I was preoccupied with Linda's discovery of a broken reflector post on the shoulder of the road.

I was thinking about the accident from the previous night, hypothesizing that a cousin of Eileen's named Elmo was driving home after an exhausting evening guzzling beers and bragging about a dove-hunting trip. He'd managed to keep from nodding off until his cell phone rang and Eileen began excitedly relating an anecdote about a friend of an old kindergarten friend. The road took a turn, but Elmo's car did not. He awoke when his tires hit the gravel, just in time to drop the phone, slam on the brakes, snap a reflector post, and holler, "Jeepers!" as the headlight of his SUV disappeared in a mist of shattered glass. "I know, I couldn't believe it either," Eileen's voice replied from the floor. Veering sharply back onto the asphalt, he braked again to avoid repeating the mishap on the opposite shoulder, and then in a state of heightened wakefulness continued on his way as the chattering Eileen continued on hers.

I decided that this was how the accident must have happened, even if I couldn't prove that one of Eileen's relatives was actually involved. But my reconstruction failed to impress Victor, who seized the opportunity to indiscreetly seize my calf.

You might think that a duck bite is an inoffensive nip. Certainly a Muscovy's beak doesn't compare with the jaws of a crocodile, pit bull, or African grey parrot. But there's a lot going on behind it. Other domesticated ducks—from the practically goose-size White Pekin to the diminutive Call Duck—are shy offshoots of the familiar wild mallard. But except for a few changes in coloration, the Muscovy barrels into the barnyard with his primal wild Muscovy roots intact. He's a nightmare version of a duck, a Frankenstein's fowl with a lurching, menacing walk, heavily clawed feet, muscular wings, and a thuggish demeanor that fits his fleshy red face mask. He hisses like a snake, pants like an obscene phone caller, thrashes his thick tail like an alligator, throws back his head and grins like a horror movie villain, and likes nothing better than to sneak up on you and inflict a painful hematoma. And we had three Muscovies: Victor and Hamilton, who traded places as top dog, and Ramone, who showed surprising reserve with us despite his bluster.

When Victor bit me, I whirled around with the broom, pressing it against his chest and shoving him away. Instead of retreating, he came straight at me and grabbed a beakful of my pantleg. "What's wrong with you?" I demanded, pushing him harder with the broom. He reeled backward, flapping his wings, flashing his yellow eyes, and charging with outstretched neck. I didn't strike him with the broom. I used it to slow his momentum as he came at me; then I pushed back, intending to show him who was boss and discourage him from ever attacking again. But he fluttered in the shadows, set his toenails against the cement floor, and launched himself again. Each push from me stoked the fires of his increasing rage, and his emotion ignited mine.

The light from a single overhead bulb gave the barn a theatrical ambience. While the other birds probably didn't as much as glance up from their food dishes, I imagined that a gallery of hens perched on the stanchions and ducks settled in the straw watched us like the patrons of a cockfight. Both of our standings were at stake. Victor kept coming at me, and I kept pushing him back. Our conflict had begun as a struggle for dominance, more ritual than reality; but from the escalating intensity of Victor's lunges, I saw that he was now protecting himself from a perceived threat to his safety. And he had read my anger correctly. I would just as soon have grabbed him by the throat if I thought that it would stop him.

The whole time our fight was taking place, a tiny voice in the background clamored against the clatter. At first, I easily blocked it out. My reptile brain generated red noise as I focused on avoiding getting bitten. But finally the words came through with moral clarity. The voice asked, *Do you realize you're having a shoving match with a duck?*

I'm not thinking right, I answered. *Since my father died, I've gotten as nutty as Eileen. And, by the way, have we been introduced?*

Interrupting my internal dialogue, Victor came at me from across the floor. I lowered the broom and backed away. He surprised me by breaking off the charge, contenting himself with panting to the air, wagging his tail, and opening and closing his beak. I couldn't tell if Victor was dancing a victory dance, but somehow I didn't think so. To my left, Hamilton started hissing, but he bypassed me, waddling up to my opponent and joining him in an elevation of snaking necks.

I loved these ducks. That's what bothered me so much. For ten years, I had lived closely with animals. I didn't expect them to act like people and was frequently happy that they couldn't if they tried. I was patient with them. Guilty about the whole idea of confinement and control, I did my best never to flaunt my advantages of holding the keys to the larder and the cage. Despite my oodles of empathy for them, it had taken precious little to turn me into Elaine's cousin Elmo.

"Sorry," I told Victor, who held his spot in the middle of the floor. "Sorry," I said to the hens and ducks who had witnessed my equivalent of a panting-and-hissing display.

On my way back to the house, I found Linda inside the backyard duck pen. She had set up a plastic chair next to the door and was feeding Lulu dandelion leaves at the end of an outstretched arm. The other ducks stayed away. Goose sisters Liza and Hailey were too shy to accept the food from her hand but bold enough to nibble the belt loops of her jumper. Above the murmur of goose voices I heard Linda singing, "Oh, Dear, What Could the Matter Be." Everyone seemed happy, and I suspected that the barn birds had already dismissed the kind of squabble that probably occurred among the Muscovies every day. But I was so keyed up, I half wished Eileen would call and sap my nervous energy with a few *peewees*.

A FOUR-YEAR-OLD Chinese girl met us in the foyer of the Chinese buffet in Ionia and asked us with grave formality, "Would you like smoking or nonsmoking?"

Linda's back trouble prevented her from sitting for any length of time, so we usually couldn't eat at a restaurant unless a waitress on roller skates whisked our orders to us as soon as we walked in the door. Buffets were a different matter, since we never had to wait for our food. Along with the expected Chinese dishes, the Peking Happiness surprised the diner with such Cantonese delights as squash, corn on the cob, pepperoni pizza, ham-and-cheese-stuffed mushroom caps, French-fried onion rings, and an inspired sushi roll that substituted a plug of hot dog or dill pickle for the anticipated shrimp or yellowfin tuna.

"We want to be up there," said Linda, indicating a raised area. I settled in facing Linda and a pair of televisions above the waitress station, and Linda sat facing me and a pair of televisions above the windows. One TV in each pair had the sound turned on. The other used closed captioning, allowing me to read the text of an Aleve commercial while I picked at bamboo shoots.

When Linda returned to our table from the buffet, I noticed that she listed slightly to one side, and I didn't think it was simply the weight of her plate. Her back pain had flared up again, though she didn't complain. "Henry Murphy called with the soil test results this morning," she told me as I marveled at the sheer amount of food on her dish.

"You know, they let you go back as many times as you want."

"Everything looks so good," she said, picking up her corn on the cob. "Anyway, he was quite proud of the results. He said that our soil contained zero amount of phosphorus, zero amount of nitrogen, and zero amount of potash."

"That sounds pretty low."

Problems with the closed-captioning software caused Tom Brokaw to spew a stream of asterisks, percentage signs, and exclamation points. The glitch matched the language of a heavy man in a tight fitting T-shirt one table away, who indelicately dressed down his grade school son for stuffing himself on desserts rather than entrées.

"He was quite triumphant about it. I said I didn't think it was possible to have zero phosphorus, zero nitrogen, and zero potash—my gardens wouldn't be so lush. But he was very insistent that his results were correct."

"Did you ask him about the blood-alcohol test results?"

Reaching behind her back, Linda extracted an object resembling a serving of uncooked calf's liver. The gel pack hadn't come from the store in this distended condition, but it had earned its amorphous shape by being repeatedly plopped down upon, stepped on, and, from all appearances, run over by a school bus. Its original plastic envelope had burst long ago, and Linda had encased it in a series of sandwich bags. She squeezed it a couple of times and announced, "I've got to zap my heat pack."

I was happy that the restaurant offered a self-serve microwave, or she might have had to explain to our four-year-old hostess that she wasn't smuggling in a bizarre food item that somehow hadn't made it into the buffet. Too many times I had witnessed Linda handing the visceral-looking pouch to a terrified teenager behind a fast-food restaurant counter and asking him or her to please warm it up.

"I got quite the phone call today while you were at the grocery store," I said after she'd returned with the gel pack, knocked her lumbar cushion to the floor, dropped the gel pack while picking up the cushion, and finally managed to arrange them both behind her. "My mom called. She lost her purse."

"Again?"

"She claimed that somebody had come into her house and taken it. When I told her I'd be right over to help her find it, she said, 'Joan's here already. I was just wondering if you knew anything about it disappearing.'"

A large, white, inoffensive non-Muscovy duck appeared on a commercial. "That looks just like Lulu," Linda pointed out. "She thinks you took her purse?"

"I'll bet she doesn't bite people," I said. "I'm talking about the duck. Joan came on the phone and said she'd found the purse stuck under the couch cushion. Same place she found it the other week." I gestured toward the thickset man whose sulking son refused to lift his fork. "How'd you like to have that for a family?"

"Did you tell her she needs to keep it in one place?"

"I told her, 'I'll put a hook in the front vestibule for your purse, and you'll always know exactly where it is.' But she said, 'I don't want my purse out in plain sight. Someone will come in and take it.'"

"Didn't one of your sisters say it sounded like she might have dementia?"

I'd heard that suggestion before, and I didn't care for it. "She's a little forgetful, and she's upset about my dad," I muttered to my plate.

"I didn't tell you the rest of the Henry Murphy story. I called the DNR and asked them if it was even possible for soil to have zero phosphorus, zero nitrogen, and zero potash. They told me absolutely not. You wouldn't even get numbers like that with sand, so I called Henry back and told him that he must have done the test wrong, but he wouldn't listen. He said his test was right and our soil needed lots of work."

I raised my face from my stir-fry. "We're not using him for anything anymore, are we?"

Linda shook her head. "But I think we should send the poor guy twenty dollars. Just for doing the test."

I WANDERED INTO the backyard in more of a mental fog than usual. Instead of giving the chickadees that hung acrobatically from the bird feeder the attention they deserved, I watched an epic internal newsreel about my mom, worrying what would happen to her in the absence of my father's stabilizing presence. Trying to deal with all these brand-new concerns, I had begun feeling like a duck out of water myself. The door of the girls' pen was cracked open and a body sat on Linda's green plastic chair. Through the curtain of preoccupation, I did a zombie-stagger down the hill and called listlessly, "Hi, sweetie."

Kate's face flashed me a frown; then she laughed. "Your wife said it was okay."

I caught myself blushing. "Sorry. I was talking to a goose."

She cradled Lulu in her arms. "He didn't seem to recognize me at first. Did you, Louie-Lou?"

I was embarrassed again as I noted that Lulu's blanket, bear, and mirror were wet and covered with dirt. "She's been a little confused, but I think she'll do okay," I said, though I had strong doubts about the duck's progress. Kate nodded.

"Did you take the day off from work?" I blurted out without weighing the intrusiveness of my question. "I only work mornings," I added hastily. "Unless you count what I do here as work."

"I'm an attorney with a realty company, and the nonlawyers are at a seminar," Kate answered. For a flash, I could see her as a lawyer—she did have a sharp-boned, intelligent face—but Lulu's nervousness distracted me. The duck quacked and made a move to hop off Kate's lap. Kate covered the duck's head with one hand and petted her back with the other.

Although Kate continued talking about her job, I missed the meaning behind the words and concentrated on the sound of her voice instead. Her nasal twang reminded me of the convenience-store worker who had wished me good morning a few minutes ago through the speaker on the gas pump as I filled my car. I knew the circuit worked both ways, but I hadn't yet reached the point in my life where I was comfortable answering a gas pump's greeting. I also had a difficult time separating Kate from Eileen's foolishness, which wasn't exactly fair on my part. But she had hidden a large white duck in an apartment bathroom.

"She's having a hard time, isn't she?" Kate asked me.

Eileen's unfathomable motives even affected how I viewed Lulu. I felt sorry for the poor creature, who spent much of her day pacing and calling for the owner that she considered to be her mother. Three days was an eternity in duck time, however, and I had expected her to accept her duckness and join the flock by now. While I was glad that Lulu didn't act like Victor, I wished that she possessed a little of his grit.

"She's eating well," I assured Kate. "And we did see her in the pool a couple of times. Nobody's picking on her, either. Her size intimidates the other ducks, and Liza and Hailey aren't the least bit aggressive."

Lulu started squirming again, Kate let her hop off her lap, then stood up and joined me outside the pen. I shut the door, fastening both latches and wondering whether my mom had found the house keys that she'd reported lost. Instead of running up to the fence to see where her owner had gone, Lulu wandered over to the girls preening near the back of the pool. She looked so much like our white Pekin Richie, who lived in the barn, that I wished I could put the two together. For all his gentleness, however, Richie was too much of a ladies' man to trust with the gals.

"I can tell a definite difference in her," Kate told me sadly. "She's already left me, even if she doesn't fully realize it yet. I'm glad I didn't bring Geri."

"No, I guess that wouldn't have been good," I agreed. Her perceptiveness impressed me. I had paid too much attention to Lulu's larger behavior and missed the more subtle signs that she was starting to fit in. "It's tough to lose a friend," I told her as a chickadee called his wide-awake song from the roof of our milk house.

CHAPTER 5

....

Wild Things

For the first time in my forty-eight years of life, I found myself wishing that my mother was more like a duck as I watched Lulu quickly get over the loss of her "mom." Understandably enough, my mother remained a long way from reconciling herself to losing my dad. After having tea with her and trying on a few of my father's sweaters, I decided to check with Mrs. Teany, across the street, to determine whether she was helping or hindering the situation.

I felt stupid standing on Judy Teany's porch and even worse when she insisted that I sit in a ridiculously large recliner in the living room. As its great striped bulk engulfed me, I whisked back forty years in time to the house then owned by the widowed Mabel Kuipers and my faux-pas asking, "Why did Mr. Kuipers die?" as my feet dangled from her couch. I could have phoned Judy instead of dropping by, but I needed to figure out whether she was acting strangely or my mom had been making things up. Her alleged remark about eating in the basement to avoid seeing the light in my mom's kitchen nettled me, as did my mom's recent claim that Mrs.

Teany had walked into the garage and walked out with my father's grass seeder without asking if she could borrow it.

"Would you care for a Little Debbie cake?" Judy asked. "We have maple cream sandwiches."

I thanked her, no. "Mr. Teany's gone?"

"Don went out to mail a letter. I hope he's okay." She lifted the clock from the coffee table, then set it back down on its well-worn spot on the fabric-covered mat. "You never know what might happen," she sighed with the arch of a penciled eyebrow.

I didn't remember the dark woodwork throughout the room, though it may only have seemed dark in the midday indoor dusk. She'd bunched the sheers so tightly across her curtain rods, they could hardly be called sheers any longer. They were more like paper towels soaking up the sun. This was, I realized, the first time I'd ever spoken to Judy without my mother's presence. And except for an exchange of pleasantries at the funeral home, this was the first time I'd spoken to her at all in a decade. We had a lot of catching up to do.

"Maybe he was stopping for shrimp," she concluded.

"Do you ever go to the Wooden Bridge Fish Market? Up on Plainfield."

"Oh. I thought I heard a car door." After a moment, she looked at me expectantly.

"The Wooden Bridge Fish Market."

She smiled as if I had complimented her.

The problem with determining whether Judy had run off the rails was that nearly everyone struck me as provisionally sane at best. I too readily read a character disorder into Judy's display of a teapot-shaped wall plaque with a hanging wooden tab that could be flipped to indicate whether GRANDMA was HAPPY or UNHAPPY. I found myself wishing that my sister Joan could have tagged along to provide balance. My dad would have made me laugh. A year earlier, he had told me, "That Judy Teany has been sending money to televangelists. I think she's afraid of the end of the world." This definitely struck me as loopy, but I couldn't link neurosis with pilfering gardening implements—otherwise my barn would be swollen with stolen lawn mowers.

Our halting conversation dramatically improved when my dull comment about how the neighborhood had changed over the years led to a good story about my dad. "I came home from the bank one day and saw your poor father trapped by Mr. Brink while he was trying to wash his car," Judy told me. Brink was the barely coherent old bore from the next block who had made a habit of sneaking up on my father while he was doing yard work and informing him, "That's how I got my start," as the launching point for a rambling discourse about his sales career.

"I was so sorry for him," Judy said. "Your dad was way too nice to tell the old coot to buzz off, like Don would have, so I rushed inside and called your mom and told her, 'Bette, stick your head out the front door and tell Bob he's got an important phone call.' He was so pleased that I'd rescued him, he invited us over for a highball later."

"I remember that," I laughed. "From then on, we sort of kept watch on him and always called him in when Mr. Brink surprised him. But he didn't like it if we made it really obvious, even though Mr. Brink was too far gone to catch on. He started talking to bushes not long after that."

We continued reminiscing for a while, recalling the stark or pastoral names of neighbors who had moved away or passed away: Gray, Glass, Edge, Rotz, Meadows, and Greenfield. Finally I asked her, "I was wondering if you'd seen my mom recently."

With a deep intake of air, she raised her large body from the couch as if the subject was too important to address while seated and headed toward a window. "We just think the world of Bette."

"She mentioned something to me about a grass-seed spreader."

"Anything of ours she's free to use, of course."

"You don't have one of hers?"

"No, but Don could spread some seed. We've got a regular hardware store in the basement. He should be home any moment if you want to ask him for help."

I joined her at the window. When she pulled back the curtain to gaze out at the curb, the daylight nearly blinded me. "You don't eat dinner in the basement, do you? The one with the hardware store."

"Why, no." She let the curtain slip through her fingers.

I pulled it open again. "You can't even see her kitchen from here, can you?" I squinted at the bright stripe of Judy's front sidewalk.

"What's that, dear?"

"My mom's kitchen. You can't see into her kitchen from here."

I noticed her attitude shifting from one of concern over my mother to vague wariness about me, but I didn't feel comfortable repeating the quote from my mother. "I just meant, I was wondering if you could sort of keep an eye on her."

"We always do," she beamed. "We liked your dad so much. It's sad thinking about your mom all alone now over there." She astonished me by making a clicking sound as she pretended to turn off a switch on the side of her head. "So I just don't think about it."

I CAME HOME CONFUSED. Maybe Judy Teany had swiped my mother's grass-seed spreader after all. My parents hadn't used the grass-seed spreader for years, and my mom certainly didn't need it now. So why would she concoct a fantasy about the

underemployed, unloved grass-seed spreader instead of the far
more popular hose, rake, broom, string trimmer, hedge clippers,
bucket, hoe, or shovel? My head hurt to think about it. Fortunately
an endless succession of animal chores prevented me from prob-
ing the bottomless pit of my mom's and Mrs. Teany's idiosyncra-
sies too deeply.

As soon as Linda cleared the table after dinner, I sat down on
the plush and beaten chair next to Stanley Sue's cage, never imag-
ining that the chair was keeping a secret from me. Stanley Sue
dropped the peanut that she had been cracking, climbed down
from the top of her cage, and stepped onto the arm of the chair.
Using her beak to anchor her upper body, she clambered down
to the cushion to stand next to my leg. She could have flown the
same distance in one-tenth of the time, but she always chose the
mountaineer's approach.

"Would you like me to scratch your head?" I asked her. She bent
her head as if to let me, and when my hand descended, raised it
again as if to bite. This was all part of a nightly ritual, but the unusual activity inside the chair was not.

Across the room, Linda admonished Dusty, "Be nicer to your
Donald" as he lunged at the vinyl Donald Duck figure he had
long ago decapitated. "Who's this?" she asked, squeaking a bar-
bell-shaped dog toy with a monkey's face on each end. "Is this
your Opie?"

I sat forward in the chair. My attention was riveted on Stanley
Sue, who had begun to preen with precise jerking motions that
reminded me of our failed mechanical bird sentry. She showed
impressive control over her feathers. She spread her tail as easily
as I would spread my fingers, reached back with her beak to grab
some oil from her preen gland, then applied it to the feathers on
her back, which popped up like rows of shingles in a windstorm.

With quick strokes she smoothed and arranged one feather after another. Finally she lowered her head in a sign that she would allow me to rub her neck. As I brushed her skin with my finger-tip, she made nibbling motions in an expression of satisfaction. I started to lose myself in her. I fell into the fish eye facing me, jumped to the curved plane of her upper beak, and was about to wrap myself around her grey reptilian toes when Linda cried out, "A mouse, there's a mouse running up your chair!"

Hopping up, I extended my hand to Stanley Sue and spoke the command that every parrot owner recognizes and that every parrot must obey. I said, "Step up," ordering her to step onto my hand. She ignored me, turned, and climbed the chair arm, then scaled her cage bars to the door and popped inside to eat a sun-flower seed.

I'd gotten over my fear of mice the year I had moved to this house and discovered that the basement was a favorite sightseeing spot for hornets, spiders, earwigs, snakes, chipmunks, squirrels, the occasional well-traveled Norway rat, and, most of all, mice. I still hadn't embraced the concept of vermin jumping out at me, though. So I lifted the cushion warily, beheld an unpleasant secret inside the chair, and felt the blood drain to my feet.

"What?" asked Linda. "What?"

A writhing mass of tiny pink bodies beckoned "hello" from a hole in the upholstery that mama mouse had excavated. For all I knew, the entire chair was stuffed to the bursting point with wriggling, sightless entities that resembled mammalian slugs. I replaced the cushion and turned toward the rain that was rolling off the leaves of our hackberry tree and had darkened the plumage of the goldfinch on our feeder.

"A mouse nest," I stammered, though this failed to do justice to the extraordinary sight. Had the mice been dead, my shock

wouldn't have been so great. It wasn't just that a test-tube culture
of rodents bloomed in our dining room. It was that I'd seen the
creatures in a distressingly helpless state of being. I'd inadvertently glimpsed an unpleasant process usually hidden from human eyes, like the secretion of bile by the liver or the production
of canned cat food.

"Don't hurt them."

"I'm not going to hurt them. I don't want anything to do with
them. But they can't stay here."

Linda looked at me in shock. To her way of thinking, if there
was anything worse than stumbling upon undulating, pop-eyed,
furless larvae in a dining room chair, it was depriving the pop-
eyed, furless larvae of their opportunity to undulate. "Well, we
have to let the mother finish raising them, at least."

A tinkling crash came from behind us. We knew the sound, so
neither of us took any notice. Dusty had climbed from his cage top
to the plant hanger attached to the windowsill, snagged the much-
abused wind chime, and thrown it to the floor. He would do that
two more times before calling it a night.

"You do see a problem with that, don't you? When she's finished
raising them, they'll make themselves at home, and the next thing
you know, we'll have mouse nests in our mattress."

Linda put her hands on her hips, eliciting a squeak from Opie
between her fingers. "We can't let them just die."

"How about if we move the nursery to the barn?"

Linda decided that this would be okay as long as she tagged
along to make sure that mother mouse didn't abandon her chair
in transit. I hadn't seen the mom when I'd raised the cushion,
and by the time I flipped the chair sideways to fit it through the
front door and lurched it down the porch steps without a sign of
her fecund form, I decided she must have high-tailed it while I'd

been begging Stanley Sue to step up. We moved briskly over the slippery grass, but just as I huffed and puffed my way around the massive evergreen within sight of the barn door, Linda hollered, "Stop, stop! There she goes, put down the chair."

I was happy to oblige. Although the chair wasn't exactly heavy, I was even more of a lightweight and gratefully set it down. The rain increased intensity, gleeful for the chance to drench a pair of mouse abusers.

"We have to leave it here so that she knows where it is," said Linda.

"In this?" I flicked the wet hair from my eyes. "For how long?"

"At least overnight."

I couldn't really argue with her, since I didn't see the value in returning a mouse-infested chair to the dining room. The next thing I knew, Linda had taken my hand. "Dear Lord," she said, closing her eyes and bowing her head. "Please let the mouse find her babies in the chair." The enormousness of the moment humbled me. Despite all of the people who had preceded us over thousands of millennia of human history, I was confident that no one had ever spoken such words in prayer before.

THE BABY MICE would probably stay dry. Their nest was deep within the chair, and the rain had started to taper off. But some of the hens in the pen behind the barn stood outside complaining about the downpour instead of marching through the open door. During pleasant, sunny weather, these same contrarians typically huddled indoors in the gloom, muttering to themselves. The worst offender was a buff-colored Buff Orpington named Buffy. After I had shooed the other soggy chickens into the barn, Buffy remained perched on a rock, wearing a quizzical expression that revealed either profound philosophical insight or

vacuity noteworthy even by poultry standards. She finally straggled in just before I closed the doors and began scattering kitchen
scraps on the cement floor. The other birds fell upon the treats
with gusto, but Buffy sauntered through the lettuce, peas, and
macaroni working out algebraic equations in her head. Then she
turned and pecked at a bar of light from the window.

Hamilton the Muscovy darted from the shadows to try to attach
himself to my calf. He was the new king of the barn. My old neme-
sis Victor had started to molt, and Hamilton was taking advantage
of Victor's depleted energy level by crowning himself and banish-
ing his rival to the back of the barn. I discovered Victor hiding behind our old pottery kiln. His scraggly wings bristled with quills
that would soon flower into pure white feathers. Squatting beside
him, I took a sandwich bag from my shirt pocket and turned it
inside out to deliver a few chunks of watermelon. He ate the fruit
greedily and with a tolerance for my presence that I half took to
be gratitude. If he recalled our recent brawl with the push broom,
he didn't let the memory get in the way of his favorite treat. But I
didn't stay too close to him, out of respect for his pride — and his
reach.

A scuffle brought me to my feet. Shy Muscovy Ramone was
running panicky figure eights in the center of the barn with
Hamilton's beak clamped to his tail. Even Buffy took notice and
flapped to higher ground. Blocking their progress with my infa-
mous broom, I managed to grab Hamilton, pull him off Ramone,
and pin his wings to his body so that he wouldn't knock me out
when I picked him up. Snaking his neck backward, he put a vise
grip on a fleshy fold of my forearm before I could safely set him
down again. I shook the arm that he had bitten, and he took the
movement as a provocation until I stepped back and reached for
my plastic pitcher. I distracted him by scattering bits of bread. As

the other ducks and hens converged on the fresh goodies, Hamilton came up with the idea of terrorizing Richie by preventing him from getting to the food.

I tossed a handful of bread directly under Hamilton's beak, then flipped a few pieces over Richie's head. Hamilton ignored the bread near him and advanced on Richie's share instead. I stepped between them with the broom, then turned to present Richie with a private helping. But in the waterfowl world, big birds just don't help smaller birds. Instead of viewing me as his rescuer, he sized up my height and my general birdlike characteristics as evidence that I was bent on chasing him as well. He retreated, softly quacking Pekin curses at me.

I said good night to Victor behind the kiln, leaving him the last few morsels of bread before snapping off the barn lights. I hadn't intended to revisit the chair under the evergreen, but it exerted an irresistible pull. I had all I could do to keep myself from lifting the cushion to determine the fate of the wrigglers. But some secrets were better left concealed, especially when they presented me with a minor moral dilemma.

If I lifted the cushion and discovered that mother mouse hadn't come back aboard, out of a misguided notion of truthfulness I would feel compelled to report the bad news to Linda, and it would bother her all night. And if the mother mouse had returned, lifting the cushion might spook her and cause her to abandon the nest for good. I couldn't completely disregard a third possibility, either. If I lifted the cushion and somehow found yet another copy of the *National Audubon Society Field Guide to North American Weather*, it would be as serious as seeing a peanut-shaped spaceship piloted by an African grey parrot. I'd never be able to go back into the house and resume a normal life. So rather than lift the cushion and risk disappointing Linda, disturbing the mouse, or displacing myself from my home, I imitated Buffy instead. I stood near the chair in the rain and quizzically regarded the cushion with what I hoped would be a thoughtful look, though the dim expression on my face probably wouldn't have fooled anybody.

WE WERE GLAD to be rid of one batch of babies. The starlings had finally left, which made Linda happy. The orphans had come to her in plastic margarine tubs from rehabber Marge Chedrick, graduated to a small cage on the porch, and ended up in a tabletop flight cage at the foot of the basement stairs. Dark grey blurs shot back and forth behind the wire whenever Linda charged down the steps. You couldn't count the dark grey blurs, but occasionally one would perch and turn into a bird. Screeching and vibrating its wings, the starling would beg for food with its beak wide open. Just as Linda guided the syringe into its mouth and began squirting in the feeding formula, the bird would jerk its head away and get slimed with ocher goop. One by one each bird was fed and cleaned. Two hours later, the whole process started again.

To thwart mealtime escapes, Linda would drape a sheet over herself and the cage while she crouched with the feeding formula. "Say *cheese!*" I'd say, since she reminded me of an early-twentieth-century photographer. Despite her precaution, a bird often slipped through the cage door and past the sheet to motor misguidedly around the basement. Pet carriers, a discarded vacuum cleaner, heaps of clothes, a forgotten juicer, boxes of Christmas tree ornaments, and two circular knee-high fences defining rabbit exercise areas hindered the recapture despite Linda's deft swishes with a trout net. Inevitably the escapee would gravitate toward a small cutout in the perennially unfinished drywall and vanish behind the west wall. Twice I'd tacked a screen over the opening, and twice the screen and tack had fallen down, due to an elusive invisible force called sloppiness.

Eventually the bird would reemerge and fly to another inconvenient part of the basement—such as the clothesline that held our winter clothes—and from there flit to the pipe above the washing machine or the windowsill near the pottery supplies shelf, with Linda close behind. When the starling grew tired of its separation from the others but couldn't work out the matter of getting back, and when Linda was on the verge of giving up the pursuit, the bird would suddenly shoot past her just as she had raised her net into the air, and a soft but satisfying impact plus subsequent squawk would indicate that she had caught the escapee. Two hours later, the whole process started again.

"You're going to Marge's to get more birds?" I asked Linda as we ate Saturday breakfast. "You just got rid of these." She'd had three batches of starlings over a period of five weeks, and had just begun reclaiming the chunk of her life that they had eaten up.

"She's not giving me starlings this time. These are Baltimore orioles."

That made all the difference in the world. The most beautiful bird song I had ever heard had issued from the double syrinx of a Baltimore oriole. While his peers were also in splendid voice as they defended their breeding territories, this particular bird was the operatic tenor of the yard, with a gliding, flutelike, harmonically complex arc of notes that would stop me in the middle of my chicken chores as I scanned the treetops in search of him.

A visit with Marge was always so intensely chaotic that it made our place seem about as exciting as the Department of Motor Vehicles. At first glance, George and Marge's house was of a piece with the other 1930s-vintage homes in their urban neighborhood.

But to stroll through the gate to the Chedrick's backyard was to
leave behind a typical community where the squirrels ran up a
tree as soon as you got out of your car, and blue jays squawked
harsh warnings that you had intruded on their space—and to enter a tiny raucous world where squirrels scampered unconcerned
across your feet, and blue jays squawked as they landed on your
head.

A flock of Canada geese honked hello. We made a wide detour
around the swan that was justifiably pissed off to have swallowed a
fisherman's hook, line, and sinker, which had festered in its throat
until the kindly zoo vet Dr. Hedley surgically removed the mess.
We were also on alert for a nervous wild turkey or an abused emu
with a grudge, though the current fraction of the twelve hundred
birds and mammals that the Chedricks took in, nursed, and released over the course of a year prowled the property at ease.

"Watch it," Marge warned as we caught up with her in the
building behind the house. I assumed that she was cautioning
the person on the other end of her cordless phone until a flash
of wings propelled a gangly being from its roost on top of a towel
at the window to the moving platform of my shoulder, and an
impossibly elfin green heron probed and pecked my hair with its
sharp forceps of a bill.

"He's imprinted on people. I don't know what we're going to do
with him."

With a thrust of his pipe-cleaner legs, the pigeon-size heron
hopped from my shoulder to Marge's, and she reached behind her
to pet his neck. "Near the mouse food," she told her caller. "See the
rat food? Now look next to it."

I couldn't guess the context of the conversation. Before I could
open my mouth to ask, she disconnected caller one to talk to
caller two about picking up an injured Cooper's hawk. "Careful,"

she said as the heron popped back onto my shoulder. "He'll go for your eyes. He likes anything shiny."

"Are you talking about the hawk?" I asked. She vigorously shook her head. I vigorously shook mine, and the putative eye plucker puttered back to his window seat.

Linda slipped into the room next door to coo at a white racing pigeon that had crash-landed in someone's backyard. Marge followed with the phone to make sure that Linda didn't stick her finger through the bars to pet a recuperating muskrat in another cage. "We wear gloves with that guy."

"She's talking about a hawk," I informed Linda.

Marge covered the phone with her hand. "I'm talking about the muskrat. And the porcupine, too."

Things weren't any less zoological inside the house. Crowbar the crow, who had lived fifteen years caged in a pet shop, enjoyed his unfettered freedom to the max by chasing volunteer Chris across the living room rug she was attempting to vacuum. After I poked my nose into a bedroom to greet a pair of house finches not quite at home in a house, Linda reported that I had missed seeing Crowbar drag a slice of pizza from the kitchen countertop, dunk it in Muff the dog's water dish, and stash it beneath the china cabinet. "Maybe he'll do it again," I suggested with undue optimism.

As the phone kept ringing and the answering machine kept answering, Marge provided us with a running commentary. "Call the humane society," she muttered to herself as a caller droned on about a cat in a tree. "A rabbit person for you," she shouted to Chris above the labored whine of the vacuum cleaner and the cheery whine of a teenage girl. "I can't be everywhere," she informed me when a man with a cigarette voice requested help catching a duck some eighty miles away. From past experience, I knew she would get back to most of the callers, but not before she had explained to us why one of the four Baltimore oriole fledglings wore a snappy adhesive-tape legging.

"Oh, listen to that," she told me as their clamorous two-toned peeping abated only after she'd fed the lot. "This one has to go back to Dr. Hedley later in the week to get his cast removed. He had a fractured leg but seems to be doing nicely."

WE SET THE ORIOLES on our dining room table, and their tree-frog peeps filled the downstairs. Stanley Sue paid no attention to the quartet. Perhaps because they were closer to his end of the room, Dusty studied them with cocked head and cool intelligence blazing in his black pupils. While he typically enjoyed nothing more than sinking his beak into my ankle, he showed unique tolerance toward smaller birds, even to the extent of leaving un-molested a parakeet that would wedge herself through the bars of his cage to explore his food dish. In fact, he often imitated Linda's sighs of affection for the starlings and other baby birds, comment-ing, "Aw!" when she fed them within view.

I often puffed myself up and told people that garden-variety starlings deserved rescuing every bit as much as colorful and me-lodic songbirds. "No bird's life is worth any less than any other's," I'd proclaim. Yet I fell deeply in love with the orioles, and so did Linda. We both declared them to be our favorites of all the birds she'd raised. In stark contrast to the starlings — or even baby blue jays, which are unexpectedly well mannered — the orioles didn't shriek at feeding time. Nor did they flap frantically around inside their cage as starlings did, in the manner of bats swirling out of a cave. They patiently waited for their turns like people in line at the savings and loan.

You certainly couldn't accuse a young oriole of gluttony. Af-ter the tiniest squeeze of the syringe, the bird would snap shut its beak as if to say, "Oh, really, no, I couldn't swallow another dollop," then retire genteelly to its perch for a peep and a spot of beauty sleep. And what a beauty a baby Baltimore oriole was, with its olive-brown head, barred black-and-white wings, and patch of burnt yellow on the breast. And that's not to mention the white strip of adhesive tape that adorned the bird that Marge had dubbed Gimpy.

WHEN I WALKED into the barn that evening, I formulated a new hypothesis about the strange animal noises of the preceding winter. I hadn't heard mysterious creatures whooping after all. They were crying, "Poop!" and preparing our hens and ducks for a late-summer poop-up-the-barn contest. The coaching had certainly worked. Even though they had full access to the outdoor pens, the fowl had fouled the cement floor instead, and they had done so with such gusto that I vacillated between clearing out the dung with a push broom and hiring a crew with bulldozers. On my own I managed to slop the slop into the center trough and slosh it down the hill before the EPA showed up with a cleanup order — and just as the hens began to wander inside to cluck their complaints about the treats I'd brought them.

I was pleased to see that Victor had finished his molt and beamed resplendently in fresh wing plumage. Still a bit weak from the energy-sapping process of shucking off old feathers and growing new ones, he hung back from the other barn birds as I doled out veggies and chunks of bread. Hamilton hissed, panted, and stalked me in alpha-bird mode, even attacking the head of the broom when I interpolated it between us. Frustrated at his failure to reach me, he feinted in Victor's direction then clicked his jaws at Ramone, who managed to lurch out of his way and keep his tail feathers intact. If Hamilton's anger-management skills continued their sharp decline, I'd have to switch Victor and Ramone to the smaller pen where white Pekin Richie's randy son Timmy lived. I might be forced to house Richie with them, too, and hope that Timmy wouldn't go romantic on him. Though Hamilton usually contented himself with tormenting his fellow Muscovies while leaving the others alone, lately he'd started launching himself at any creature that wandered too close. Not even a chipmunk was safe.

A fluttering at the window caught my attention. Two large butterflies—an eastern tiger swallowtail and a giant swallowtail— flicked their wings against the pane of glass, struggling to get outside, presumably before Hamilton picked on them. I had seen these species only once in the last few years and certainly not practicing the buddy system. How they had teamed up and managed to founder like Laurel and Hardy inside the barn mystified me. This sort of trifling but genuinely flashy event was tailor-made for interpretation as an omen. Trouble was, I had no notion of what two butterflies trapped against the glass meant, especially since I intended to intervene and save them. Was this a cosmic truism about the fragility of life or a signal that the barn windows needed a good scrubbing? Was it an obscure warning about my mom or a hint that we needed to keep a butterfly net with the hens?

Armed with my plastic pitcher, I gently scooped up the swallowtails and set them loose in the field. The tiger flew off with vigor, but the giant wearily flapped to a ground-level leaf on a sprig of wild catnip, adding layers of complexity to the symbolism.

I was musing about whether we should expect Moobie to sprout wings anytime soon when I walked into the barn and spotted trouble brewing. Hamilton was dogging Victor, preventing him from getting to the nightly treats in a repeat performance of his tormenting of Richie. When I stepped between the two Muscovies, Victor demonstrated his mental superiority to a White Pekin by advancing upon my slight but towering form to lustily scarf up every piece of bread located within the radius of my broom. Hamilton hissed and glowered at us from a distance.

"You are one smart duck," I told him. "How would you like to come and live indoors?" He answered my query by leaving a significant deposit on the cement.

LINDA HANDED ME the phone when I came up through the basement. "It's your mom," she told me with a glint in her eye that added: Watch out.

"You didn't happen to see my keys when you were here," my mom said.

"You called me about that earlier," I reminded her. "We decided you had probably put them in your purse."

"Where's my purse?"

I looked to Linda for moral support, but she had wisely retreated to the shower. "As of this afternoon, it was under the couch cushion."

She set the down the phone and made a quick search. "It isn't there."

"You lifted up both cushions?" I asked. At least she didn't run the risk of uncovering a mouse nest. "Then try next to the humidifier at the bottom of the stairs."

The phone clunked against the tabletop.

"No, I don't see it."

"Check the bread drawer in the kitchen," I suggested. "That's the latest hiding place."

The phone took another bounce.

"I don't know where I put it," she lamented.

"The only other spot I can think of is the bottom shelf of the china cabinet."

This time the receiver tumbled to the floor and thunked twice as it hit the side of my dad's hi-fi cabinet.

"It's there," she told me after a moment. "I'm really glad I called you."

"And are the keys inside your purse?"

"The what?" she asked.

"Your house keys. The keys you're looking for."

Once we had confirmed that my mom's keys were safely safety-pinned to the lining of her purse, her voice took on an uncharacteristic edge. "I don't mean to criticize you, but I would like you to bring back the electric hedge trimmer you borrowed without asking. I want to touch up the shrubs in the front."

This time it was my turn to ask, "The what?"

"The electric hedge trimmer. You took it over a week ago."

"Gee, no. I did borrow the trimmer last fall so that Linda could hack away at our spirea bush, but I gave it back to Dad a couple of days later. I haven't taken it since then."

"Well, I think you did," she answered sharply. "Don Teany saw you putting it in your trunk, and I need it back."

"He did not!" I exploded. "Don never told you that."

I only lose my temper every few years, push-broom tussles with ducks aside. But quite inexplicably, my mother's accusation threw me into a rage, and the overstimulation short-circuited my brain. It was if another person, one I couldn't hear distinctly, were shouting at my mom. If any of the words registered with me, I forgot them as rapidly as they sputtered out of my mouth and disappeared into the soupy black neocortical muck. They involved some blather along the lines of how could you accuse your one and only son of stealing from you, what would Dad think if he could hear you now, and other such bellowing of a wounded beast. The outburst literally shook me. I could barely hold the phone steady.

With tears in her voice my mother asked, "Honey, what did I possibly do to hurt you this much?"

"What do you mean, what did you do?" I sniveled. "You accused me of stealing your hedge trimmer."

"Oh, honey, I would never say anything like that."

"You did. You said I took your hedge trimmer."

"I would never say anything like that," she repeated.

"You did," I insisted with decreased enthusiasm.

As the fog of emotion began to slip away, I realized that my anger had been triggered by fear. Since my father's death I had cheer fully repressed the increasingly obvious signs that something was wrong with my mom that couldn't be shrugged off as the short-term effects of grief. Forgetfulness was one thing. Most people over forty grapple with their own name from one hour to the next. But fabrication was far more serious, and so was her increasing paranoia that people were walking off with her possessions. As best as I could, I made my apologies for being a wretch, and she graciously accepted them. It bothered me that I'd exhibited more patience with a duck than I seemed capable of extending to my mother, and I couldn't quite figure out the reason why.

Fortunately, Linda had been singing "Camptown Races" in the shower and had missed my darkest hour except for a dull rumble beneath her chorus of doo-dahs. After I'd calmed down a little, I phoned my sister Joan. She phoned my sister Bett. My sister Bett phoned me. And we all faced the sad reality that my mom had fallen down a rabbit hole and the bottom was nowhere in sight.

• • •

I HELPED LINDA release the Baltimore orioles, though they weren't exactly chomping at the beak to join the world of the wild. I carried the cage outdoors, climbed the stepladder to the top of the milk house, set the cage upon the flat roof, and opened the wire door. Polite as ever, each bird waited for the others to exit first. "After you." "Oh, no, I wouldn't think of it." "Age before beauty." "I may just call a cab." When it became clear that they wouldn't budge without encouragement, I waved my hand "good-bye" behind the cage to scatter them. One at a time the orioles hopped out and flew up to the tree overhanging the milk house. Gimpy, now lacking his leg bandage, left last, after a wistful survey of his enclosure. We had always been able to tell him apart from his siblings by a tentativeness to his movements, and it now expanded to full-blown uncertainty as he clung to a cluster of leaves and refused to go any farther.

The other three birds leaped from branch to branch, peeping as they moved from the heart of the tree to its spindly extremities. The bravest oriole teetered for a moment at the end of a woody finger that pointed toward our swamp, then flung itself into space as if from a diving board. Two more birds followed in wobbling flight and disappeared into foliage at the bottom of our hill.

"Maybe the babies know that the grown-up orioles are by the river," Linda said. "But I wish they would have waited for Gimpy."

Whenever we released birds in our yard, we would leave the cage on the roof for the entire day with a plastic jar lid of food sitting next to it. Most of our orphans had grown so sick of motel food that they didn't hang around for the buffet. But after making himself at home on a small section of tree limb, Gimpy worked up his courage sufficiently to flutter down and peck at diced grapes and whole mealworms. By evening, he still hadn't budged from the security of the milk house and tree. As darkness descended, so did he. When Linda went outdoors to bring in the cage, she found Gimpy perched on top of it.

"I think he wants to come in for the night," she told me.

But if leaving his cage had required significant coaching, entering it again was beyond the oriole's expertise. Twice I climbed the ladder in hopes of luring him through the door with food, but each time my head popped into view, he flew back up into the tree.

"I don't know how we're going to get him," I complained. "And considering how he's acting, he definitely shouldn't spend the night out here."

"Gimpy!" Linda called. "Come on, Gimpy."

I gave her a you-gotta-be-kidding-me look. "He has no idea his name is Gimpy."

"Gimpy!" she called again, ignoring me.

I was about to get the trout net from the basement when, right on cue, Gimpy landed on the ground a few feet from Linda. He readily allowed her to scoop him up and put him in his cage, and he ate heartily once she had carried him upstairs to the dining room.

"He's not afraid of living in the wild," I said. "He's afraid of missing out on the deluxe shuttle service."

After breakfast, Linda went through the entire exercise by herself: climbing the ladder, setting the cage upon the milk house, shooing Gimpy out the door, and providing a blue-plate special for him to peck at throughout the day. By the time I returned from work in the early afternoon, his food already needed replenishing. It didn't take me a moment to spot him on his perch seven feet above the roof, though I marveled at how readily his brown-green coloration blended into his environment. Beyond the issue of camouflage, however, he wasn't exactly evaporating into the natural world. By the evening of his second day at large, he had expanded his wanderings only as far as a slightly higher tree limb.

"Gimpy!" I called over and over. "Gimpy, come down to your cage."

"What's the matter?" asked Linda from the basement door.

"Gimpy won't come in."

"That's good. We want him to stay outside."

"He's not ready. He's a sitting duck for an owl or something."

"He looks just fine to me."

"You try," I suggested. "He likes your voice."

"Gimpy, do you want to come in?" Linda asked the oriole. If the small smudge against the darkening sky considered the question, he didn't show any sign of answering.

Compared to the problems we were having with my mom, my initial mild concern over a Baltimore oriole shouldn't have worsened into worry. But the miserable phone call of a few days earlier had activated the iron gong of anxiety. Any tiny tremor that ordinarily would have quickly faded into silence set the huge gong rumbling again. Every nerve ending in my body seemed to tingle, especially in my stomach and head. I couldn't sleep. I felt myself sitting on a branch surrounded by cold black space that predators knifed through with ease.

What if we found Gimpy dead on the ground? What if we discovered nothing but a patch of feathers? What was happening to my mother? Had my dad seen the early signs and checked out early? And why I had stopped taking my antianxiety medication? Things had seemed even and straightforward when I'd weaned myself from my daily pill, but I began to wonder if I was physically capable of leading a normal life without brain-altering biochemistry. A real shock might send me completely up a tree.

The next morning, we watched as Gimpy dove down to the milk-house roof, supped on grapes, grabbed a mealworm in his beak, and zoomed far up into the tree. That was the last we saw of him. Linda took his disappearance as proof that he had finally adapted to the wild outdoors. I wanted to agree. But I had trouble interpreting absence as anything other than absence.

CHAPTER 6

·····································

Fowl Weather

Trudging into the dining room after a nap, I was shocked to discover a far worse spectacle than a nest of baby mice. Our animals should have been safe while I snoozed. Through hard experience we had learned to stagger out-of-the-cage shifts so that an unarmed Howard couldn't foolishly attack the slash-billed Stanley Sue, hedgehog-size bunny Bertie and lumbering Walter couldn't pull out gobs of each other's fur, and the formidable Dusty couldn't cut a swath through the defenseless minions, whose numbers included me. The complex scheduling did a good job of protecting our critters, but bizarre disasters trumped planning every time.

I stopped dead a few steps into the room. Stanley Sue was perched on top of Bertie's cage, near the windowsill that she had long ago chewed into pulp. She cocked her head when she saw me and flashed her eyes "hello." Bertie stood inside his cage grooming his ears with his front paws. Everything seemed hunky-dory, until I mentally processed the severed rabbit tail that rested at a jaunty angle on the linoleum. I guessed immediately what must have happened. Bertie had been sleeping with his rear pressed against the front of the cage as usual, and the sight of the cotton-ball tail thrust through the wire had apparently proved too tempting for a parrot to ignore, even though Stanley Sue had ignored it for over a decade.

The dismal scene turned my limbs into windowsill pulp, and I nearly ended up on the linoleum alongside the tail. Linda usually handled the medical emergencies with our animals, while I performed the vital task of hovering in the background and moaning, "What are we going to do?" But her escalating back problems meant two visits to the chiropractor per week. So while Linda got a backbone manipulation from Dr. Potente, I got a reality adjustment from Stanley Sue, who stared at me while vigorously nodding her head in excitement, displeasure, or both. Bertie continued bathing his ears with such nonchalance that I picked up his tail to assure myself that the amputation had actually occurred. The pom-pom was vaguely cone-shaped on the end that had once connected to his body. A tiny dot of blood flecked a muscle no larger than the diameter of a toothpick. The rest of the tail consisted of fur.

"Sweetie, are you okay?" I asked with an unsteady voice as I interrupted Bertie's toilette to pull him out of his cage. He didn't act as if he had been emotionally attached to the snipped-off appendage, grunting indignantly as I carried him into the bathroom and examined him under the strong artificial light suitable for spotting defects in the floral wallpaper. The pinching action of the parrot's beak must have kept the injury from bleeding. I didn't detect any sign of trauma except for the dull throbbing inside me.

Plunking Stanley Sue back into her cage, I directed a few sharp words at her. I considered taking away her treasured bell as punishment, but I didn't figure it would make sense to her. Though unfailingly gentle with Linda and me, she apparently regarded a rabbit or smaller bird as just another object to chew on.

Fighting the urge to return to bed, draw the covers over my head, and brood about what an irresponsible pet owner I'd turned out to be, I let gravity pull me down the basement stairs. Next to the unused wood furnace I found a few scraps of metal screening with a half-inch grid that neither bunny ear nor parrot beak could poke through. Scissoring the panels to proper proportions, I fitted shields to the front and sides of each rabbit cage to thwart future bird attacks. As I wired the pieces in place, I lamented the fact that I had shown more understanding with Stanley Sue than I had with my poor mother, who would never bite off a rabbit's tail. Somehow I understood the futility of losing my temper with a parrot, but I hadn't transferred that to human beings.

That evening I roiled with pangs of guilt while watching a tailless Bertie frolic in the living room. Though Linda calmed me down by pointing out that the loss didn't seem to bother the bunny, she couldn't resist wondering out loud, "Why would Stanley do something like that?"

"Why would my mom insist I stole her electric trimmer?" I asked, nudging the focus back to my suffering. "It's some mysterious force of nature at work."

"We've got to make sure she can't hurt one of the bunnies again."

"I put that screen around the cages. That will do the trick."

"Because she could really injure Bertie or Walter," Linda continued. "That's probably how Walter ended up with his abscesses. We can't let Stanley bite the bunnies."

"They should be safe with the screen around their cages."

"What if she pecked out one of their eyes?"

"She can't do that with the screens on their cages," I observed with growing futility.

"I don't want any more abscesses," she said. Then, before I could bring up the screens again, she asked, "Have you seen my reading glasses?"

That was my cue to walk out of the room. As a kind of pointless tribute to Bertie's hindquarters subtraction, I saved his tail in a sandwich bag, which I taped up and temporarily stashed inside the top drawer of my dresser.

"What are you going to do with that?" Linda asked.

"Dig a hole in the backyard and throw dirt on top of it. He'll be the only rabbit we've ever owned that we've had to bury twice."

"I just don't get why these weird things keep happening to us," she muttered a little later as she clicked off the lamp on the bedstand. That, of course, was the question that kept me awake long after Linda had ceased her nightly routine of hopping out of bed to set the air purifier on low, opening the window, setting the air purifier back to high, knocking over ceramic figurines on the headboard as she searched for her lip balm in the dark, shutting the window, turning on the fan, putting on a warmer nightgown, and shifting the air purifier to low. Each time she leaned over the side of the bed or flung herself off the mattress, she yanked the covers from my body, and I didn't dare hold on to them for fear that a hearty tug from her would spin me like a top.

Different kinds of people tended to attract certain types of events into their lives. I came to this decision during a brief interval when the covers still covered me. Some folks stumbled over money every time they left the house, like a friend of Linda's who won the lottery so often, they considered replacing Jackson's face with hers on the twenty-dollar bill. Other folks specialized in tragedy, settling on major-appliance breakdowns, scofflaw relatives, or medical maladies with hyphenated names as their ongoing torment. For reasons I could never comprehend, I drew weirdness to

me like water into a straw. The granddaddy of all bizarre events,
I reflected as I lay in bed waiting for the quilt to desert me again,
was the telephone call I had once received from the space people.

One night during my junior college days I'd found myself unable to concentrate on the poetic prose of my political science text-
book. Instead I dug into a science fiction story about a man who
could mentally tune in to a kind of galactic two-way radio. At the
drop of a thinking cap, he could intercept telepathic communi-
cations between advanced civilizations located in distant Milky
Way zip codes. A mind meld with aliens appealed to me, especially when compared to trying to divine the logic behind political
processes in Washington. So after finishing the story and pulling
the sheet up to my neck at a time in my life when nobody but me
would whisk it away again, I attempted to contact whatever extra-
terrestrials might be tuned to earthling brain-wave frequencies.

I hypnotized myself into a state of relaxation that I had learned
from reading, of all things, a 1950s issue of *Popular Science* magazine plucked from a flea market. I marshaled my puny thought
energy, waited for my inner ON THE AIR light to blink on, and trans-
mitted a plea for the space people to contact me. "I'm ready to join
you off-planet in a life that doesn't involve memorizing members
of Congress or being humiliated by the girl who sits next to me in
biology class. Please reply. Over." I lay still, palpitating as I concentrated on my thoughts for a response from Regulus or an answer from Antares. Nothing came, and I finally drifted off to sleep
awaiting a vaguely Rod Serling–esque voice inside my head.

A few hours later, the jangling telephone woke me up. A woman
asked, "Is Richard there?" as electronic tones burbled in the background. Her question scared me silly. That same day I'd received a
Unitron telescope catalog in the mail, which I'd whimsically sent
for under the name Richard Plantagenet. Nobody knew this fact

other than the mailman and a Unitron employee, and I figured that postal and telescope personnel had better things to do at two A.M. than bother me. I wanted to ask, "Richard who?" But if I did and the voice supplied the appropriate last name, I would be alien food. So I chickened out by replying, "There's no Richard here. Who are you calling?"

"I'm calling you, Bob Tarte," she told me.

I couldn't have been more frightened had I actually believed in the saucer people. "You've got the wrong number," I told her and hung up.

The experience taught me several lessons. Never poke my nose into the cosmic equivalent of citizen-band radio. Never request catalogs under the name of a deceased British regent. And, of course, never assume that my mother was any more askew than a son who lived with one foot in a fantasy world. The memory of alien telephony reminded me that I needed to do something special for my mom to make amends for that *other* annoying phone call, the one where I had shouted at her, and I needed to do it soon.

THE FOLLOWING SATURDAY, I mulled over potential restaurants for lunch with my mother as I ambled down the hill toward the duck pens. Judging her taste in food wasn't easy once I'd factored in the oddball meals she'd treated us to over the years, such as ham balls in orange-flavored gravy and chicken casserole with a crust of saltines that expanded to take on the characteristics of ceiling tiles. Fortunately, my mom was so easy to please, I could take her to the Kmart snack bar for a corn dog and she would say, "This is nice." I wanted to do a notch better than that, but I didn't want to spend much money. Maybe she'd be so thrilled that I was treating her to a meal that she would actually insist on paying. This thought buoyed me as I started to unlock the girls' pen and noticed that the atmosphere wasn't right. Instead of honking and quacking at the sight of me and the prospect of an insect safari in our yard, the ducks and geese were eerily silent at my approach.

A glance into Stewart and Trevor's pen sobered my mood. I went back into the house, exchanged a few quiet words with Linda, then went out again and gently lifted the latch on their gate. Linda had no peer when it came to treating sick and injured animals, but I didn't want her to have to face what had happened to our handsome Khaki Campbell boys. For once I was grateful for a life spent avoiding reality, as a psychological black hole mercifully slipped between my eyes and the bodies of our ducks while I wrapped each in a towel, then buried them under a shade tree.

When I had finished, Linda joined me at the graveside. Holding my hand she told Stewart and Trevor how sorry she was for what had happened. I reminded her how they would sometimes waddle up to me when I stretched out on my back in the soft summer grass and nibble at my shoelaces. Linda mentioned how much they had enjoyed spending time in the yard with the female ducks. Their offshoots, Carla, Marla, and Darla, testified to that fact. We also talked about the day a few years earlier when we had brought them home from a woman who had lost her job and couldn't afford to keep her pets. Then we let go of each other's hands and wiped our eyes.

I rattled through the top floor of the barn until I located another section of wire screening. Once again I fetched the tin snips and a spool of wire to belatedly remedy a problem. The boys' enclosure itself was secure. However, we'd added a storage shed behind the pens that was intended to function as winter waterfowl housing. The girls and boys could walk through a pair of corridors and enter separate enclosures in the shed to escape subzero outdoor temperatures—but even in the coldest weather they preferred frolicking in their wading pools instead. The builder who had constructed the shed hadn't secured the corridor on the boys' side properly, and a raccoon had apparently dug under the fencing. I had known about the defect, but I hadn't bothered to fix it, figuring that no animal would be able to fight its way through our rock-impacted soil. I had also expected that our geese would raise a ruckus and wake us at the first sign of any attempted break-in. But they hadn't made a peep during the night. We found out later that birds often react in silence when they can't escape a predator in their midst.

In one respect, we had been lucky. If the raccoon had wandered into the shed after killing Stewart and Trevor, it could have climbed over a squat barrier to reach the girls' side of the pen and killed every one of them as well. But instead of consoling me, the close brush with a mass extinction plunged me into a deep hole, and I considered phoning my mom to postpone our lunch. "She'll understand," Linda assured me, but I couldn't face the added guilt of standing her up.

"I'm just paying bills," my mom told me when I walked into the dining room. Sure enough, her dining room table was coated with a thick paper icing of envelopes, bill statements, junk mail, old receipts, and folders that my sister Bett had labeled "Bills to Pay," "Paid Bills," "Auto Insurance," "Health Insurance," "Funeral Expenses," and "Death Certificates." The implied spiral from unpaid invoices to death seemed excessive, as did the amount of clutter for what turned out to be exactly three bills due: cable TV, natural gas, and a *Good Housekeeping* subscription. I wrote out three checks in record time. Using other people's money always energized me, and the exercise helped take my mind off the miserable start to the morning. As I cleared the table, it dawned on me that these were the same three bills my mom had been in the process of "paying" a week earlier.

"Why don't I just take care of your bills from now on," I suggested.

"You don't need to do that," she said, but I could tell that the idea appealed to her.

We decided on a neighborhood restaurant frequented by members of her church. As she ate a chicken-salad sandwich and hailed an elderly woman in a tweed dress whose face and clothing I remembered from the funeral home, I told my mom about the accident with our ducks. Although my affection for poultry perplexed her, she was genuinely sympathetic. "Try not to think about it," she advised me, which was rather like advising an ant not to live underground.

We reminisced about my dad as we each ate a scoop of ice cream. This inevitably led to my favorite story, mainly because I steered her in that direction. Shortly after moving back to Grand Rapids from Washington, D.C., at the end of World War II, my dad had asked the clerk at Dodd's Record Shop for a copy of Sammy Kaye's song "Remember Pearl Harbor." My father, who had worked for the Pentagon during the war, was as patriotic as anyone. "But he hated that song," my mother chuckled. "He said it was commercializing on a tragedy." Once he had paid for the 78 rpm phonograph record, he snapped it in half on the spot and politely handed the pieces to the clerk. I laughed out loud thinking of my mild-mannered dad acting so audaciously, but that wasn't the payoff to the tale.

"It must have been ten years later that your father went back to Dodd's to buy a different record. I think it was something by Steve Allen. When he brought the record to the front counter, the woman looked at him and said, 'You!' "

I was hoping that my mom might follow this up with the improbable story about the time my dad had been hauled off to jail in his pajamas—but the memories of married life saddened her.

We drove home in silence, brooding about our respective losses, big and small.

LINDA SURPRISED ME by implicating a television program in our bad luck. She didn't exactly blame the show, which was about a woman who communicated telepathically with animals rather than space aliens. But I had just pressed play after feeding Moobie a heart-shaped cat treat when Linda interrupted the episode to tell me, "I had this horrible thought, and I feel like I have to say something about it. I can't get it out of my head that Stewart and Trevor might have died because maybe God was punishing us for watching a show about a psychic."

I hit the pause key to underscore my puzzlement. "Now, what was that again?"

"The Bible says that God disapproves of divination and false prophets."

My eyes darted from the freeze-framed psychic's friendly face to Linda's pained expression. Moobie's head popped up in expectation of another cat treat. "Does that mean we can never watch the show again? I thought you enjoyed it."

From her faux-sheepskin rug on the living room floor, Linda considered the issue. Moobie walked over and tapped her leg with a front paw, demanding another heart-shaped goodie. "She's not exactly fortune-telling, I guess, when you come right down to it," she decided.

"No," I agreed. "Reading the mind of a kitten isn't the same as divining what the cat is going to do tomorrow, though with Moobie it would be an easy prediction."

"'Eat. Sleep. Drink water. Get petted. Beg for treats,'" Linda muttered as she rose from the rug to snag the can of cat treats from the entertainment center. "I guess it's okay to watch it," she said. "You know how I am. When I get obsessed with something, it usually doesn't go away unless I say something. You're lucky you don't get obsessed with things."

"That's one problem I don't seem to have," I told her with a total lack of conviction. As a matter of fact, the snipping off of Bertie's tail followed by the snuffing of Stewart and Trevor had spooked me to such a degree that I inwardly flinched whenever I walked into the dining room, backyard pens, or barn, for fear of the disaster that I might encounter next. Whenever the phone rang, I worried that my mother might be calling to claim I had absconded with the gas cap for her snowblower.

"She certainly isn't doing anything evil," Linda added. "She's helping people and animals."

I pressed the play button as a way of signaling my concurrence and wondered if I could find other devices to do my talking for me. The next time I was angry, I might boil a pan of water. At any rate, I was relieved to start the show moving again. While staring at the petrified image of the psychic, I had briefly imagined I'd noticed a glint of malevolence in her eye.

I didn't know what I thought about the woman in terms of paranormal powers. When it came to human subjects, I believed that mind reading was the cheap stunt of carnies and evangelists, but my pessimism took a dive when it came to mental melding with a duck or beagle. The idea of someone speaking up for creatures that most people regarded as disposable possessions hit my emotional center with the force of a Muscovy charge. Anyway, I didn't suppose that God would fling his wrath upon folks who watched the wrong TV show, especially when sitting through most shows was punishment enough. But Linda had increased my general uneasiness. A possible connection between pet deaths and television viewing gave me yet another reason to worry, no matter how illogical the cause.

After the finale of the show, in which the host relayed reassuring messages from pets frolicking in the next world to their former owners sobbing in the studio, I walked into the bathroom with Moobie hot on my heels. I didn't want an elderly, overweight cat breaking a leg hopping down from the sink, so I had broken her of the habit of drinking from the faucet by holding her water dish as she stood on the toilet seat. The plan had been to convince her to accept water from her own dish—and she would, as long I held the bowl aloft. Moving deliberately, I could even lower the bowl to within a millimeter of the floor as long as I clutched it in my hand. As soon as dish touched floor and fingers disengaged, Moobie would fix me with a withering expression that said, "How am I supposed to drink now?" Never mind that we had frequently caught her slurping muddy water from the pot of a freshly watered plant. Her own bowl was taboo unless I suspended it in space.

She raced me to the bathroom the next evening just before I headed out to the barn, exercising impressive fussiness by drinking first from one edge of the dish, then sniffing and shifting her head to several other carefully chosen spots in search of the optimal lapping experience. But I didn't let this prolonged annoyance bother me. My mood had jumped several notches as the bright sunshine of the day had dispelled the superstitions of the previous night. A catbird sang its scratchy song from a tree overhanging an abandoned cattle trough. A floral scent politely glossed over the smell of a spoiled and broken duck egg I'd tossed into our field a few days ago.

From the darkness of the barn interior, I strode merrily outdoors into Timmy's pen to shoo first him, then Ramone into their bachelor quarters. I hunted for a while before happening upon chickens Buffy and Brenda crouching behind a wickedly pointy thistle. Brenda's sister Helen had inserted herself into the heart of a stinging nettle patch that had zero effect on her, but every nerve ending in my featherless hand hit the fire alarm when I brushed up against the leaves. After rousting her into the barn and determining that there were no more stragglers, I visited Richie's pen. When I stepped outside, the Pekin bobbled inside with annoyed wing flaps and grousing *duck, duck, duck* mumbling. Victor and the rest of the hens slowly followed. Hamilton refused to budge, which surprised me. He usually couldn't wait to launch himself at me, yet through a thicket of weeds I could just make out his upright form at the fence between the pens.

"Come on, Hamilton," I called. "C'mon, buddy. Time to get your treat." As I made my way through the bushes it became clear why he didn't respond.

His feet hung limply an inch or two above the ground. I couldn't simply whisk his body away with a towel, as I had with Stewart and Trevor. I had no alternative except to closely study the small but stabbing horror of his fate. It was as if the fence had grown around him. His neck threaded in and out of one heavy strand of wire, while his beak and the bottom of his skull were wedged into a second. I cursed and cried as I swept the flies off his bloodied head and struggled to pry him loose. His yellow eyes fixed me with a cold glare while I went about the grisly work of releasing him. I thought I might have to cut the fence apart.

We had moved Ramone to Timmy's pen a week earlier, when Hamilton's aggression toward the shyer Muscovy had escalated into violent explosions. We hadn't seen any harm in the two of them hissing at each other with a fence separating them. But an enraged Hamilton had apparently flung himself at his rival, caught his head in the wire, and strangled himself as he fell. I finally managed to coax Hamilton loose. Buffy pecked the dirt near my boots, uncertain whether my activity ought to involve her. I laid him on the grass behind the barn and compulsively stroked his back. Nothing similar had ever happened before, but failing to foresee any possibility for injury, no matter how remote, was a serious breech on my part. I didn't know what to say to him. What can you ever say to a dead duck? Feeling entangled by my own body and caught inside an inexplicable cycle of loss, I steered myself toward the house to get a towel from Linda.

I PUT OFF WATCHING the next episode of the animal psychic as long as I could without being too obvious about my dread of the show. Two episodes in a row followed by two pet disasters had seriously undermined my faith in the laws of causality. Linda had tossed aside her objections to the show and started asking me when we were going to see it again. We usually watched only one TV program a night, preferring to read books or groan in exhaustion after a day of animal chores.

"There's a special on tonight about the history of the hamburger," I told her. "Let's watch that instead of the psychic."

"We don't even eat hamburgers."

"Either that or I'd like to see *The World's Most Luxurious Truck Stops*."

Had it been simply a matter of admitting my superstitiousness to Linda, I could have lived with it. Far more alarming was the notion that I had suddenly slipped into a world where dark undercurrents had risen to the top like worms after a rain, and the worms were now in charge. I'd had a taste of this deep anxiety over intangible but seemingly real forces in my college days—also known as my dodging-telephone-calls-from-extraterrestrials days. My friend

Cole had developed a fascination with his Ouija board, and we whiled away long hours giggling and transcribing gibberish from supposed spirits. On one fateful occasion, Cole challenged an entity who called himself Gatsby to predict which *Star Trek* rerun a local television station would air at eleven-thirty that night. The newspaper listing hadn't provided a description, so this seemed like a reasonable test for even the most menial of disembodied beings.

"MOBSTERSPIECEOFTHEACTION," the board spelled out.

Neither of us could connect the underworld with the *Enterprise,* so taking this as just another of Gatsby's nonsensical missives, Cole guffawed, and I followed suit. We swallowed our mirth when eleven-thirty rolled around and the teaser at the beginning of the program presented Captain Kirk, Mr. Spock, and expendable crew members visiting a planet whose society was based on 1940s Hollywood mob films. The opening credits trumpeted the episode title as "A Piece of the Action."

I barely slept that night, worrying that Gatsby and his cohorts had a bird's-eye view of every twist, turn, and pillow hug I made. A haze of unreality clung to me for days, a dizziness resembling the onset of a head cold. I was constantly conscious of the idea of bumping elbows with dead souls who had nothing better to do than fritter away eternity performing clairvoyant stunts for college students. That didn't speak well about the quality of life in the afterlife, and the experience skewed my residual belief in the neat cosmology of my Catholic upbringing. Only the triumph of reason and an explanation from Cole when I visited him the following Saturday restored my faith in an orderly universe—a universe populated by English-speaking aliens with Roman haircuts and double-knit Starfleet uniforms.

"We're both rational people," Cole assured me. "We both know that a spirit named Gatsby doesn't exist. He's just an amplification of our subconscious thoughts. All of *them* are," he added with a significant glance at the Ouija board, which crouched on the card table, pretending that it hadn't caused me all kinds of emotional trouble.

"So how did our subconscious thoughts know what was going to be on *Star Trek*?"

"I watched it the week before," Cole replied. "That means I undoubtedly saw the preview for 'A Piece of the Action' but wasn't paying attention. The information registered in my subconscious anyway, and it came out when we asked the board the question."

"So that's all there was to it," I said with relief. "Let's ask Gatsby about tonight's *Hogan's Heroes*."

Linda kept asking about the animal-psychic show. The evening finally rolled around when I couldn't face a documentary about harvesting peat moss. So I gritted my teeth, grabbed a mental handful of Mr. Spock–style logic, and informed Linda that we would indeed be watching the program. Popping in the tape, I soon found myself enjoying an episode about a Californian ostrich who wanted the psychic to tell his owner that he strongly disapproved of the smell of his enclosure.

"I hope the psychic doesn't visit us," I said to Linda. "Think of how Penny would complain about her litter box."

"You're supposed to be changing that. The whole upstairs stinks."

"It's not that bad," I said. "I'll burn a stick of incense."

The show ended, as usual, with the psychic relaying messages from deceased cats and dogs to their owners and, as usual, I caught myself sniffling. Our Netherland dwarf bunny Bertie sat on my lap while I petted him. His brother Rollo had been the lap rabbit, but after Rollo had suffered a heart attack in the office of a loudmouthed emergency veterinarian eighteen months earlier, Bertie had grown increasingly affectionate with us. "Rollo's ghost must have told him he'd enjoy being petted," I'd joke to Linda. But now the deaths of Stewart, Trevor, and Hamilton, the weeping pet owners on TV, and my anxieties about the show ganged up to clout me with a feeling of great vulnerability on behalf of all our animals.

"You sure have been a nice bunny over the years," I told Bertie as I hugged him on the way back to his cage. "We'll sure miss you when you're gone."

That was exactly the wrong thing to say. The next day, Linda called me at work and said, "Sweetheart, I don't want you to get too upset, but Bertie doesn't look very good this morning."

"He was running around the dining room an hour ago," I protested.

"I know. But you have to remember that he's an old rabbit, and it might just be his time to go. I really don't expect him to last the day." Fifteen minutes she called back to tell me that Bertie had died.

Bertie's death ruined me. I could barely string two thoughts together, unless they were the same thought. But as we were burying him, I still had the presence of mind to lumber into the house, rummage through the top drawer of my dresser, and grab the plastic sandwich bag I had stashed away. Back at the grave, I delicately positioned the tail behind Bertie's body in a rough approximation of where it belonged.

ONE THING HAD ALWAYS bothered me about Cole's explanation. Sure, he could have watched the previous week's rerun of *Star Trek* and let his attention wander to the inside of his eyelids during the preview. And, certainly, the coming attraction could have embossed itself on his unconscious for retrieval by the Ouija board later. Trouble is, the *Star Trek* previews definitely, decidedly, and absolutely did not include the title of the upcoming episode. I confirmed this shortly after Cole's supposed solution. Gatsby—whoever or whatever he was or was not—had somehow come up with "A Piece of the Action" on his own, and that "somehow" still nettled me twenty-five years later.

I brooded on this and the animal psychic while sitting in a field behind the barn, listening to the complaining twilight song of an eastern peewee. Since Bertie's death, I'd gotten into the habit of wandering outdoors after a few minutes of watching our nightly TV show. "You don't like not having Bertie on your lap, do you?" Linda asked me. I hadn't realized that this double negative of a condition was precisely what agitated me. I had figured that *The Crocodile Hunter* and programs about balmy, exotic islands had begun to rub raw my nerves. But she had gotten it exactly right.

Our black cat Agnes made sure I didn't keep a lonely vigil out in the weeds, midway between Hamilton's grave and the hillock where I'd discarded spoiled eggs. Indoors, Agnes practiced aloofness. She often reacted with an indignant yowl if one of us petted her, then vigorously tongued the fur we had disturbed. Outdoors, she treated us as guests in her wide-open home. She cheered me up by jumping onto my legs, rubbing her head against my chest, purring, and rolling around. And her welcoming didn't wear off in a moment or two, in the manner of most cats. For the half hour that I fixated on Bertie and Captain Kirk alfresco, Agnes treated me to bountiful pleasantries.

Walter took his friend's death even harder than I did. Although the two rivals couldn't share a room without a wire barrier between them, they had sniffed and nuzzled each other through the mesh. The height of enjoyment for Walter was plopping himself down on the linoleum and pressing his bulk against the front of Bertie's cage when the dwarf bunny was inside. The absence of his buddy affected Walter's appetite. Despite our agreement that we wouldn't get another rabbit—a bunny's modest life span ensured a tragedy every seven years or so—Linda and I decided that for Walter's sake we needed to pick out another long-eared wire-chewing rug wetter.

"Do you know any rabbit breeders?" I asked Linda when I came back into the house. Agnes had accompanied me, but at first glance and snarl at Moobie, she turned to the door and demanded to go outdoors again.

Years had passed since we'd paid money for a pet. Most of our animals had come to us in need of a good home through channels that miraculously sprang open once word got around that we were suckers. But we decided that we wanted oodles of rabbits to choose from in order to pick out a suitable chum for our Checker Giant and a laptop companion for me. Hundreds of choices were what we preferred, and we received exactly that with our visit to Paul and Magda and their bustling backyard warren. Linda had discovered them via the frequently untrustworthy business-card-on-a-bulletin-board technique, which in the past had introduced us to junk men who wouldn't haul junk and handymen who promised to take on Any Job, No Matter How Large or How Small, as long as it wasn't ours. But Linda had found Paul and Magda's card at the ever dependable Blue Ribbon Feed Company, where I weighted down my Ford Focus each Saturday with fifty-pound bags of poultry feed, rabbit pellets, and wild-bird seed. So I experienced only minor rumblings of trepidation on our drive to nearby Ionia.

My head rattled with scattered thoughts when I said hello to Magda. Three nights earlier, as a personal challenge to the supernatural powers of videotaped television shows, I had watched another installment of the animal psychic with Linda, all but daring the magnetically charged particles inside the cassette to mess with us again. The following morning, I had expected a catastrophe, but none had come. And no cataclysm arrived the day after that, just a clunk when Ollie fell two inches to the bottom of his cage after chewing through a wooden perch. The black cloud that had pressed down on us for a month had finally begun to dissipate. We weren't merely shopping for a bunny, I realized. We were ushering in a brand-new epoch of pet happiness and well-being.

As Magda showed us around the complicated complex of cages behind the house, she spoke in such a quiet monotone that in my distracted state of half-a-mind, I thought I was hearing the hum of distant farm machinery. Although my own personality could hardly be described as dynamic, compared to the resolutely low-key Magda, my pores oozed charisma. But once I had ratcheted myself down to a near-sleepwalking condition, I detected Magda's subtle enthusiasm for her rabbits as she stopped here to greet a Mini Lop and refresh its water, and paused there to encourage a nursing Mini Rex mother.

I counted six rows of enclosures divided into thirty cages each and elevated three feet off the ground for easy maintenance and to discourage predators from sniffing around. Everything looked spotless. I don't approve of keeping pet rabbits outdoors. They enjoy human contact, and the elements can be hard on them. But these bunnies seemed exuberantly healthy, and the cages all included shelters from cloudbursts. Magda's excessively tall husband, Paul, bent at the waist to assure me that the majority would find homes long before the summer ended. It struck me that you could double the cage elevation and Paul would still have to stoop to reach the rabbits, which was probably why he concentrated on the sales pitches instead.

"This English Lop won a blue ribbon at the 4-H fair," he said. "We let the little neighbor kid enter her. We raised her and did everything except put our names on the entry."

Instead of questioning the ethics of cheating at a youth fair, I piped up, "She certainly looks friendly."

"All our rabbits are friendly." He twitched his nose in a manner that seemed endemic to bunny breeders. "That's one of the main traits we go for. We don't keep ones that bite."

"What happens to them?" Linda asked reluctantly.

"We sell them at the flea market to people who don't know any better."

Deciding that the sales pitch should be left to Magda after all, I asked her to show us the dwarf rabbits. We'd barely started down the first row when Linda pointed excitedly at a tiny grey bunny. "Is that one old enough to take home? I just love him. Look at that little face."

"He's already weaned and eating dry food," said Magda.

"I don't know. He seems awfully small."

"We've sold smaller rabbits than that one," Paul volunteered, though that would have made them nearly microscopic. I'd seen larger hamsters, but the diminutive size added to his appeal.

"If you're sure it's not too soon to take him," Linda told Magda, and take him home we did. Linda fretted a bit about how quiet he acted in his cage, and I wondered why he wasn't taking to his pellets like most rabbits. We wrote this off to his tender age, as we did his lack of enthusiasm when we set him on the couch with us after dinner.

"At least he isn't peeing all over me," I pointed out, recalling the opinion our first rabbit, Binky, had expressed when I'd held him for the first time.

After letting him sniff around for a few minutes, Linda put him back in his cage and covered him for the night. The next morning, she was up before I was to check on our newest resident. I sat on the edge of the bed, waiting for her to bring us each a cup of coffee per our usual routine, but instead she came back into the room right away.

"Sweetheart," she told me, tightening her robe. "Now, don't get too upset. But the little bunny died."

I couldn't generate any enthusiasm for hauling myself out of bed. I didn't do well with death. I didn't do so well with the chaos of life, either. That didn't leave much in between except for sleep, and I couldn't sleep twenty-four hours a day, despite my most valiant efforts. The best I could do was to haul myself to my feet and in a haze of sleepwalking obliviousness try to drag myself through the rest of the day. But that didn't prevent Bobo from finding me anyway, as sure as a tail finds its rabbit.

CHAPTER 7

....

Bobo's Back in Town

I saw her name on the caller ID, but I still picked up the phone. The numbing succession of pet deaths had dulled my memory of Eileen Kucek's madness, and I imagined that talking about what had happened might help me pull out of my soggy mental state. At first, the conversation stayed on track. With judiciously timed clucks, Eileen listened to the sorry saga of the loss of Bertie's tail—then the larger losses of Stewart, Trevor, Hamilton, Bertie himself, and the nameless bunny. When I finished in a wounded voice and left an appropriate space for more elaborate squawks of sympathy, Eileen was silent. Then she asked, "Now, you don't eat any of them, do you?"

I couldn't believe I had heard her correctly. Dusty was shrieking about a dirty bowl of water that been clean moments earlier, until he'd soaked his pink cookie in it.

"You don't eat any of the ones that die?" she repeated.

"Does this seem funny to you, Eileen?"

"Oh, no, not at all," she assured me. "Lots of people who love animals raise them to eat."

"We certainly don't," I snapped.

"Linda ate Mrs. Piggle-Wiggle."

Her knowledge of that unexpected fact shocked me into silence. Decades before Linda became a vegetarian—and long before she ever crossed my path—she and her first husband, Joe, had indeed reared and eaten a pig. "I've never told you anything about that," I said.

"You must have told Dave O'Connor," she answered as Dusty unleashed another shriek.

"Dave O'Connor? From eighth grade? I haven't spoken to Dave O'Connor since 1966."

"Well, you must have said something to one of his friends, and then he mentioned it to me. I can't remember. Things like that just get around."

"Well, considering that we've lost several of our treasured animals, this is hardly the time to be bringing up Mrs. Piggle-Wiggle," I told her, with as much indignation as I could pack into a sentence that ended with "Piggle-Wiggle." Then, with a hot flush of satisfaction, I slammed down the phone.

Hearing from Eileen reminded me why I'd been dodging even well-intentioned folks. An old college friend had left a message on our answering machine when she'd come to Grand Rapids to visit her dad, but I'd been too depressed to return her call. Any attempt at catching up would inevitably degenerate into my tale of woe. If I couldn't be certain that the person on the other end of the line would smother me with condolences, I didn't even want to attempt a conversation.

I wasn't the only sedentary mammal in the house wallowing in depression. In the past, after we'd return Bertie to his cage each evening, huge Walter would shake off his typical torpor for a blobby gallop into the living room. Buzzing excitedly, he would mark any object within reach with the scent gland on his chin. He'd chin the plant stand, chin the ugly recliner chair, chin the even uglier coffee table, and inevitably chin my lovely foot. Then he'd discreetly retire to the corner for a vigorous pee on the plastic mat that surrounded his litter box. Since Bertie's death, though, Walter confined himself and his prodigious bladder to the dining room, sitting pensively under the table and only occasionally venturing in with us after dinner.

The afternoon that I carried him to his exercise pen in the basement, he didn't notice brand-new brown rabbit Rudy right away. Ignoring his feed dish, he flopped down on the cement and exhibited no interest in moving. Rabbits supposedly possess a keen sense of smell, though I couldn't count the number of bunnies who'd sniffed right past the carrot I was holding for a fruitless search of the rug. Rudy's scent and the click of his toenails on the floor also failed to make an impression with Walter at first. Suddenly, an ear twitched. His eyes snapped into focus, and he scrambled to his feet. Humming and grunting, he butted the wire barrier with his head, then darted back and forth like a caged leopard eager to sink its teeth into the tot with a lollipop. But these were hums and grunts of love emanating from a rabbit that didn't discriminate based on gender. He would gleefully hump anything that moved or just as readily scuffle with it, and little Rudy had instantly restored our Checker Giant to soaringly happy levels of testosterone.

Magda had exuded blandness when Linda had called her earlier that same day with the news that the little grey bunny had died during the night. "You have no idea how upsetting it is to wake up to this, especially after what happened to our ducks and then to Bertie."

"You can come over and pick out another rabbit."

"We are both just sick about it, and we don't understand how such a thing could have happened. You told us he was old enough to leave his mother."

"We never let our rabbits go before they're weaned," Magda drowsily assured her. "He should have been okay, but he is covered by a thirty-day guarantee. You're entitled to an exchange."

"Bob's been a complete wreck since we lost Bertie, so you can imagine how he felt having to bury another little guy. He just came in from the backyard, and he doesn't look very good."

"I don't make you bring in the body. We trust you." And that was for the best, since digging up the rabbit would have put another crimp in our morning. We were running short on towels, so I'd made an executive decision that an animal that hadn't survived twenty-four hours on the premises didn't deserve the full Cannon salute. I had wrapped him in a light blue washcloth instead—which fitted him perfectly—before interring him next to Bertie in the busiest pet cemetery in western Michigan.

"Well, what do you think he died of?" Linda asked.

"It's never happened before, so I couldn't tell you."

I stood beside Linda the whole time she was on the phone, hoping to absorb some vicarious condolences. "What did she say?" I asked Linda after she'd hung up.

"She wasn't what you would call extremely apologetic."

"She isn't extremely anything," I said.

In fact, she was extremely deadpan when, a few hours later, we stood in her garage as if rooted to the spot by an evil spell. Linda repeated how upset we were at the death of the grey bunny, then mentioned it a couple more times without budging from the shadow of Paul's station wagon, until Magda finally took the hint and conceded, "Yes, it's too bad." Suddenly freed from our enchantment by those magic words, Linda, Magda, and I glided out of the garage and into the backyard. I glanced back as a curtain swayed in the kitchen window. Apparently Paul's sales expertise didn't involve returns and exchanges.

While Linda busied herself describing the kind of bunny she wanted to the somnambulant Magda, I marched up and down the rows of cages, searching for an animal encased in a blinding ball of light signifying the peak of imperturbable good health. I paused next to a large duck pen to absorb the wondrous spectacle of Muscovies engaged in peaceful coexistence. Linda's shouts brought me out of my reverie. Working my way back toward the house and Paul's furtive peeks through the glass, I found Linda nuzzling a bouncy brown rabbit that was the spitting image of a wild cottontail. On the ride home, we named him Rudy.

"I'M SUNK IN DEATH, and I can't get up," I told my friend Bill Holm. Just as I had lobbed this comment to him, the frazzled man behind the cash register of the Weigh and Pay restaurant took my dish and placed it on a scale. "Things aren't going well with my mother, either. It used to be that immersing myself in the animals gave me a break from worrying about her, but that doesn't work when the pets are dropping like flies."

"Those are expensive potatoes," Bill said as I paid for my meal. Sure enough, he ended up getting charged far less for the heaps of chicken he had shoveled onto his plate than I ended up laying out for my spuds, veggies, and cod. "You more than anyone should realize that bird bones are hollow, and hollow means free at the Weigh and Pay. And did you know cod is also known as the Gleason of the Sea?" I looked away. Conversations with Bill were inevitably peppered with references to Jackie Gleason, Harry Nilsson, Raymond Burr, Judge Judy, or other celebrities whom he considered admirable yet absurd. "See, I'm also getting a lettuce salad. Lettuce is almost weightless. They may end up owing *me* money for this meal. You, on the other hand, may have to get a duck-pen equity loan."

Judging from the scowling faces of the senior citizens who had been bused in from a nearby assisted-living facility, I suspected that either the skewed food prices had triggered instant nostalgia for institutional fare or they had overheard Bill.

"What do you think, guys?" the cashier asked as we rooted through containers next to the register for two sets of clean silverware. "Personally, I don't think it's going to fly."

"Me neither, but you'd better not let the boss hear you," said Bill.

The cashier snorted. "You mean my father? We've had this discussion many, many times. He tells me every Korean-owned corner grocery store in New York City sells take-out food by weight, and its all the rage out there. 'Lowell ain't New York City, Dad,' I tell him."

"It's more like Tbilisi," Bill replied.

"Yeah, well, at least I got my way with the music." He beamed, pointing to the ceiling speaker as we scurried to a booth. On second thought, I decided, the weighty prices hadn't caused the sour expressions at the two center tables. It was the heavy slab of Aerosmith and AC/DC on the local headbanger station.

After I brought Bill up-to-date on the animal psychic and pet death coincidences, he uttered the chilling phrase "Bobo's back in town," then startled me with the news that he and his wife, Carol, had encountered the man named Love 22 during a recent trip to Key West.

"You met the actual Love 22?" I asked with my fork poised motionless in the air.

"Yes. He was doing some kind of bad street-performer routine, and he handed me one of his twenty-two-dollar bills. I was stunned into speechlessness, and I felt weak and ashamed for not speaking with him. The next day, we ran into him again, on the beach. Bravely, I approached him and told him about the article we had written."

Decades earlier, Bill and I had penned a tangled narrative for *Fortean Times,* a British journal of unexplained phenomenon, about a rash of strange coincidences we'd suffered involving clowns and the number twenty-two. The plague had started with our sighting of a car in Grand Rapids bearing the inscriptions BOBO THE ROLLER CLOWN and TAKE A CLOWN TO LUNCH just after we had filmed a home movie with Bill wearing a clown headpiece and sitting in a bathtub while contemplating the globe. The siege of convoluted circus synchronicities included newspaper articles about a clown-like figure named Love 22, who was prosecuted for handing out "counterfeit" twenty-two-dollar bills. After this assault, we routinely blamed a cosmic force, Bobo, for the frequent far-fetched coincidences in our lives.

Bill winced. "When did we write that article — 1982? It took Bobo almost twenty years to come up with the punch line."

"At least it wasn't twenty-two years." I shivered. "What did Mr. 22 say about the article?"

"He wasn't the least bit interested in it," said Bill. "He's so immersed in his own twenty-twos that independent verification means nothing to him at all. Besides, he looked a little worried, like maybe he thought I was a stalker or just more insane than him."

"I wonder if the animal psychic would be the least bit interested in our pet deaths. Maybe I can get her to pay my psychiatric bills."

"Are you going back on Zoloft?"

A few years earlier, when Stanley Sue had briefly fallen ill, I'd examined my ongoing problems with depression and, at the urging of a neurotic psychiatrist, had decided to try a brain-altering pharmaceutical. When the Zoloft had stopped working for me a couple of years later, I'd quit rather than hopping up to a higher dosage

"I don't think so. But I need something. I can barely drag myself through the day."

Bill started questioning me about how it felt to be profoundly depressed. Garden-variety malaise was a way of life with him, but not my twin specialties of debilitating gloom and paralyzing anxiety. Just as I had launched into a gloriously self-pitying description of my ruined psyche, the restaurant owner's son slid into the booth next to Bill.

"Food okay, guys?"

"Excellent chicken," Bill remarked, edging away from him. "It's worth its weight in gold."

"Yeah, well, I want to get away from this whole weighing idea. People are suspicious of it. They glare at me like I'm pulling something over on them. Look, look at that. That's just what I'm talking about. She's not supposed to be doing that."

I turned to watch as a large woman examined her plate on the scale and shuffled back to the buffet. Using her spoon she started scraping nonmeat ballast back into the food bins. The owner's son buried his head in his hands just as his dad wandered out of the kitchen, wiping his palms on his apron. He stared in befuddlement as the woman continued emptying her dish with decreasing regard for returning the food items to their proper locations.

"Bo!" the father called when he noticed the vacancy behind the cash register. "Bo. You're needed up here, pronto."

Bo swung his body away from our table and groaned as he

strode toward the front of the restaurant, leaving Bill and me staring stupidly at each other.

"Tell me his name isn't Bobo."

"Whatever medication you go on, get extras for me," Bill said.

I RETURNED HOME from the Weigh and Pay just in time to check on Rudy and Walter in their change-of-scenery exercise pens in the basement. Walter's loop of fencing was stapled to the baseboard to keep him from shoving it across the room, while Rudy's smaller circle was fastened to Walter's with twisted wire. When I greeted Walter, I found him snuffling at the floor, wondering what had happened to the smaller rabbit. I wondered what had happened to him, too, and delicately conveyed my concern to my wife.

"Linda, quick, get down here," I bellowed. "Rudy's disappeared!"

The wooden steps shook—the entire house groaned—as Linda thundered down a stairway made from inch-thick hardwood. It would be one thing if she were elephantine. But despite her small size, she wielded such vast reserves of physical energy that any material object in her path stood in deadly peril. Possessions owned and operated solely by me cheerfully tolerated years of use with no ill effects. But Linda snapped the plastic handles of her vacuum cleaners in two, yanked the shower door off its tracks, collapsed her side of the bed, reduced her dresser drawers to tilted, immovable trays, and generally wreaked widespread destruction with the smallest twitch of her little toe. Metal sprinklers flew apart. Portable radios shed their antennas. Door keys bent at forty-five-degree angles. Oceans evaporated. The moon fell from its orbit. I wondered from time to time why I hadn't been pulverized.

After the stairs had ceased to undulate and I could hear again,

Linda pointed to a spot beneath the potter's wheel. "He's right here."

"How did he get out of his pen?"

"I don't know. But you're a good boy, aren't you?" she told Rudy as he allowed her to scoop him up and plunk him back in his enclosure. When I checked on him a few minutes later, however, he had managed to liberate himself again.

To determine how a dog or cat had tricked me, I'd have to hide inside the wall and hope that Fido or Fluffy repeated the stunt as I pressed an eye against a peephole. Not with a rabbit, though. Rabbits lack the slightest shred of inhibition when it comes to repeating a naughty deed in full public view. While I watched, Rudy edged his nose under the bottom of the loop, lifted the fencing slightly, and wriggled his body beneath it. Then he plopped down next to Walter's enclosure and cleaned his ears with his front paws.

Emerging from the workroom with a bale of twine twice the size of Rudy, I secured the eight o'clock position of the loop to the leg of the potter's wheel. Next, I tacked the three o'clock and six o'clock positions to a two-foot-long section of two-by-four, which I laid on the floor inside the pen. The result was a vaguely egg-shaped enclosure, which I hoped would remain secure around the clock.

For the next three days, Rudy and Walter shared their after-dinner basement exercise together while apart in their separate loops. On the fateful fourth day, I tiptoed downstairs after dinner without disturbing or displacing a single molecule of staircase wood, only to find that Rudy had managed to vacate his pen. I bent down and tested the weight of the board and the vigor of the potter's-wheel mooring with my nose, then a finger. The loop refused to budge.

Hunkered down next to Walter's cage, the little brown rabbit scratched his head with indifference until I snatched him and returned him to his pen. With impressive nonchalance, he proceeded to demonstrate how he had made his escape. I saw it, but I could hardly believe it. Scurrying his little legs at hummingbird-wing speed, he clambered up the thirty-inch-tall fence as effortlessly as you or I might ascend an anthill in an auto. This time, though, instead of parking himself near Walter, he zoomed across the basement, steering toward the workroom and the door to the great outdoors, which, thankfully, was tightly shut, climbproof, and burrow-resistant.

After I returned him to his pen, I called Linda downstairs. Once the house stopped pitching like a dingy in a typhoon, Rudy obligingly repeated his Houdini routine. "I guess they can't be in the basement any longer," I said with a wan smile. Surrendering to the tiniest difficulty always cheered me slightly.

"I'll get a sheet," said Linda.

"What good's that going to do?" I asked, but she was already bouncing the giant bowstring of the stairway. To the rumbling tone of nearly subsonic B-flat, she galloped back with a sheet that could no longer do duty covering Dusty's cage because of the peppering of holes inflicted by his beak. But after she had wrapped it around a length of the loop, it worked fine converting the scalable surface into a comparatively smooth wall. Rudy sniffed and pawed the sheet for a few moments to determine if it could be tastily munched in the manner of our woodwork, carpet, or electrical cords. Then he made an attempt to climb his favorite spot and warmed my heart by immediately giving up rather than trying a different location. Linda's quick solution seemed to do the trick.

• • •

As I HERDED the ducks and hens into the barn, it dawned on me that Victor hadn't lunged at me for weeks. I could stroll from the water spigot to the outdoor wading pools without worrying that he would blindside me, and I no longer needed to arm myself with a push broom for self-defense. Victor seemed to remember my kindness to him with the watermelon, or perhaps he had come to think of me as a spindly food dispenser rather than a rival. I hated to admit it, but as much as I missed Hamilton, the absence of the aggressive Muscovy improved the emotional climate of the flock. Even shy Ramone had literally come out of the shadows to mingle with the other ducks.

Returning from the barn, I noticed a rabbit that could have been Rudy's twin on the hill behind the backyard fence. The unusually tame critter unhurriedly hopped away when I attempted to approach it. I imagined Linda laughing when I described how I mistook a wild rabbit for Rudy. But as I turned toward the house, I discovered that I had left the basement door open and remembered I'd last seen Rudy studying the sheet in his basement pen. Creeping dread overtook me, turning to full-scale panic as I hurried through the door and with a few strides reached Rudy's empty enclosure. Safely stuck inside his loop, the less agile Walter lifted his head and fixed me with an indignant stare that said, "It serves you right." I scoured the basement, checking Rudy's favorite spots near the potter's wheel and beneath the tables in the misnamed workroom, but I couldn't find him. Back outside, I couldn't locate the brown rabbit again, either.

I hit the stairs with a clatter that Linda would have envied if she hadn't been shocked by the lunatic who burst into the kitchen. "Quick, help me, I left the back door open. Rudy isn't in his pen. We've got to catch him, hurry!" Bug-eyed and panting, with my hair all but standing on end, I was the embodiment of a cartoon depiction of hysteria.

"He's right here in his cage," she informed me with a level of blandness that would have done Magda proud. "I was about to bring Walter upstairs when your mother called, asking if you had taken her keys. I think I'll bring him up now."

It took me hours to get over the shock of thinking that Rudy had escaped outdoors. I slept poorly, while phantoms shaped like Stewart, Trevor, Bertie, Hamilton, the little grey bunny, and an accusatory Rudy slid underneath my eyelids and flitted about in the blackness. My dad made an unbilled cameo appearance with Benny Goodman. My mom and I wandered a maze of rabbit-pen loops, trying to find our way to my grandmother's kitchen. The next morning, I asked Linda to make an appointment with the doctor for me.

THE SIDE EFFECTS of the antidepressant sneaked up on me as I drove to work. I'd been taking the pills for three days without any noticeable results, which was a good thing, since instant relief from an existential dilemma would have made me suspicious. My osteopath had recommended this particular medication because of its effectiveness against anxiety plus the fact that none of his other patients had suffered an adverse reaction. None of his other patients had suffered visits from the hose demon, Henry the master gardener, or Bobo the Roller Clown either, so this didn't exactly let me off the hook.

I popped in an ancient Van Morrison CD as I turned onto the East Beltline. While I wasn't what you'd call jaded to the charms of music even after reviewing hundreds of discs for publication, I had reason to doubt that "Moondance" alone could suddenly slow my cellular activity to that of a hunk of granite. Fortunately, my transformation into inanimate matter didn't impair my ability to drive. I had become part of the car, sort of an extension of the driver's seat with arms and legs. Once I reached my workplace, getting to the door presented unusual difficulty. Instead of locomoting my body, I dragged the building toward me with each step, and having to rotate the planet beneath my feet added to my sluggishness.

I felt medicated, but without the pleasures that the word implied. My sensory apparatus had been dulled. Perceptions lagged behind stimuli like a movie with an out-of-sync soundtrack. When my friend Ron moved his mouth to greet me, I heard his hello a split second later. When I opened my jaws to return the salutation, a brief but noticeable pause elapsed before the drool flowed in reply. My thought processes seemed normal enough, so writing catalog copy for my client proceeded at the typical glacial pace. But avoiding ossification required me to lurch to a standing position and visit Randy at his workbench in the bowels of the shipping room for cup upon cup of seriously caffeinated coffee.

Back home after lunch, I was grateful that the direst effects of the drug had dissipated, but to prevent myself from declining into total torpor I had to keep moving around. Only move around and do what? Physical exertion and I had never seen eye to eye. I happily encouraged Linda to hire college students for stress-inducing projects such as barn cleanup, duck-pen gravel maintenance, and lacing my shoes. Occasionally, though, an odd job would motivate me. The task I had in mind didn't seem that debilitating if I did only a teeny-weeny bit of it each day. Given the nice fall weather, I surmised that the work could even be — gasp — not entirely unfun.

Although we lived within five hundred feet of the Grand River, we rarely stood on its bank. Spring rains flooded the hollow beyond the back fence, blocking our path. By summer that same lowland turned into an impassable malarial swamp. In the fall, when the wet finally evaporated, neck-high weeds barricaded the way until heavy winter snows battered them down. While I was powerless against the elemental forces of rain, snow, and biting insects, I was merely weak when it came to combating vegetative growth. Armed with a grass whip and careful vigilance for poison ivy, which a string trimmer would readily atomize and spray onto my face, I could conceivably, slowly, lazily cut a path to the river.

Wild birds were my motivation. They had fascinated me ever since my move to the country from downtown Grand Rapids more than a decade earlier. Dealing with the challenges presented by our Jekyll-and-Hyde Ollie, avian geniuses Stanley Sue and Dusty, and stubborn dove Howard convinced me to consider their outdoor cousins as more than flighty darts with colorful feathers. The months we'd spent with orphan European starling Weaver, who had learned to talk as well as a parrot, suggested that each and every bird that teetered on a tree limb or bobbled on the ground possessed a charismatic personality. So I started learning songs and field marks in my usual haphazard way. But Linda and I hadn't investigated the "riparian habitat" of our river, where we might glimpse shorebirds, ducks, and other dabblers, plus the occasional migrating warbler. Fall was migration time, and time was wasting, so I started on the path by lopping down the first few weeds.

I also started on a second antidepressant a week later. Despite the bouts of outdoor exercise, I still had enough pent-up anxiety under my skin to power a small city, with sufficient stores of uneasiness to light up the suburbs, too. A fellow music writer who also fought with fear and gloom had suggested a particular medication, though I felt sure that he consorted with a higher-quality inner demon than the clunk that slummed inside me. My osteopath agreed with the drug choice and presented me with a sleekly packaged introductory kit. Nestled inside four rows of plastic bubbles, twenty-one minimum-therapeutic-dosage pills lorded it over seven smaller half-dosage pills, as minimum-therapeutic-dosage pills all too often do.

"Most of our patients skip the first row of pills altogether," my doctor told me, but if anything I wanted to cut the half-dosage pills in half.

Since side effects from the first antidepressant hadn't kicked in until I'd taken it for three days, I downed my training-wheels dose of the second medication without a second thought. No neurological calamity struck during the drive to my workplace. After I'd worked for about an hour, though, I stopped to chat with Ron and caught myself wondering whether I was awake or dreaming—not the strongest indication of mental health. I couldn't quite categorize the particular flavor of dissociation from reality. Then, while sitting at the computer, I experienced what could best be described as a lightning strike inside my skull. For a fraction of an instant, the external world fizzed in a hot flash of white noise and static. While the bulk of my nervous system was busy superheating, the lazier neurons that had been caught playing canasta in the back room contented themselves with shooting electrical jolts through my limbs. All of this happened so quickly, I imagined that I had imagined it. When it occurred twice more, I drove home during a lull between voltage peaks and climbed into bed, where I spent the remainder of the day.

Oddly enough, the following morning I felt better than I'd remembered feeling for months, or even years. "It's as if the medication burned off all my anxiety," I told Linda.

"You're not taking that again, are you?"

"Absolutely not. But it's almost worth going through every few months or so."

THE PATH TO THE river evolved with inexplicable ease. If I had all the athletic prowess of a rusty gate, at least I could swing my arm like one and with the addition of a grass whip eventually hack down a weed. Waving my skinny appendage to and fro, I allowed the weight of the L-shaped sickle to inch my body toward the water in much the same fashion that a pendulum advances the hour. The activity was so mechanical, I turned into a perpetual-motion device. Even after my brain decided I should stop, my swinging arm exercised a mind of its own, repeating, "Cut more weeds."

Within a few days, I had chopped, sliced, diced, and, especially, minced a six-foot-wide avenue down the hill, across the spongy matter of the swamp, into the poison ivy–strewn margin of the woods, and ultimately all the way through the trees to the Grand River. I saw little logic in hiking the path with Linda only to stand single file at the end and remark, "Yup, that's the water. Could you please move your head?" We needed space to spread out upon our arrival, so over the next several days I carved out an airy oasis seventy feet long and fifteen feet deep. But once at the river, we'd still need a way to get down the bank to the water's edge without rubbing up against enough poison oak, poison sumac, poison ivy, stinging nettles, belladonna, and amanita mushrooms to wipe out Tbilisi. The grass whip kept whipping. Still, it was better than the nervous tic I'd been cultivating over the past month.

My enjoyment of being in the woods was heightened by the fact that I had never benefited from more than fleeting exposure to nature as a child. Once a summer our family might drive to Cannonsburg Park for a picnic, but we would cling to the picnic table like ants, venturing into the woods only if they lay between us and a playground. I still wondered what I had missed compared to folks who had chased birds and butterflies for decades and knew a dragonfly from a damselfly. Houseflies were my milieu.

My grass whipping finally paid off big. I normally wouldn't have noticed a single, silent brown bird hiding in the leaves. But the hush at the river's edge—the lush green that muffled the whoosh of traffic—allowed me to pay attention to tiny things. Tree bark, I marveled. *Tree bark.* The brown bird looped out over the river, then flew back again. As I moved to get a better look, it replayed its boomerang flight. Finally I caught the silhouette of its crest, the wedding band on its tail, and a high-pitched squeak that a locust wouldn't have envied. Embarrassed not to have recognized a cedar waxwing, I glanced at the next tree down the line, where another waxwing performed a mirror-image routine. It was the same on the opposite bank. Up and down the river, four or five birds at a time went airborne as these berry eaters dined on flies on the fly. Not to be outdone, a belted kingfisher hit the water with a crack and, after settling on a snag, erupted in a long, rolling, mirthless, chattering laugh, lamenting his failure to catch a fish. He should have tried the bugs.

When Linda joined me the following evening, the bell tones of a song sparrow serenaded us, along with the splash of turtles that hopped off their log when they spotted us. I wanted the cedar waxwings to surprise her, but we had barely planted our heels next to an oak when a pair of crow-size birds zipped by with folded necks, splayed orange legs, and grumpy *kuk-kuk* calls. "Green herons," I gasped.

"No!" said Linda.

We'd once glimpsed a solitary green heron at a marsh on Lake Erie. A pair in full view in our own liquid backyard was as mind-numbing as being back on antidepressant number two. Honks replaced the receding squawks as a dozen Canada geese wheeled close, pulled up landing gear at the sound of Linda's cries, then touched down in the water behind a grassy island one hundred yards upriver. Their clatter scattered a flock of killdeers, which squealed their name as they took flight.

"Who knew all this went on down here," I said.

"You'd never know our house was just back there."

Except for the whine of a farmer's tractor and a truck that blew its horn like the salute of a gargantuan swan, we might as well have been stranded in the wilds of Manitoba. For as far as we could see, the riverbank shielded our eyes from any man-made structures, though a quality doughnut shop wouldn't have been entirely unappealing. The beauty drew us back evening after evening. We kept close tabs on the larger birds that clustered around the tiny island, watching for Linda's flock of Canada geese, a trio of juvenile sandhill cranes with shaggy brown backs, a skittish great blue heron, and—if we had been very, very good and had eaten all our vegetables—a magnificent bald eagle bathing in the shallows.

"What's that on the rocks?" Linda asked. I swept the opposite bank with my binoculars. "There's two of them!" she exclaimed. "Right there. Just a little bit down from us."

I had grown so used to goggling at big birds at a distance that I hadn't noticed a couple of diminutive peepers right under my substantial nose. "Sandpipers," I muttered. Bobbing and teetering as they walked and probed the mud for food, they resembled a toy maker's whimsical creations. I was about to express my amazement that we'd find sandpipers on our river when an unearthly call grabbed my jaw and dropped it to the ground. Linda shared the same dumb expression of astonishment as we listened to a resonant piping that rose from a low, throaty croak to the suggestion of a woodwind at full tilt. If you crossed a clarinet with an exotic percussive instrument, you might create a similar call, but only if a master musician played the theme as a matter of life and death. The call repeated again and again, dazzling us with every replay.

"Could that be a heron?" Linda wondered.

A great blue heron perched upriver on a stump halfway to the island. Leaving our neat little clearing behind, I found myself racing through the brambles and poisonous plants trying to locate the soloist. As I drew opposite the heron, the volume of the sound diminished.

"It's not the heron," I wheezed when I'd trudged back to Linda. "It must be some other bird on the other side of the trees across the river."

As soon as we got back to the house, I retreated upstairs, flipped past the Madagascar CD with its call of the indri lemur, and selected a disc of bird songs. A few minutes after I had gone downstairs to tell Linda that the cosmic bugler was a sandhill crane, the phone rang. Ignoring the warning of the caller ID, I lifted the receiver anyway.

"Just checking in," said Eileen brightly, as if we were old friends rather than old classmates. "I just wondered what was new."

"What's new," I harrumphed. I didn't know what to say at first. Then, in an unexpected burst of goodwill, I suggested, "You really should come over some evening and walk down to the river with us."

CHAPTER 8

······································

Golden Orb Weaver

Linda and I had started taking a palm-size two-way radio on our solo trips down to the river. That way, if I saw an interesting bird while Linda was scrubbing cages in the dining room, I could radio her, "There's a pair of spotted sandpipers by the big tree, but no eagle," and Linda would answer, "What? I can't hear you. Your voice sounds funny."

I had hoped to get my daily peek at a tiny flock of migrating yellow-rumped warblers that moved along the riverbank in the late afternoon. This attractive brown fall bird with yellow patches had previously carried the dignified title of myrtle warbler. But pranksters in the American Birding Association had renamed it for a potentially embarrassing body part to keep the white-breasted nuthatch, red-bellied woodpecker, and bristle-thighed curlew company. I could usually spot the warblers in the trees only by homing in on their sharp *pik* call, but some idiot was polluting the aural environment by running a string trimmer. It didn't take me long to realize that we were that idiot.

I tried to radio Linda from the river to ask her what was going on, but she didn't reply. Either she was right on top of the puttering two-stroke engine or she had dropped her walkie-talkie into a wading pool. Heading back toward the house, I stepped over the backyard fence and wiggled a finger at our student helper Mr. Bean, who flicked off the Ryobi and vigorously waved.

"Oh, Mr. Tarte," he shouted just before I had managed to scurry out of conversation range. I reconciled myself to waiting for him at the basement door. "I wonder if I might ask your advice," he began. "There's a girl at college that I want to take out on a picnic and ask her to go steady. Do you consider Fallasburg Park to be a romantic spot?"

"Just keep away from the dumpsters," I suggested. "If the aroma doesn't chase her off, the yellow jackets will." When he nodded as if seriously considering my remark, I asked him, "Is this someone you've known a long time?"

"This will be the first time I've dated her."

"And you're asking her to go steady?" I thought that going steady had fallen out of fashion when *The Adventures of Ozzie and Harriet* had left the air, but social mores proceeded at their own pace at the local Bible college. I couldn't resist the obvious. "Why would you ask someone to go steady on a first date?"

"I can't get her to talk to me," he said, shaking the string trimmer to convey his agitation with a slosh of its gas tank. "She spends most of her spare time with the other Indonesian students. But if we were going steady, I could see her on a regular basis."

"I guess that makes a certain kind of sense." I glanced at the cloudless sky in the wild hope that the sun might go supernova and interrupt our exchange. Instead, to my horror, I heard myself prolong the moment. "What happened to that Korean girl?"

"She's too busy with her Korean girlfriends. But I'm sure I have a chance with this one. Do you think it would be too forward if I bought her a ring?"

Substituting for a cosmic calamity, Linda burst around the corner, allowing me to slip into the workroom while she distracted him with a barrage of questions about his string trimming. The last noise I heard before easing the door shut with a soft but fulfilling click was Linda: "You didn't cut down the weeds around that big yellow spider, did you?"

I gave her a few minutes to sort out whatever the big-yellow-spider matter might involve. Then, fearing that Mr. Bean had entangled her in his gooey web of dating-etiquette questions, I followed Judy Teany's lead in rescuing my dad from old man Brink so many years ago. Clicking the two-way radio, I informed her, "Telephone, Linda." Apparently, I hadn't lied. As soon as she clomped up the stairs, the phone rang as promised.

"It's your mother," she told me, passing me the receiver and glowering because I had called her into the house just for that. Then she raced back outdoors to resume her conversation with the hired helper who had earned his secret nickname via his resemblance to sad-sack comedian Rowan Atkinson.

I didn't know what to make of the phone call with my mom, who seemed levelheaded, if forgetful, as we chatted about her intention to winterize the Buick and the color of Mrs. Teany's latest wig. Then she announced that in November she would be working at the polls, which she hadn't done for almost a decade. She had last applied two years earlier but hadn't been called in, presumably because her old boss had noticed her problems concentrating.

"How did you find out you'll be working?" I asked.

"It was the funniest thing," she said. "I was taking a walk to the end of the block, and down by Aberdeen School I saw a piece of paper on the sidewalk with my name on it telling me to report to the polls. I don't know how it got there."

"Where did you find that paper?"

"Just down the street. It might have been closer to church. I can't remember."

The phone call alarmed me. Before calling Joan to discuss this latest development, I peered out the window and noted Linda and Mr. Bean still embroiled in conversation. From his slumped posture and his longing glance up at the sun, I gathered that my wife had gained the advantage.

"I FEEL SO SORRY for that spider," Linda told Joan as we sat on her enclosed porch.

Joan made playful kazoo noises with her mouth as she picked up Beethoven from the cement floor and deposited him inside a cardboard box. "Where did your dolly go?" she asked him, even though, like many pure white ferrets, he was as deaf as a deceased composer. Before she could completely remove the stuffed doll, the outraged weasel grabbed it by the arm and yanked it back inside his box.

Her husband, Jack, came out with a piece of popcorn and handed it to me. "Busy Bird will land on your lap if you hold this very still. She loves popcorn." Instead of paying the slightest particle of attention to me, the house sparrow scolded Jack with a level of invective that only a bird could muster. "She hates it when I wear my glasses." He said this on the sly from the side of his mouth, so that the sparrow wouldn't overhear.

"What about the spider?" Joan asked.

While we tended to have animals dumped on us by other people, Joan and Jack stumbled across them as they tried to go about their lives. Driving to work one morning, Joan had noticed a

sausage-shaped, white furry form scampering under a van in front
of her at a traffic light. The next thing she knew, she had become
a ferret owner. Jack had scooped up an abandoned baby sparrow
in the driveway after the parents had shoved the featherless pest
out of the nest twice. He undertook the daunting task of raising
the chick into a sassy adult that preferred lording it over the other
pets to sparrowing outdoors. Elsewhere in the house skulked a
rescued wolf-dog amalgamation, a couple of adult cats, and three
growing kittens that had recently materialized half-starved in the
yard—though you couldn't tell they had ever suffered to see the
spoiled things now.

"I'm scared to death of those big yellow spiders," Linda told
Joan. "I can't even stand to look at a picture of them in a book."

"Golden orb weavers," I added.

"Every time I go out to the barn, I have to look the other way, because it terrifies me just to see that spider by the door. But one of the
college students cut down all the weeds around her web, and now
there aren't enough insects. I don't know how she'll feed herself."

"She's a spider," I pontificated. "She'll take care of it."

"That is worrying, about Mom," Joan said.

"Where did Dusty Marie go?" asked Jack.

Joan pointed to the snaking coils of plastic tubing that covered
the floor of the porch and concealed the second ferret. "I don't
believe she found that piece of paper about the job at the polls,
either. It really concerns me, Bob."

Swiveling at the sound of Busy Bird pecking her cage bars, I
caught sight of the building across the street; large letters painted
across the bricks proclaimed FOSTER GRAVE VAULT CO. I flinched to
face such an unvarnished reminder of where my father currently
resided. "I didn't tell you about Mom's visit last week," I said to
change the subject inside my head.

"What happened?"

"To start with, she couldn't remember how to get to our house and had to write down the directions."

"She almost hit someone," Linda added.

"Even then, she had trouble following the instructions and ended up coming a roundabout way. When she was leaving, though, she pulled out into the road directly in front of an oncoming car, swerved to miss it, and nearly clipped the postman's station wagon."

"She nearly hit the postman," Linda said.

Joan's attention drifted to Beethoven in his box. He lay on his back holding a tennis ball in his paws, like a sea otter about to crack an urchin's shell for lunch. A few inches from him, the plastic tube wiggled as Dusty Marie navigated the tunnel. "She probably shouldn't be driving, except around the neighborhood, maybe."

"Next time we ask her over, I'll just pick her up."

"Or we'll come and get her," offered Jack.

"Watch this," said Joan. Standing in the center of the porch, she recited in a singsong voice, "Busy Bird, fly, fly." The sparrow launched herself in circles around the room, landed on top of her cage, and puffed herself up with pride. "If you think that's something," Joan told us when we had finished laughing, "you should hear her sing her heart out to a Journey CD."

I hadn't come to appreciate animals until I married Linda, in 1990, and even after that they had crept upon me unawares. But Joan had long enjoyed the company of all manner of creatures, wild and tame, and so had Jack. A female squirrel that they had hand-fed and befriended once made a special trip down the tree to the picnic table to show off her babies, and a pigeon they had rescued a few summers ago hung around the yard for weeks. As we drove home, I expressed my deep regard for the two of them to Linda. "Those people." I shook my head and sighed. "They're even worse than we are."

IN ADDITION TO HER talent with animals, Joan had invented the purse finder.

Tens of thousands of years ago, disparate cultures scattered around the world had developed basic inventions like the plow, the irrigation ditch, and the collapsible umbrella entirely independent of one another. Similarly, when my mom started losing her purse on a regular basis, my sisters and I almost simultaneously came up with the idea of planting some sort of noisemaking device in her handbag. I got the ball rolling by buying a gizmo off eBay designed to help people locate a TV remote control that had slipped behind the couch to keep the stray beer cans company. I triumphantly stuck the beeper inside her purse and from across the room pushed the red button on the transmitter. A faint but clear high-pitched tone harangued us from the handbag. But when I stashed the purse beneath a cushion or buried it at the bottom of mom's sweater drawer, the alert tone turned into an ineffectual lisp.

Meanwhile, from a pricey high-tech gadget catalog, Bett ordered a fancy-pants Never Lose Anything Again doohickey that turned out to be a glorified redesign of the TV-remote-control finder. The manufacturer must have used the same cheap signaling microchip. We couldn't detect the telltale beep unless the purse hid in plain sight surrounded by several cubic feet of open air. In a stroke of near genius, I considered subscribing to a paging service. That way, when Mom lost her handbag, Bett, Joan, Linda, Stanley Sue, or I could simply punch in a phone number from the comfort of our home or cage, and the pager tone would reveal the latest hidey-hole. But none of the pagers that I investigated on the Web boasted of having the type of high-decibel tone that the job required. So I abandoned the idea.

While I soldiered on with a device that emitted a feeble, quavering tone when it detected the distinctive sound of a handclap—or a door slamming shut, or a fork clicking against a dinner plate, or a parakeet chewing a millet seed—Joan came up with the breakthrough notion of using a wireless doorbell. About the same size as a pack of cigarettes, and about the same weight, too, if the pack were made of heavy plastic and contained a trio of AA batteries plus electronic circuitry, it did add major heft to a handbag. But, boy, was that sucker loud. Joan could stow the purse beneath the mattress in an upstairs bedroom, and from the living room downstairs we could hear the friendly *bing-bong*. To keep doorbell and pocketbook from going their separate ways, Joan wrote across the front and back of the unit in large letters with an indelible marker: PURSE FINDER—KEEP IN PURSE.

"A purse finder," remarked my mom with a mixture of interest and suspicion. "What will they think of next?"

For weeks the purse finder worked brilliantly. My mother would phone and confess in sorrowful tones that somehow, quite remarkably and unexpectedly, she seemed to have misplaced her purse, and what was she going to do? Joan or I would hightail it over to the house and retrieve the push-button unit from its Mom-proof hiding place in my dad's file cabinet, behind his collection of road maps. Within moments, a reassuring chime would lead us to her purse, tucked behind the dehumidifier at the bottom of the stairs, concealed inside the slide-projector box in the bedroom closet, or nestled in the bread drawer with a boatload of paper bags, wrapped in a mystery inside an enigma. Then we'd stand back and wait for the praises.

• • •

LINDA HADN'T EXAGGERATED her fear of the golden orb weaver spider. Up north at her cabin in Morley, I had once teased her by asking, "Have we ever seen this kind of vireo before?" And then, instead of showing her a photo of a bird, I thrust a picture of the black-and-yellow spider at her. She shrieked. I laughed. Oh, the fun we had.

I had always assumed that she was overacting for the sake of our mutual amusement. But when I found her in the pumpkin patch a few days after our visit with Joan and Jack, she insisted, "I really am terrified of them. When I was little, I saw one in the grass in my mom's backyard and thought that it was dead. I couldn't stop myself from touching it out of a sort of morbid fascination. But it wasn't dead, and it came at me like this." She held her hands at chin level and wiggled her fingers at me. "I was absolutely traumatized, and after that, I never wanted anything to do with them again."

"But you're not exactly afraid of insects," I observed as she plucked a squash bug off a pumpkin, examined it in the light, and discarded it over her shoulder.

"Bugs, snakes, salamanders, they don't bother me at all. There was a ditch in front of my mother's house, and I practically lived in there. I would collect snails in a bucket, and when I found those big male ones, I was in absolute heaven. I kept them in a Shedd's peanut butter pail that had dirt and grass in it, and I would check on them every day."

"And are we keeping *that* in a pail?" Having selected a squash bug that met with her approval, she cupped it in her hand.

"No, it's for the spider."

"You're kidding."

"I called Mrs. Martini today, and she told me that spiders won't eat insects with hard shells, and I'd been putting Japanese beetles in her web. But she won't touch them."

"Mrs. Martoni."

"Martini, Martoni." Her voice trailed behind her as she marched toward the golden orb weaver. "The web scares me almost as much as the spider does."

I had to admit that if the spider didn't look sinister enough with the black-and-yellow tribal mask painted on her back, the toothy zigzag down the center of her web clearly suggested danger. Linda screeched to a halt as she came up on the weaver. From two feet away she aimed her insect, tossed it at the web, and missed.

"Your hand is shaking too much."

"Feel my heart. It's beating like crazy." Her bug had disappeared into the tall grass beneath the web, and she couldn't find it. "Now I've got to get another one." Next to the web and tacked to the side of the barn with wisps of silk, the spider had spun three brown cocoons each about the diameter of a nickel. I didn't see how they would survive a hearty gust of wind, much less a typical Michigan winter, notorious for its inhospitality toward arachnid egg sacs. You can hardly sit down in a restaurant in the middle of January without hearing someone at the next table comment, "I don't know about them spiders' eggs in this awful cold."

"How many tries does it usually take you?" I called after Linda.

Deciding to undertake an insect safari of my own, I slipped inside the barn and, ignoring the disdainful glare of our Rhode Island Red hen Rosie, headed for the dusty windowpane where I had discovered the swallowtail butterflies during the summer. Sure enough, a quartet of flies bounced against the sunlit glass in search of a way out. One of the four didn't bounce so much as weakly flail. It had become caught in the national historic ruins of a web whose owner had vacated the site years ago.

"Sorry," I told the fly as I grabbed it by a wing and carried it outside.

Linda still hadn't returned from her search for the ultimate squash bug, so I proceeded to attach my insect to the web. While I didn't share Linda's terror of the large spider, I was nervous that at the first tremor of a silken strand, the golden orb weaver would awaken from immobility and launch herself onto my hand in the blink of a fly's eye. Instead, I had plenty of time in which to learn that adhering a now deceased *Musca domestica* to the web of an *Argiope aurantia* required more *Dexteritie manual* than I possessed. Finally, after turning the web into a small trampoline but still not raising the hackles of its builder, I managed to adhere a single hair of the housefly's leg to a microscopic picture-hanging hook attached to the living room section of the web.

The next afternoon I checked the web only to find that my fly had fallen off. Linda had replaced it with a bug that met with the spider's approval. Encased in silk, it dangled within millimeters of her jaws. "Oh, no," Linda moaned.

"What's the matter? You wanted her to eat the bug, didn't you?"

"Not that." She waggled a finger at the cluster of cocoons stuck to the side of the barn. It took me a moment to realize that a fourth egg case had joined the other three.

"Well, that's good news, isn't it?"

"No, it's not. If she's still having babies, I'm going to have to start feeding her twice a day now."

LINDA WASN'T THE only one troubled by an irrational fear. When we sat down to eat dinner that evening, Dusty crawled down the bars to warily pace the floor of his cage and refused to climb back up to eat the vegetables that he loved. He didn't seem sick. Moments earlier, just before I had walked into the room, he had been imitating a train whistle and repeating his favorite phrase, "What does the duck say? 'Quack, quack, quack,'" in an embarrassingly perfect imitation of my voice.

Our furnace man, Greg, had recently been working in the basement while Dusty talked about the duck and inquired over and over again, "Who's the big grey bird?" After Greg had finished tuning up our oil burner and I was writing him a check in the living room, he asked, "Was that you I heard talking upstairs?" I had always considered Greg to be a genius, but I realized at that moment that he probably didn't hold a similar opinion of me.

Linda and I tried to figure what could be spooking a macho bird like Dusty. He kept staring at something from the bottom of his cage, but when I tried following his line of vision, I came up blank. His focus shifted whenever I got up from my chair to investigate, and he eyed me eyeing him.

"Dusty, eat your green beans. Do you want Jell-O?" Linda asked.

"Is there anything new in here that might be scaring him? Whatever he doesn't like isn't staying in one place." I walked to the window and scanned the treetops for a hawk or crow.

"Maybe he sees a ghost. Is Agnes in here?"

"She's sleeping on the couch."

We finished our dinner, fruitlessly cajoling him to eat as we went along. Not until I was standing at the sink, scraping my leftovers into a dish of table scraps for the ducks and hens, did Linda's mood brighten. "He's climbing up to his food dish. Good boy."

I peered around the bulkhead that separated kitchen from dining room only to witness his retreat back to the cage floor. An odd thought hit me. Popping into the bedroom, I peeled off my bland black-and-grey sweater and replaced it with an even blander yellow-checked shirt. Upon my return to the dining room, Dusty treated me to his typically unfathomable "squid at the bottom of the sea" glare. But then he made his way up to his perch and tore into his bowl of vegetables.

I asked Linda to follow me into the bedroom and showed her the offending sweater. "You know how Dusty won't chew on some of those leather belts you bring home from the thrift store? The ones that have a kind of snakeskin pattern?"

"He's terrified of them."

"Look at the stripes on the sweater."

"They look like snakeskin!" She shook her head. "Maybe he thought a big snake had hold of you."

"I doubt it. He'd be celebrating if that happened."

"But isn't it odd that he would have a genetically imprinted fear of snakes, even without ever having seen one?"

The telephone rang in response, triggering my cellular-level antipathy toward telemarketers, but the caller ID informed me otherwise.

"Mom just called," said Joan. "She's lost her purse again."

"I can't possibly drag myself over there tonight."

"I can't go either, Bob. You know how upset she gets no matter how often this happens, but I think I calmed her down. I'll get it tomorrow with the purse finder. I just wanted to let you know that I talked to her in case she calls you next."

I PULLED INTO MY mom's driveway right behind Joan, treating the phone call as an excuse to visit both of them at once. I had hoped my mom might have already located her purse — possibly in the course of hiding the electric hedge trimmer behind my dad's old hi-fi console in the den — but as soon as we walked through the door, she met us in the vestibule and gravely announced, "Somebody came in while I was eating breakfast and took my driver's license."

"You found your purse?" Joan asked.

"My driver's license is in my purse."

Joan gave my mom a hug and assured her that she had simply mislaid her handbag. I bragged that I would find it before the tea water even had a chance to boil, and sure enough, before the kettle hit the stove, the familiar *bing-bong* chimed in the dining room as I pressed the doorbell button. A moment later I stood holding one of my mother's shoes and fixing a stupefied Buffy-the-hen gaze at the purse finder nestled inside it.

"Mom," I told her gently, "see where this says, PURSE FINDER — KEEP IN PURSE. Why do you think you put it in your shoe?"

"I didn't put it there," she answered. "Somebody's trying to drive me crazy."

"Don't worry about it," said Joan. "Everyone loses things."

"We always found your purse before you had the purse finder, and we'll find it again," I said.

"You always found *what* before? I don't ever lose my purse."

While my mom finished heating up a can of soup for Joan, the two of us decided that I'd search the familiar hiding places. If I came up empty, Joan would join the hunt after savoring her lunch-meat sandwich. My mom tended to use a favorite cubbyhole for several days in a row, then abandon it for a more obscure location. But once in a while she would break loose of habit and revisit an earlier niche. So I had plenty of spots to check. Armed with a flashlight, I poked my nose into and underneath the chairs and couches, paid a courtesy call on the narrow space behind the dehumidifier, then said my quick hellos to my father's writing desk, the vestibule closet, the china cabinet, and the kitchen cupboards.

"Why are you looking in the bread drawer?" my mother asked me. "I never keep my purse in there."

Joan and I exchanged the look.

Upstairs, I roused the slumbering dressers in two bedrooms, levitated the mattresses, crawled under the beds, briefly closeted myself, took a pessimistic peek into the wastebaskets, made a private trip to the bathroom, and finally trundled down the hall to my old bedroom, now a sewing room. So much had changed over the years, and especially in the past several months, I was grateful to note scant traces of my former presence. Long ago my parents had refinished the floor, eradicating the water stains caused by my six-hundred-pound saltwater aquarium, plus the char mark where a stick of burning sandalwood incense had prostrated itself before my Donovan and Dylan posters in 1969. Only a few of my knick-knacks remained, including a hunk of petrified wood and a small ceramic pig. I reached behind the rows of paperbacks in a fleeting hope that an old copy of *Playboy* might somehow still reside there. No magazine. No purse.

This was new, and this was strange. My mother had apparently progressed from merely stashing her handbag out of sight to seriously concealing it. I enjoyed a flicker of triumph when I unearthed a brown purse from a laundry basket in her closet, but I recognized it as one that she hadn't used in years.

"I didn't have any luck," I told Joan.

"Well, it can't just have walked away on its own," declared my mom.

Joan asked me if I had removed everything from every drawer upstairs. When I answered no, picturing myself floundering in a heap of my dad's clothes and my mother's costume jewelry, she resolved to go thoroughly through each piece of furniture on the second floor—including the linen closet, which hadn't been excavated in so long it probably still contained the Bronze Age remnants of my crib bedding. I followed her to pitch in, but she stopped me. "It's better if one person takes care of it, so we don't get confused about where we've looked." I took this as a merciful dismissal.

• • •

I SLIPPED AWAY from my workplace an hour early the next morning. Joan hadn't turned up anything in her search other than the stuffed dog Malcolm, which I'd vomited on as a tot. My mom had dutifully cleaned him up, but in my eyes the accident had altered the bed companion, who involuntarily retired to a cabinet nook among tea cozies from my mother's 1937 trip to Cuba. I unlocked the front door, and on the verge of tears my mom intercepted me in the living room. "I did a really stupid thing," she said. "I lost my purse."

"I know. We've been looking for it."

"I had it last night."

A dull chill hit me. Joan and I could find ourselves playing a game of musical chairs with the handbag if my mom had, in fact, remembered where she had stashed it and then hidden it a second time. That meant that every single place that we had already investigated was in play all over again. I searched the downstairs couches, chairs, and crannies, explaining the sorry situation to Joan when she arrived. While she and my mom enjoyed a can of soup and a lunch-meat sandwich, I repeated the previous day's performance upstairs.

"This isn't going anywhere, Bob," Joan said. "I'm going to start looking in the basement."

The basement was our version of the Library of Congress, if you substituted cheese boxes filled with hardware for books, cartons of old paint cans for bundles of rare manuscripts, and ephemera dating back to World War II for government librarians. "She wouldn't put her purse down there," I said. When Joan responded by giving me the look, I gamely replied, "I'll search the den." Under normal conditions, I couldn't imagine poking through the cluttered room where we had played as kids to keep out of our parents' hair. But it was child's play compared to ransacking the cellar.

Two hours later, the sad scraping sounds and ominous crashes from below gave way to meditative silence. I assumed that Joan had finally given up, but she called out proudly, "I found it!"

"Where was it?" my mom and I shouted in unison from different corners of the house.

Joan kept mum until we had joined her downstairs near the clothes dryer. Underneath a hulking wooden utility table—whose chipped grey paint revealed chipped white paint revealing a green base coat—stood a wooden trunk handed down from my dad's mother and containing who knew what. On top of the lid sat a neatly folded electric blanket from the Eisenhower era. Joan slid her hand into it and retrieved the missing handbag to great acclaim.

For two days my mom had been as upset as I had seen her since the funeral. But while Joan and I remained rattled and exhausted from the search, my mom gained tranquillity in direct proportion to the number of sips she took from a cup of surprisingly palatable ten-year-old jasmine tea that I'd met in the den while reacquainting myself with a set of old cocktail glasses. Joan spoke sleepily about her ferrets. I managed to croak out a few sentences decrying my having to hold the water bowl for Moobie. My mom held the floor with an effusive recap of a telephone conversation with one of her friends from church. When she finished, she met Joan's bleary stare and asked her, "Now, were we looking for something?"

THE LEAVES SPIRALED down from the trees, making it difficult to spot any yellow-rumped warblers in flight, had any flitted around for me to spot. The leaves flecked the surface of the river, and through the bare trees on the opposite bank I noticed for the first time a cultivated field. Near our little pristine island, a picnic table stuck its fat nose into the primeval setting, but still no doughnut shop appeared. A song sparrow sang a halfhearted autumn song. A few woodpeckers and a brown creeper climbed the spindly maples as if searching for the orioles, buntings, grosbeaks, and flycatchers that had gassed up and zoomed south, collectively carrying my mother's purse.

I didn't even bother bringing the two-way radio to the river. I hardly needed it to communicate with my wife. As soon as Linda spotted my wispy figure trudging birdlessly toward the house, she called for me to meet her behind the barn. "She's back!" she hollered before I had even halved the distance between us. Four miles away, two nuns in downtown Lowell scanned the shelves of the BookAbout for Brother Cadfael mystery novels. The older of the pair dropped a Grisham novel in surprise. "Who's back?" she asked the other.

"Look, sweetheart, look." Linda couldn't have been happier had I fixed the broken window in the bedroom. "Look who came back again." Cemented to the center of her web as if she had never left was the golden orb weaver that had disappeared in the middle of a cold snap ten days earlier. "I can't believe I'm saying this, but I really missed her."

"So, does that mean you're not afraid of her now?"

"Are you kidding? I'm absolutely terrified, but I came to kind of like her in a way."

A phone call to Mrs. Martini-Martoni verified the fact that once a spider vacated its web at the end of the season, it would be highly unusual for it to return. She hadn't ever heard of an *Argiope aurantia* spinning more than one or two egg casings, either. But within a few more days, our weaver had added a remarkable fifth cocoon to her collection.

"She sure is devoted to her babies," Linda told me.

"Let's hope at least one of her egg cases makes it through the winter."

Constructing the final cocoon had physically depleted our spider. Her once round abdomen had shriveled to a fraction of its former size, spoiling the painted-mask effect on her back. After taking a single fly that Linda had tossed against her web, she refused to eat again. Yet day after day she remained fixed to her zigzag, in accordance with some mysterious schedule of her own. One Saturday morning, the temperatures had plunged so low overnight that the water pails in the barn had skimmed over with ice. *Surely she couldn't have survived,* I thought, and I made so bold as to brush her leg with my finger. When she failed to respond, I gingerly touched her body, causing her to spring to life and in a burst of motion zip to the bottom of her web and hide in the grass.

"I shouldn't have done that," I told Linda. "I made her use up the little bit of energy she still had left. I'm sure I killed her." By the next morning, though, she had returned to her usual place.

Almost two weeks from the day that our spider had made her unexpected reappearance, Linda found the web empty when she did her morning chores. This time the golden orb weaver did not come back. "I looked for her in the grass," Linda told me. "I checked the cracks in the cement wall for her, too."

"Were you going to bury her?"

Linda gave me a look worthy of my sister. "I wouldn't bury a spider. I just wanted to see her again."

At least the spider never had a purse to lose. I wouldn't have relished the thought of calling Joan over to the house, telling her, "Well, it's not our mom, it's another mother that Linda's been looking after, and could you whip up another of your wireless doorbell contraptions? But this time we need it to be a wee bit smaller."

CHAPTER 9

....

Somebody Left Something Somewhere

I couldn't imagine who would be blasting a gun behind our house in the black of night. During daylight hours, beer-sloshed deer hunters occasionally popped off a few unsteady rounds at squirrels on the state land next to us. But the explosions I heard from my upstairs office came from just beyond the backyard fence, and there was nothing but ice all the way to the river's edge. Unseasonable spoutings of rain, consequent flooding, and subsequent zero-degree temperatures had turned the woods into a frozen lake. I couldn't figure out who could possibly be back there.

I heard a splash between rifle cracks. Fearing that a deer might have fallen through the ice, I trotted down two flights of stairs to the basement, suited up for a visit to a frigid moon, and trained my puny flashlight on a plain of steely grey and white. As I stood at the back fence, a dull noise midway between a crash and a clatter—like a picnic table dropped down an old stone well—echoed and warped weirdly a few hundred feet away. Closer to me, the darkness snapped. The eastern horizon hit a walnut with a brick. Out west, Paul Bunyan's great-great-great-grandson split a willow tree in two.

Normally, I'd no sooner stay outside in the cold than I'd stay outside in the sun, but the cracking sounds of the expanding ice amazed me. I remembered Linda telling me about hearing this very same thing when she had lived up north in a cabin overlooking Morley Pond. But the bangs and pings of the frozen Grand River had never come within earshot of our house before. If I couldn't have bird songs in January, and if I couldn't ever seem to catch the northern lights, I could at least marvel at this eerie percussion until the bloodcurdling temperature drove me back indoors.

Stepping over the fence, I walked down the hill to the lip of the ice. A popping greeted me, followed by a low ascending note. I shivered on top of my shivering as the strangeness of the scene took root. Ever so politely, the familiar world was crumbling around me. This was exactly the kind of night that a howling primate would relish, and for all I knew a giant hominid might be watching me from the crook of a tree with dinner on his mind. Fortunately, I didn't believe in the local Sasquatch. I could also ignore a dead vaudevillian named Gatsby who telegraphed *Star Trek* titles through the Ouija board, and I could even disregard Bobo the Roller Clown, with his circus train of garish coincidences. But I couldn't look Buffy the hen in the eye and convince myself that the mighty force of reason was anything more than a trickle, out of touch with the great current of life. If my mom, who had always been our family's wellspring of common sense, could begin to come unraveled, what lay in store for any of us?

On this cheery note, I gathered my jacket around me and sloshed back to the house against a sound track of things breaking. From the bathroom window, I could still hear the frozen fireworks out back. The largest cracks extended all the way to Linda's faux-sheepskin rug on the living room floor, and we hoped they would splinter off into the bedroom to lull us to sleep.

The moment the bedroom light went dark and Linda's thrashing died down—after the air purifier, heater, and lip balm had each received its nocturnal throttling—a chipmunk, red squirrel, or bison inside the wall hurled itself at the plasterboard inches away from my ear. With a thump and a scuffle it sunk its claws into the gypsum and scrabbled loudly up to a hidden perch that gave its activities the resonance of a band-shell performance, then began exercising its teeth on what sounded like shards of ceramic tile. If you were to shake a metal box filled with ball bearings with every ounce of your strength, the energetic chewing would have easily drowned out any clatter you could muster.

In past winters, I had fought back. I would batter my fist against the wall, raising such a ruckus that the cats would streak into the basement, the parrots would squawk from the dining room, and plaster would rain down from the bedroom ceiling. After just enough of a tranquil interval had passed for me to wrap an adhesive bandage around my hand, while Linda calmed the critters and vacuumed white dust from the floor, the dental exercises would start up fresh and invigorated, as if the chipmunk, red squirrel, or musk ox had benefited from the brief intermission.

So I did nothing. Typically the concealed billy goat would fall into a reverie of comparatively quiet meditative nibbling after several minutes of munching on plate glass, but the intruder had come to us in an inordinately cheerful mood. It couldn't resist augmenting its remarkable crunching with friendly clawing scratches upon the plasterboard. I did my best to fall asleep despite the din. The odd acoustics of the bedroom made the chomps and scrapes inaudible a mere twelve inches in any direction from my pillow—and from Linda's rhythmic breathing, I could tell that she had plunged directly into unconsciousness.

After a while, the chewing and grating took on an almost hypnotic quality, and I hovered just above a state of sleep upon my padded bench inside a sawmill. As I dozed, the tooth-and-toenail sound track disturbingly transmogrified into words. "You don't do enough for your mother," the raspy voice accused me. "You care more about your animals than your mom."

That was enough to send me to the couch in the living room. I paged through an old copy of *Reader's Digest,* but the "Humor in Uniform" funnies failed to divert me for once. I felt immensely grateful for my two sisters, who had shown unflagging consideration for Mom. From the moment my mother's memory problems had worsened, Joan had repeatedly called and faxed the doctor with reports of her behavior. Routine office visits had failed to uncover a condition that Dr. Doering might treat, but finally Joan and Bett had talked Mom into taking a mental-proficiency test. We had pinned our hopes on this. Amazingly she sailed through the short-term memory exercises.

"She did better at memorizing a list of words than I did," Joan had said.

So instead of diagnosing the Alzheimer's disease that Joan, Bett, and I had feared, and starting her on medication that might slow its progress, Dr. Doering informed Joan that Mom suffered from mild dementia. Since dementia could have a variety of causes, he couldn't prescribe a treatment beyond diet and exercise. Dissatisfied, Joan contacted a geriatric specialist and described Dr. Doering's approach. The specialist told Joan that Mom's doctor was following proper protocols and that he wouldn't necessarily do anything differently.

A faint scraping from the far wall interrupted my brooding.

Apparently my conscience had less power to nag me in the living room, because the commotion was too weak to keep me awake. The perpetrator wouldn't be a clamorous squirrel or caribou but one of the endless series of mice that invaded the nooks and crannies of our house with the tenacity of a hidden purse. I did what I could for my mom, I told myself. I visited her twice a week, paid her bills, and alternated with Joan taking her to Sunday Mass. Bett, who drove up about once a month from Fort Wayne to spend a weekend at the old house, enjoyed a natural rapport with Mom that eluded me. I felt closest to Mom not when I struggled to make conversation but when I shut off the outdoor water faucets for the winter, lugged the trash out to the curb, or pounded in a nail to accommodate an indoor thermometer. One afternoon, following an exhaustive round of thermometer hanging, I curled up on her couch for a nap. She tossed an afghan over me. A few moments later, as she puttered around in the kitchen, I heard her humming. This passed for quality time between us.

I had to wonder why it sometimes seemed easier for me to respond to an animal in distress. Apart from helping with essentials, I was uncertain how to provide my mom with whatever else she needed. Showing love was the obvious approach, but I didn't know how to switch to caregiver mode after years of having been mother-henned. That was the crux of things, and my mom's declining mental condition muddied matters further. With animals, no such psychological complexities applied. They had no expectations, no emotional baggage, and their vulnerability made responding feel like second nature, especially since an animal couldn't ask for help—though it would gleefully let you know when it had made a home inside your walls.

• • •

WE WEREN'T THE ONLY victims of home invasion. Our neighbor Roswitha sat reading the *Grand Rapids Press* at the kitchen table when she heard a tapping at the door. Snowy branches waved to her when she turned in her chair and glanced outside, but no one hailed her from the porch. When the tapping came a second time, she got up and opened the door. Accompanying a blast of cold air, a pigeon walked into her living room. It marched across the rug and started pointedly pecking at the nap.

"This bird was obviously asking me for help," Linda's German-born friend told her on the phone. "And, oh, was that guy hungry. I put some sunflower seed on the doormat and, *dit, dit, dit,* he ate up every bit of it. But now I don't know what to do with him. Can you come and get the bird?"

Pigeons didn't hang out in our neck of the woods. They preferred spaces with a view of open ground, as opposed to our usual weed-choked swampy thicket. For similar reasons, we didn't get European starlings or house sparrows, either—two species of so-called nuisance birds, whose roles as pests were eagerly taken on by squawking Ollie, foot-biting Dusty, and bell-ringing Stanley Sue. A solitary pigeon wouldn't casually leave its flock to visit our area, unless the bird had found itself in serious trouble, which worried Linda. Suiting up for the perilous trek across the frozen wastes of the front yard to her car, she drove down the hill through wind-whipped ice fields to Roswitha's house on the river, then retraced her eight-hundred-foot drive back to the house.

"She seems okay," she said as she examined the towel-wrapped bird in our bathroom.

"There's a tiny little scrape on the edge of the wing," I said.

"She was flapping around in the carrier," Linda told me. "She probably did that then."

Satisfied that the bird had most likely gotten separated from its fellow pigeons by a hawk or owl and lost its way, we decided to feed it, keep it overnight, and release it the following after- noon — forgetting for a tiny, yet crucial moment a hard-and-fast rule about taking in wild birds in cold weather. That rule would flutter back to haunt us soon. Not wanting to introduce any avian cooties to our healthy indoor birds, we installed the pigeon in a cage in the office off the living room, where Linda studied the Bible, did her church's bookkeeping, kept track of her housecleaning business, and charred the ceiling with a decorative candle.

"That bird is lucky to be indoors," I said.

As Linda prepared dinner, I bundled up to head out to the backyard duck pens. I should have known better than to ven- ture outside of the house when every wild beast in the woods was trying to sneak indoors. In the past week, the overnight low had plummeted to three degrees. To keep the slushy water in the two wading pools from congealing into gigantic ice discuses by morning, I needed to slosh out the water with my trademark push broom. Months ago we had moved the girl ducks to Stewart and Trevor's pen, and I emptied their pool first, noting that almost as soon as I leaned the broom against the wire, the wet bristles froze to the pen floor. Latching the door behind me, I trudged to- ward the entrance to the geese's adjoining suite. As I opened their door, I remarked to myself that I ought to move carefully, since the ground beneath my feet seemed to be glare ice.

The bare boughs of the apple tree wheeled overhead as a distant comb of cirrus clouds raced toward the opposite horizon. A fat conjunction of three stuck-together snowflakes hovered in front of my nose, reversed direction, and hopped onto an eyelash. My legs flailed like flags in a stiff wind. My arms stretched in search of a solid surface. Bobbing in a warm salt sea, my mind tacked leisurely between a tropical island called Uh-Oh-Here-I-Go and a bone-colored coral reef populated by blood-red fish. A blue whale surfaced directly under me. Bad luck. Its stiff spine jolted me at both poles.

I believe, I told myself, *I believe I'll just lie here for a little while. I believe that's what I'll do.* Status lights winked on one by one. A foot untwisted. A hand uncurled. I accounted for my ribs. The right elbow felt numb. Was that a stone beneath my head? A skin of water on the ice soaked into my pant legs. *Just relax.* I stared up at the apple tree. *Just enjoy this fine brisk afternoon from ground level.*

A menacing rasp raised me partway up. Liza—the African goose that Linda and I had nursed through a serious illness on our front porch, carried in our arms for four weeks when she couldn't walk on her own, and fed fresh dandelion leaves plucked one by one on hands and knees from our lawn—Liza, yes, *that* Liza, opened her serrated beak, waggled her thin pink tongue, and hissed at me. Her sister Hailey joined in. I struggled unsteadily to my feet. "It's okay," I assured them, hugging the doorpost, wheezing, slamming the door shut, and hobbling back to the basement, the push broom my cane. My head chimed the hour as I limped upstairs.

"Something's upsetting Stanley Sue," Linda told me from the stove. My wife had missed my brief aerial ballet, but the parrot had taken it in from her perch on top of Walter's cage. She waggled her head at me in disapproval. "Maybe she saw a hawk," Linda added, dumping onions into a pan.

Stumbling out of bed the next morning, I didn't need a thermometer to tell me that the mercury hadn't simply plunged overnight, it had fallen off a cliff. The tip-off came when Linda tried to coerce the kitchen faucet to issue water. The prescient individuals who had constructed our house in 1907 had apparently enjoyed a draught of cold water so much, they had created a special basement air space within the east wall with the foresight that the next generation of residents would route water pipes through this otherwise useless passage. My preference was that we wait until July and the frozen-water problem would take care of itself, but Linda displayed her usual impatience on this issue.

If nothing else, balancing on the rim of the laundry tub allowed me to take a fresh inventory of my aches and bruises from my parrot-witnessed spill of the previous afternoon as I jammed the nozzle of a hair dryer into the frigid air tunnel. The vibration of the motor jarred the blow dryer loose from its niche and knocked it into the dry laundry sink, providing me with a second daybreak test of elbow flexibility and knee-joint range of motion. As my body began to slow to hibernation metabolism, Linda shouted downstairs to inform me that the waters flowed freely once more — leaving the thawing job finished except for the painstaking picking of Styrofoam insulation pellets out of the back end of the hair dryer.

A warm front crashed into western Michigan while I sat at my workplace writing catalog descriptions of home-theater gizmos. Ordinarily I would have welcomed any mitigation of the cold. But the heat wave hijacked a cargo of moisture from Lake Michigan and returned it to us as a huge dumping of snow.

I considered taking advantage of the bad weather and the throbbing in my limbs as an excuse for putting off a visit to my mom. While I didn't expect to do another backflip on a patch of glare ice at the entry to her house, I worried about being emotionally upended by her bad mood. But the roads had been reasonably well plowed and, truth be told, I didn't feel any worse than I ever did.

My visit hit a snag when I turned off a clean north-south artery onto the clogged east-west vein of my mother's street and immediately embedded my car in a trackless waste. After trying to inch

forward toward my mom's driveway and failing to gain even a millimeter of progress, I found myself unable to reverse and rejoin
the other corpuscles puttering along. A ten-year-old boy wearing a
fluorescent orange stocking cap slogged to my aid from the house
on the corner and silently handed me a snow shovel. He seemed
unwilling to do the excavation for me, even after I had grabbed
his cap as a bargaining tool. After not that many sweaty minutes,
I managed to clear the crown of the road and, with my mother's
house in view through the driver's side mirror, set off for home with
my newly acquired shovel dripping untidily on the upholstery.

"I felt terrible. I was only a half a block away, but I didn't dare
just leave my car in the middle of the street," I told Linda.

"Visit her tomorrow. It's supposed to be sunny."

"That reminds me. Is this a good day to release the pigeon? Or
should you do it tomorrow morning?"

"We forgot something," Linda said. "You can't subject a bird to
anything greater than a twenty-degree temperature drop when you
release it, and we've had the pigeon indoors where it's warm."

"What does that mean?" I asked, although I knew the answer
all too well.

"It means she has to live with us until the spring."

MY MOM'S STREET still hadn't been plowed the following
day, but enough SUVs had barreled through to provide a choice of
tire ruts to follow. As I stomped the snow off my boots in the vestibule, my mother told me, "The furnace isn't working." An ineffec-
tive wiggle of the thermostat wheel in the living room produced no
response from the giant basement octopus. Downstairs, I squinted
at the beast from several angles under the light of a bare bulb,
trying to determine which scary-looking valve from the Calvin
Coolidge era held the least promise of blowing us sky-high.

"Dad would sometimes push that red button," my mother finally pointed out.

Inside an inky black shadow near the isinglass faceplate crouched a lozenge-shaped utility box that some mustached gent had undoubtedly installed during the Herbert C. Hoover years while converting the behemoth from a coal to a natural-gas diet. A promising yet intimidating red button whose dustless surface spoke of frequent use begged me to depress it, but I hesitated. "This button?" She nodded. "You're sure this is the one?" After determining that no competing button concealed itself to ridicule me later, I reluctantly gave my mother's choice a stab, figuring there were worse ways to leave the planet. A startling chuff of safely contained fire rewarded my bold action.

"There we go!" my mother cried. "Now we're cooking with gas."

Her use of that old catchphrase from the Harry S. Truman era led me to ask her about her youth as I paid a few bills at the dining room table and drank a cup of tea. She didn't find a sure footing for spinning a tale until my mention of her 1937 trip to Cuba brought an excited glow to her eyes.

"Well, I think I told you before that I went with four other girls, including May Heaver, who was my boss at Mueller Brass in Port Huron, and her cousin Kathy, who was an epileptic. But I probably didn't mention that when we landed in Havana, we were met by Mr. José Ollio himself."

"Who's José Ollio?"

"He was the head of the José Ollio Company," my mother beamed. "He was an important man, but he gave us gals the royal treatment, because he did a lot of business with Mueller Brass."

I didn't mind that I had heard most of the Cuban anecdotes before. I loved the idea of my mom as an adventurous girl just out of high school taking a trip that her father didn't approve of. Many years later she convinced my dad to forgo their annual four-thousand-mile-long asphalt oval in favor of a trip abroad instead. He ended up enjoying the bus tour of England so much and relished sharing stories and influenza bugs with his fellow bus passengers to such a degree that encapsulated trips to Spain, Germany, Morocco, Thailand, and China followed.

I mentioned to my mom that I was fond of Cuban music, and she told me that José Ollio had taken them to Havana nightclubs. "The orchestra would play one set of American songs, then after an intermission they'd play Latin numbers." She also mentioned a cab driver who had committed an unnamed naughty indiscretion that resulted in all five of the girls bolting from the taxi at a traffic light.

"How did you find your way back to the hotel?" I said, laughing.

"I don't remember that," she said. "I think we just waited for another cab."

My mom's good mood carried over until the following afternoon, when her furnace stopped again. Bett remembered that a close friend of Mom and Dad's used to inspect furnaces for the City of Grand Rapids and knew the older models inside and out, so she gave him a call.

"Mike found the problem," Mom told me on the phone after dinner. "He even had the right part at home, and he said he was saving the box to remind him of the part number in case it goes ka-flooey again."

All seemed well until the phone rang an hour later and my mom asked me, "The next time you stop by, would you please bring back the package that was on the countertop? I didn't get a chance to open it yet."

"What package would that be?"

"I don't what it was, but Mike dropped it off."

"You're thinking of the furnace part he replaced," I told her.

"Is that what it was?"

"He didn't even leave it. He showed you the box and took it with him."

This answer satisfied her for about forty minutes. "I'm sorry to bother you again," she said. "But I need the package that you took from the countertop." When I ran through my explanation about Mike and the furnace part, she insisted that he had also dropped off a package for her. While we talked, Dusty muttered in the background in a perfect imitation of my telephone manner, "Uh-huh. Oh? Hmm. Okay. Bye-bye," until I hung up.

"Maybe he did bring her something, and she hid it," Linda suggested.

Just to be on the safe side, Dusty and I called Mike and asked him if he had indeed left anything with my mom. He told me no, but he suggested that we consider replacing the furnace. He didn't think he'd be able to fix it the next time it went ka-flooey.

BUSINESS HAD APPARENTLY gone ka-flooey at the Weigh and Pay. As Bill Holm and I approached the cash register with our food plates ready for the scale, Bo pointed at a sheet of paper taped to the wall announcing a new pricing policy in a rainbow of computer typefaces. "No more of that weighing bull," he informed us. "I finally convinced Dad to just charge one price like a normal buffet, so go back and load up your dish."

I shook my head. "I don't eat very much." In an apparent concession to Bo's father, golden oldies from the 1960s showered us from the ceiling speaker in place of heavy metal.

"I'll be back for seconds," Bill told Bo as we headed for a booth along the wall under the scrutiny of the only occupied table in the restaurant. From the expressions on the gawkers' faces and the lettering on the yellow bus parked outdoors, these were residents of a home for the developmentally disabled who had never witnessed anyone eating food before. Each forkful that rose to my mouth received silent scrutiny from diners that weren't doing much dining themselves. A taste of my au gratin potatoes suggested a reason why.

"They're doing interesting things with leather these days."

"You should try the chicken," said Bill. "It's older than Eric Burdon."

Between slowly swallowed mouthfuls, I described the recent spate of phone calls from my mother. "The accusations are unrelenting. In the past, she'd call me once or twice suggesting that I'd stolen something of hers, and that would be it. But I've heard from her every day this week about the package I was supposed to have taken."

"Wouldn't it be easier to bring it back?"

"I would if I could. But this has got to be about my father, and I'm a miserable substitute. Maybe that's what's supposed to be in the package."

"The missing ingredients—so to speak?" Bill poked unhappily at a dollop of macaroni and cheese. "It certainly doesn't need more salt."

I spoke quietly so that the vigilant Bo didn't overhear. "Any word from Bobo?"

"Just 'Beep Beep.'"

"Why 'Beep Beep'?"

"That's the question. Carol and I were driving to her brother's house, and she had the radio on. It was playing Nilsson's 'Don't Leave Me.'"

Here we go, I thought. *Another Nilsson rant.*

"You know, his parody of dramatic loss-of-love songs."

"Yes, I kind of remember it," I mumbled to my mashed potatoes.

"I was amazed to hear it. It's so funny. He was such a tortured man—so skilled and emotive in so many styles and forms, yet at the same time he hates them for their clichés and their grip on him. His stuff is so very serious and funny and ironic and arty. It's so derivative and so original all at the same time, and the tension ended up killing him. That's my theory, anyway. I was kind of tingly hearing it, and it has that part where he just wails to the woman who dumped him, 'Beep-beep, bip-bip yeah,' — you know, from the Beatles 'Drive My Car,' as if that's going to win her back somehow. It's an amazing performance. Then that awful 'Dust in the Wind' by Kansas came on, and as I changed the station, I said to Carol that one song I hadn't heard in years was 'Beep Beep' — the one about the little Nash Rambler trying to pass the Cadillac — and you can guess what song came on next."

As if on cue, Bo interrupted us by honking, "How's the food, guys?" But his display of enthusiasm dissipated as he plopped down on the red leatherette bench next to Bill and groused, "This weather isn't helping us at all. If things don't start to turn around, we'll be lucky to stay open another month."

The weather grew steadily more dismal as we consoled Bo with a few oblique phrases while eating around the worst parts of our meals. By the time we had jettisoned our substance-laden plates in the trash receptacle, snow covered Bill's blue Jetta. We could barely see the road in front of us on the two-mile drive back to my house. "Don't you think you had better head home?" I said. "Spare yourself further exposure to the perils of the world at large?"

"You wish," he told me. "Not when there's good television to watch."

To Bill, "good television" meant finding the Inuit-language Canadian channel on our satellite system and watching a Frobisher Bay resident cook an apparent lump of animal fat over a campfire. "That looks better than anything we ate," he said. "At least it didn't sit around for a couple of weeks."

Safely isolated from the glare of our personalities, Linda lay in the bedroom talking on the phone with the door closed. After a while, she came out to ask, "Did you hear something?"

"It sounded like a pop," said Bill.

"It sounded like an accident," Linda said.

Spread out across the windows of the front porch, we strained to find signs of a wreck through the swirling snow and darkness. "Maybe the ice is cracking again," I offered. Then an SUV slowed and turned on its emergency flashers. As it pulled onto the shoulder, its headlights illuminated a car sitting sideways just off the road. Steam poured out of the pulverized engine section. A teenage boy and girl stood in the ditch with dazed expressions. As one man from the SUV approached them, another ran past them toward our barn.

Throwing on their jackets, Linda hurried outside to talk to the teenagers while Bill followed the man into the darkness. He returned quickly. "It looks pretty bad," he said. "There's isn't much left of the other car."

I dialed 911 as Bill went back outdoors. "Can you check to see if anyone's hurt?" the operator asked me.

"There's not much left of the car," I parroted.

"We need to know if we should send an ambulance."

Bill ducked his head through the door as I stretched the telephone cord toward the porch. "The guy in the red car is unconscious," he told me. "We can't get at him."

"Send the ambulance," I said.

"The people from the other car seem to be okay," Bill added.

Linda had joined us again. "This woman who lives in Ionia just around the corner from the Chinese restaurant said the people in the white car passed her on the curve. She said they were passing everybody."

A man in a dark blue stocking cap came into the glow of our outside light. "Call an ambulance."

"It's on the way."

Bill returned to the car with the man trapped inside, while Linda crossed the road to talk to a few more people who had joined the gathering crowd. I suited up and stood in the front yard. The man with the blue stocking cap set up flares and started directing traffic. I stared down the long curve toward Lowell until I saw the first flicker of emergency-vehicle lights and heard the sirens. When I came back into the house, the phone was ringing.

"I'm sorry to bother you so late," my mother said. "But when you get a chance, could you bring back the package that Mike left for me? I never got a chance to look at it."

"There's been an accident outside," I told her. Flashing red lights swept the living room walls as a fire truck rumbled into position. "I talked to Mike already. Remember? We discussed this earlier today. He told me that he didn't leave anything at your house. There isn't any package."

"It might not have been Mike," she said, "but somebody left something somewhere."

I couldn't really argue with that. It was as succinct a summing up of the seeming randomness of events in life as I had ever heard. "Call Joan and ask her about it. Maybe she knows something." I certainly didn't. In fact, I knew a little less about the world every day.

I went back outdoors. The snow had begun to let up a little. Headlights lined the road in both directions as far as I could see. "I'll never get out of here," said Bill's voice from behind me. While firemen worked on the crushed car, an ambulance driver convinced the teenage boy and girl to go with him. As he ducked his head and climbed into the back, the boy held his elbow to his chest as if he had been hurt.

Bill followed me inside. "Beep beep," he said.

CHAPTER 10

....

Underwater

My mother's house was drowning in little slips of paper. She could have worked for a fortune cookie company, although most people, upon finishing their moo goo gai pan, might have been perplexed to crack open a cookie and encounter the message "Bring back my aluminum mixing bowls." One note caught my eye as I hauled myself upstairs to hunt for the sixteenth pair of scissors we had bought her. Poking out of the back of my dad's antique-style clock on the archway overlooking the living room was the merest hint of the corner of a yellow sticky-note. I popped open the battery compartment to find a memo from four months earlier, which reported, "Purse is behind the humidifier, 12/29." If my mom couldn't remember where she had hidden the purse, I wondered how she could recall where she had hidden the reminder about her purse.

Returning downstairs sans scissors, I spotted a spiral-bound notebook topping a heap of junk mail on the dining room table. At first, the taped-together advertisements commanded my attention. I had torn them into pieces and thrown them away the previous week so that my mom wouldn't confuse them with her bills and try to pay them. But she had retrieved them from the wastebasket and reconstructed them with the care of a museum curator. As I stuffed them into a plastic trash bag for immediate conveyance to the garage garbage bin, my eyes wandered to the open page of the notebook; then I sat down to read the entry in full.

"When I was talking to Linda on the phone, Bob asked if he could see the watch that my husband gave me for our anniversary," my mom wrote. "He stuck it in his pocket and took it home with him. I want that watch back. If he doesn't return it, I will call the lawyer and remove him from my will."

"What's this?" I asked my mom as she bustled around the kitchen.

"Oh, that." She casually ripped out the page and crumpled it up. "You haven't seen my anniversary watch, have you?"

"The one that's upstairs in your dresser drawer? Why on earth would you think I'd take that home?"

She chuckled guiltily. "I just get worked up sometimes. You know me. If I put it in the drawer, it was probably because I didn't want those little boys from next door to find it."

"Which boys?" I knew of no little boys on my mom's street at all.

"Those brats that live next door with what's-their-names. They came over again last night and kept moving my things around. I even caught one of them going through my purse, and I had to hide it."

This account troubled me deeply. Two different friends of mine had parents who had started complaining about nonexistent children shortly before suffering a serious decline. As soon as I got back home, I phoned Joan and told her what had happened.

"I'll schedule her for another mental evaluation," Joan sighed. "But, Bob, we have to be grateful for how well she's doing overall despite whatever is wrong with her."

Bett gave me similar advice. "She still gets her own meals, looks

neat and clean, keeps up the house, and she seems happier lately
than she has in a long time. The best we can do is let the doctor
know what's going on and watch for any signs that she's a danger
to herself. I'm coming in next weekend," she added, "so I'll keep
an eye on her to see if she's acting any different."

I felt better after these conversations and realized that visits
from imaginary boys weren't significantly worse than neighbors
purportedly making off with grass seeders or sons allegedly ab-
sconding with electric trimmers. And if seeing little people who
weren't there indicated a mental breakdown, then I had slipped a
serious cog two decades earlier.

A few years before meeting Linda, I had briefly dated a woman,
Jolene, who claimed to be a witch. One summer afternoon, we sat
at a card table in her living room working on her résumé for a job
as a substitute teacher that didn't explicitly require spell casting.
While struggling to fill a yawning chasm between her periods of
paid employment, I glanced around the room in search of inspiration only to notice a small person staring at me from the foot of the
stairs. For an instant, I assumed it was her Vietnamese roommate.
But when I blinked, the figure vanished.

My face must have worn the classic pop-eyed, just-seen-a-ghost
expression, because Jolene stopped riffling through her sheaf of
papers and asked, "What's the matter? Are you feeling okay?"

"Over there," I managed to squeak as I gestured with my thumb.
I decided it wouldn't be a problem admitting a strange apparition
to a witch. "By the railing. There was a little person, about three
feet tall, with slanted eyes and a bowl haircut."

I might as well have reported a ladybug on the windowsill.
Jolene turned her attention back to the résumé and in a blasé
manner said, "I left the back door wide open, and it probably wandered in from the garden."

"What wandered in?"

"A fairy," she explained, as if speaking to a child. "They help me grow my flowers and vegetables." I resisted asking her if they might possibly assist with résumé writing.

Certainly they couldn't have topped my mom in the note-writing department. I knew that Mom's mental powers had begun to deteriorate, but I hadn't expected them to take a nosedive so quickly. I felt as if my sisters and I were standing in water up to our chins, and the level would rise before it came down. That was the most profound metaphor that came to mind as I stood in our dining room staring out at the Grand River, which had just flooded its banks. A pond was forming down the hill, and while this meant the arrival of wood ducks before long, it also promised hordes of mosquitoes and a population of vicious alligators hell-bent on tearing me into pieces. Well, maybe they weren't exactly alligators. Someone had recently told me that spring peepers were frogs, but I wasn't taking any chances.

THROUGHOUT THE WINTER MONTHS, there had been two constants: wretched weather and relentless phone calls from Eileen Kucek. She had taken a proprietary interest in Lulu, and the haze of an accusatory tone hung over every conversation about the previously pampered white duck, who had become a contented member of our flock. "Are you feeding her enough fresh greens? I can bring over a few bags of kale if you're not giving her any," she had told me more than once, despite my protests that we treated our waterfowl and poultry to fresh produce every day. On another occasion she had said, "I want to make sure you're keeping her pool water clean. The last time I saw Lulu, the water looked dirty."

"That's because she brought a beakful of mud into the clean pool with her," I explained. "That's the nature of a duck. We empty and refill each of the four pools at least twice a day. But if you like, I'll try to divert the Grand River into Lulu's pen." I didn't bother telling her how easy that would be if the flooding followed its usual course.

Mostly, I let the answering machine weary its silicon heart with Eileen's droning voice. But I immediately returned her call the morning she left a message about bringing us two new geese. "The woman who owns them has to give them away, because she's moving. I've got a friend who can take ducks," she added, in a development we would soon hear more about, "but the geese have nowhere else to go. And they're really sweet."

We had the space in the backyard pens, we were crazy about geese — having recently added a new gander named Matthew — and I couldn't think of a belligerent primate I'd rather have drop by for a visit than Eileen. So after a quick consultation with Linda, I agreed. "As long as you're sure the geese would be happy living with us," I said. "Lulu's been a little grumpy with us ever since we took away her bedroom slippers."

"I'm bringing their owner-companion, Marcia, and I'll let her decide whether or not she wants to let you have them. But I'm glad you brought up Lulu. We'll talk about her when I see you."

"I can't wait," I muttered after I hung up.

While I bided my time until the promised goose-and-pest arrival, Linda buzzed into town for groceries and brought back news of our former master gardener, Henry Murphy. "I saw him walking down the street carrying his laundry, so I gave him a ride to the Ammo Shack. His bumblebee died over the winter."

"Most of them do." Stanley Sue was performing sentry duty, stalking the tops of the bunny cages. When I handed her a grape fresh from the store, she crushed it in her beak and let it fall onto Walter's back below.

"So without a car, he's not able to do his gardening consultation now."

"That's a shame when so much soil needs testing." On hands and knees I retrieved the pulped grape before Walter had a chance to eat it and foul his touchy digestive system. "Maybe he could test the water in our pond for phosphorus, nitrogen, and potash."

Linda's crinkling of plastic grocery bags offended the delicate sensitivities of our parrot Ollie, who voiced his disapproval of the innocuous noise with a series of grating chirps. Barely missing a beat, Linda covered his cage with a light blue bedsheet from the hall closet, transforming his outburst into contrite squeals. "Nobody feels the least bit sorry for you," she told him. "I wonder what kind of people would use Henry for financial services? That's what he said he's doing now. Anyway, he seemed kind of pathetic, and I said we might help him out."

"With financial services? You've got to be kidding."

"No, I offered to do his laundry once in a while."

THE APPEARANCE of two women in our backyard interrupted our discussion of Henry's professional prospects. "This is my good friend Marcia," said Eileen in a sickeningly sweet singsong when we greeted them outside. Then her voiced dropped an octave to convey the burden of her acquaintance with us as she hurriedly told Marcia, "This is Bob and Linda."

"What a nice pen," Marcia said as Eileen elbowed past us to throw open the door.

"Peewee!" Eileen called to an unimpressed Lulu, while pointedly failing to peewee the other flock members.

"It's goose paradise," Marcia proclaimed. An energetic woman in her forties, she had tightly curled hair that gathered above her ears only to terminate abruptly below them in an awkward truncation that suggested a mushroom cap. I wondered if she had made off with my mother's electric trimmer for the job. Her coif seemed subdued compared to Eileen's, though. Instead of the usual tightly wrapped bun, she had arranged her straw-colored hair into a wildly sprouting topknot reminiscent of a troll doll on a bad 'do day. The styling incited muttering among the ducks whenever she inclined her head toward them. I imagined that they associated the tuft with a raised crest, signaling provocation.

Chatting excitedly about her geese, Marcia led Linda to her van while I counted to myself, waiting for Eileen to say something ridiculous. I managed to make it to eleven.

"Something's wrong with Lulu. She's very depressed. She won't come to me."

"Of course she won't come to you. She doesn't know you from Don King," I told her, diplomatically avoiding any mention of her hair.

"Well, I was talking to Kate this week, and she decided it would be best if Lulu went to live with Henrietta."

"Or Henrietta could come here," I suggested, uncertain who Henrietta might be.

Shunning Eileen, the ducks and geese retreated into their shed, quacked and honked among themselves in hasty conference, then filed out again. Leading the flock was our white Embden goose Matthew, whom our rehabber friend Marge Chedrick had taken in from an apartment-complex parking lot and given to us a month earlier. At first sight of the intruding Eileen, Matthew propelled himself at her with outraged hissing, outstretched neck, and serrated bill poised for biting. Ignorant of basic waterfowl body language, Eileen extended a welcoming hand. She pivoted her wrist at just the right moment for Matthew's jaws to clamp onto her jacket sleeve instead of latching onto flesh.

"What a nasty duck," she observed as she backed out of the

pen. Taking exception to the dual insult, the goose pursued her and would have chomped her once again if I hadn't whisked him off the ground and deposited him in the bunny enclosure. "Lulu," she called frantically. "Lulu, are you okay?"

Linda and Marcia padded into the yard carrying a large goose apiece in their arms. Spotting the newcomers, Matthew honked a baritone saxophone solo and easily hopped over the rabbit fence to gallop toward Linda, wings flapping. Marcia's geese burst free of human embrace and with exuberant caroling joined Matthew on the grass.

"Watch out, he's dangerous," warned Eileen

Matthew, the new white female Embden, and the new white-and-grey male Embden briefly chased and pecked one another before settling down to probe the soft soil. The other ducks and geese poured out of the pens to join them in yard-destroying revelry.

"I guess they like it here," said Marcia. But the new male concerned me. The primary feathers of his right wing stood out from his body at a right angle, as if he were signaling to make a turn, in a harmless condition known as angel wing—often caused by a vitamin deficiency in a waterfowl's innocent youth. Birds with any obvious peculiarity were often picked on by stronger members of the flock. While Angel, as we soon called him, outweighed Matthew, I doubted he'd succeed in dominating him.

"Kate would like Lulu to live somewhere else," Eileen told us once the clamor had quieted down and our ears had stopped ringing.

"She's perfectly fine here," I answered.

"What goose or duck wouldn't love it?" Marcia asked.

"I spoke to her yesterday, and she feels Lulu would be happier with Henrietta, who just spent twelve thousand dollars on a duck pen."

"Twelve thousand dollars!" exclaimed Linda. "Are the fences made of gold?"

"No, but she had special chain-link fencing custom-made for the exercise pen so that a raccoon can't fit a paw through it. The roll of fencing was so heavy, it took seven men to carry it into her yard. Her ducks have also got a fully insulated Cape Cod–style cottage for their sleeping quarters that includes a fold-down bed for Henrietta. She can spend the night out with the ducks when she misses them. And there's a two-way closed-circuit TV system so that Henrietta can see them and talk to them from the house, and they can see her face on the video screen."

"Is there room out there for me?" I asked. "It sounds like quite the life."

I pulled Linda aside, and we conferred in quiet quacks. When Kate had first brought Lulu to us, she'd told us that she might be back for her one day, so we didn't really consider her to be our duck. Linda decided that she would have to check with Kate, and if it was okay with her, Eileen could come back for Lulu. After Linda explained this to Eileen, I caught myself on the verge of asking my former grade school classmate how she had hooked up with Henrietta—or, for that matter, Marcia—but realized that the convoluted answer would only depress me. I did put a question to Marcia, though. "After hearing about the golden duck palace, are you sure your geese will be happy here?"

"Are you kidding?" Marcia laughed. All five geese, including Africans Liza and Hailey, had worked their way to the garden alongside the house and begun pruning the hyacinths and daffodils.

"No, no, no," said Linda. "You leave that alone."

Eileen shaded her eyes with her fingers and gazed off into our swamp. "Where's that path of yours you've been bragging about?"

"Underwater."

She snorted. "That didn't work out very well, did it? I could put in a good word with Henrietta's contractor, if you'd like to build a boardwalk."

"Totally unnecessary," I assured her. "Why walk to the river when the river can come to us?" That gave me an idea for Henry Murphy's laundry, and I made a mental note to mention it to Linda later. We could tie a few of his checkered shirts to a tree trunk and give them a thorough soaking.

WE REALIZED THE flooding would be much worse than usual the morning Roswitha nearly lost her footing as she slogged along her gravel road. "The water's well above her knees," I told Linda at the breakfast table. Along with the rising river level came a wicked current that did its best to sweep our neighbor off the raised roadbed and topple her into the swamp. Dressed in hip waders and a nylon jacket, she used a broom handle as a walking stick to steady herself as she plodded forward.

"Whoa. She almost went over that time."

"Did you see that?" Linda asked. "A huge fish just jumped out of the water."

I lowered the binoculars. "It must have scared her."

"Don't let her catch you looking at her with those."

The next morning I scanned her road for the metal post that normally came up to my chin, which made it just over five feet tall. But the post was completely submerged. I watched through binoculars as Roswitha stood in an aluminum rowboat and poled her way up her driveway with an oar. I lost sight of her as she drew even with the poultry pen behind our barn, which so far had stayed above water.

"When is the river supposed to crest?" I asked.

"They said tomorrow afternoon on Channel 8 news."

"I'd better go down and see if the chickens need to take swimming lessons."

I met Roswitha on our porch as I was about to go outside. In order to maintain the dry-land portion of her amphibious lifestyle, she kept her car parked in our driveway. She was luckier than most of the people along the river. She managed to escape the worst effects of the flooding by living in a house whose habitable portion was confined to the second floor. But that didn't make things easy for her. I could just imagine the process of trying to step onto her outside stairway with a load of groceries without capsizing her boat. She had never struck me as a hardy soul. In another life and with a shift of a few degrees, she might have been a high-society denizen, just as I might have been a nematode. Yet she poled her gondola without complaint, and for years had taken care of her husband after his disastrous heart attack.

"How are you making out down there?" Linda asked. "Do you have time for a cup of coffee?"

"No, I've got to get to the dentist. I just stopped to see how my pigeon is doing."

"We're about to put her on the porch for the day," said Linda. "She's way too wild to keep with the other birds, but she's not happy out on the porch either. As soon as it warms up a few degrees overnight, we'll be able to let her loose."

I slipped past Roswitha, feeling slightly like a Peeping Tom with the binoculars around my neck, but I intended to squeak in a little bird-watching after visiting the poultry pen. The sheer volume of water was impressive. Only ten days earlier, when it seemed as if we wouldn't get our usual spring rains, I had wandered among the puddles and ponds of the swamp sowing biodegradable mosquito pellets in hopes of staving off the annual bloodletting. Larger areas of water got treated to a doughnut-size anti-mosquito ring, but the mud tried repeatedly to swallow my boots instead. Now, in place of the scattered bits of wet lay a fast-moving widening of the river, and I envisioned my pricey larvae-poisoning snacks—harmless to other wildlife—enjoying an all-expense-paid voyage to scenic Lake Michigan.

I couldn't circumnavigate the pen behind the barn. The flooding blocked my regular route through the brambles. I cut around the front instead, patting my old friend the satellite-TV dish good morning before angling down the bank to Roswitha's road. The water curled around the high ground of the barn. If the river rose another six feet, we'd have to consider relocating the chickens. Even if nine-tenths of the pen stayed dry, I couldn't depend on Buffy to avoid drowning in a teaspoonful of water.

I stepped into Roswitha's rowboat, which safely sat half in and half out of the river. It wasn't going anywhere without her. The stern rested solidly on familiar ground, while the bow pointed toward if not exactly terra incognita, then certainly terra indefinite. It felt strange to lose sight of the gravel driveway along with the familiar dips and ridges of the woods. It also made me claustrophobic to be barred from land I often walked. When neatly tucked within its banks, the Grand River was a marvelous companion. But for the river to awaken with a yawn, stretch its limbs, and matter-of-factly abuse its power was like discovering that the nice fellow who lives next door is actually an insurance adjuster. Fortunately, the flooding affected only the cosmetics of our property. Hundreds of people along the riverbank lived under a serious threat. I didn't understand how Roswitha could cheerfully remain in a house that had become an island, even if she stayed high and dry. Putting up with the inconvenience was one thing, but how could she possibly adjust to the strangeness?

A kingfisher on the telephone wire above my head cursed the bad fortune of trying to dive for fish in a tree-choked bayou, and his complaint pinged across the water. Raising my binoculars, I searched the brush ahead of the boat for other birds. To my left I heard the cluck of a red-winged blackbird's call note. I ignored the commoner, hoping for a glimpse of warbler royalty through the leaves. The caller persisted. He must be related to Eileen, I thought. Turning toward the noisemaker I was shocked to see an olive-backed bird with a yellow breast and a jet-black mask across his eyes. During the hot days of summer, the *witchity-witchity* song of the common yellowthroat warbler often sounded in our woods, but I had never laid eyes on the singer before. The flooding had flushed him out of the thicket and perched him on the top of the poultry pen, like Stanley Sue on Walter's cage. He regarded me warily before sailing away to cluck from someplace else.

As I OPENED THE front door, Bette Ann asked brightly, "Are we having a rummage sale?" Deprived of space in the bedroom closet, Linda's dresses and blouses had migrated to a clothing rack on the porch, whose cement floor also provided a gathering place for bags of rabbit feed, parrot seed, and kitty litter, plus the recycling bin, an exercise bike with a pigeon on its handlebars, a pair of pet carriers, and a pile of rocks.

"No, we just live like hillbillies," I told her.

"You need a bigger house." She shielded her face from Roswitha's bird as it took off from the exercise bike to flutter against a window. "Where did that pigeon come from? You're not keeping it, are you?" Linda detailed the story of the bird that taps on doors while we inched toward the dining room just in time for Howard to land on my head and coo. I lifted my hand and stroked his satiny back with a finger.

"Stanley Sue isn't out?"

"I put her in before letting Howard go," I said.

"Can't they both be out of their cages at once?" Bett asked.

"They're feuding," I explained. "A few years ago, Howard flew into Stanley Sue's empty cage and started eating her seeds. Stanley surprised Howard and tore open his back. I thought he was dead when I found him." I shook my head to think of it, inadvertently dislodging the dove. "Sorry, Howard. After Howard recovered, the first chance he got he came after her, but it's like a minnow attacking a barracuda. Stanley's got a wicked beak and claws. Howard's got nothing. The best he can do is beat her with his wings."

"I don't know how you keep up with them," she said.

I could never keep up with Bett. Though eleven years my senior, she effortlessly surpassed me in youthfulness and energy—as would a three-toed sloth, of course. She matched an uncomplaining nature with boundless enthusiasm, which raised inevitable sticky questions about her parentage versus mine, as did her ambivalence toward pets.

Stimulated by our voices, our canary Elliot erupted in glorious song. He began with flutelike glissandos reminiscent of a cardinal, then launched into a series of ecstatic trills. His gorgeous voice never failed to garner compliments from visitors.

"Be quiet! We're trying to talk," Bett told him with exaggerated sternness. "I brought a couple of documents from the lawyer."

"I think Linda made some cake. Why don't we have that first?"

"Just a small piece, Linda," said Bett. "*Small*," she repeated. "I brought the durable power of attorney and the patient-advocacy forms."

"I'm glad you know what those are, because I don't. You certainly got extra practice with Aba's estate."

After my father's death, Bett had guided our family through the thicket of legal issues initiated by the complicated trust account he had set up. More recently, when my dad's sister Aba died, Bett discovered that she had failed to leave a will. Bett immediately flew to Washington, D.C., to manage the affairs of our eccentric aunt, who had had the habit of cutting off communication with any relative who crossed her in the smallest way. Bett's sin of sending Aba a small bouquet the Christmas following my dad's passing—in violation of a no-gifts tradition—had caused her to add my sister to her zipped-lips list. Despite this, Bett had cheerfully put our aunt's final affairs in order.

"I'll bet if Aba's looking down from heaven, she's really steamed that I went through her apartment," Bett joked.

"So how did things go with Mom this weekend? How did she seem?"

"I broached the subject of selling the house," she said as Linda plunked down servings of spice cake the size of small office buildings. Neither Joan nor I would have been so bold as to mention the idea of moving, but Bett could get away with it. While I may have allegedly had my mother's electric trimmer and anniversary watch, Bett definitely had her ear.

"I'm supposed to eat all this?" she said to Linda.

"It's mostly air," said Linda.

"What did she say about the house?"

"She said, and I quote, 'I'll think about moving when I start to lose my faculties.'"

"So how will she know when she reaches the point where she doesn't know what she's doing anymore?"

"That's an excellent question, Bob. I did get a chance to check her out in the car. She drove me to Mass in the Buick, and she did fine. I'll tell you something else: she whomped me at cribbage last night."

"Maybe she'll be okay in the house for a few more years."

"Who's that on my head?" Taking his cue from the house-cat playbook, Howard inevitably gravitated toward the very people who least desired intimate contact with him. Bett was gracious about the intrusion, patiently waiting until I scooped him off her head and plunked him back into his cage.

With the dove dislodged, Bett ducked into the living room and came back with a pair of file folders. "Here's the durable power of attorney form, and here's the patient-advocacy form. I explained both of them to Mom, and she agreed to sign them. These copies are for you. They're pretty self-explanatory," she added, but because I had trouble comprehending the legal text on a postage stamp, she was good enough to explain them to me.

The context of Bett's visit to our house on her way back to Fort Wayne was Dr. Doering's recent diagnosis of Alzheimer's disease following Mom's latest mental-acuity test. While the diagnosis hadn't come as a surprise to Bett, Joan, or me, it did demand a significant shift in our thinking. It was no longer a question of wondering how bad Mom would get. Instead it became a question of how bad, how soon. We decided not to share the doctor's report with Mom, since she wouldn't have accepted it anyway. She would only have insisted that she would be just fine if people would stop taking her things. This ignorance was the saving grace of an illness that mercifully tended to conceal itself from the sufferer.

As Stanley Sue squawked in vain to be let out of her cage, we tried to make headway with the huge mounds of cake Linda had given us. "Good heavens, you've got more critters coming for a meal," said Bett. At the bottom of the hill, the first wood ducks of the season swam toward the water's edge, trailing V's behind them. When the six ducks finished fighting over the scratch feed that Linda had set out for them, we three humans waddled out to the backyard and stared at the water for a while. I wondered if Bett was having the same thoughts that I had about being inundated by worry, but I decided not to burden her with a cliché.

WHEN IT RAINS, IT POURS. I should have told that to Bett, too. A scant few hours after my sister left, Linda made an unhappy discovery about Walter. "What's wrong with his front leg?" she asked me. "It looks like he's got an abscess. I don't know why I didn't see that before."

I couldn't, in fact, see anything. Whether hunkered down or in blobby motion, Walter resembled a furry gel-stuffed pillow with front legs that were occluded by generous folds of flesh. A similar description might apply to Moobie. The two were nearly the same size, though he survived being momentarily mistaken for our massive cat thanks to the Rorschach inkblot pattern interrupting an otherwise white coat. I rarely found myself caught in a dark mood that couldn't be lightened by a glance at Walter, who seemed to exude foolishness from every pore, though he held the highest opinion of himself.

I got down on all fours on the living room rug, unintentionally encouraging Moobie to begin her campaign for a kitty treat by rubbing up against my face. As I moved toward Walter with watchful eyes, he ducked behind the chair. I curled up on the floor and waited. He thundered along the wall toward the safety of the plant stand. A couple of minutes later, large black eyes, a wiggling nose, and alert ears popped around the dragon tree to assess the threat level. Determining that I presented a target for a quick toe-biting foray, he galloped toward me making happy buzzing noises. Following a nip at my sock, he retreated to the safety of the chair.

"That right front leg is a little swollen," I agreed.

"He's got to go to the vet right away. We don't want to take any chances with an abscess."

We had once lost a sweet French Lop bunny named Bea during surgery to remove a virulent abscess that spanned her neck, shoulder, and leg, and we didn't want Walter to suffer a similar fate. Our vet, Dr. Fuller, specialized in "exotics"—the pet industry's term for any animal other than a cat or dog, including the rare and seldom-glimpsed parakeet—and had saved several of our animals from premature demise, including a turkey attacked and temporarily blinded by a flock member, and a goose that had contracted a tuberculosis-like respiratory disease. After checking Walter's leg, Dr. Fuller told me that the mass didn't have the yielding feel of an abscess. He recommended an X-ray and biopsy.

A few days later he phoned with the results. Walter had a malignant tumor on his leg, and because the growth lacked clearly defined boundaries, surgery could be long and difficult. "And even then, I wouldn't know with absolute certainty that I'd removed it all," he told Linda. "The other factor to consider is that it might already have invaded the bone."

"He's an old rabbit. I'd rather not put him through surgery," said Linda. "It would probably be too much for him."

"I think you might be right," he told her. "And this could turn out to be a slow-growing tumor."

"So he might outlast the cancer?"

"It's a possibility."

Contributing to our decision to let Walter live out his time in peace was the fact that another vet had removed two noncancerous tumors a year earlier, and the experience had stressed him to the point where he had barely eaten for several days. "Walter could do fine for quite a while," Linda said.

We didn't obsess too long about his condition. A fresh disaster sloshed in the following weekend when my old college friend Michael visited me. Sitting in the living room, we had just finished listening to bits of a CD by the Oratorio Society of Minnesota, of which he was a member. Michael was patiently pronouncing composer Kodály's name for me for about the fourteenth time when a flurry of wings and parrot squawks interrupted my Hungarian-language lesson. I ran into the dining room as Stanley Sue flew from Howard's cage and landed on the countertop.

To keep Howard and Stanley Sue apart when one or the other bird was loose, we put a towel on top of the captive bird's cage to prevent sneak attacks from above or below. I had never considered the possibility that the parrot would fight the dove through the bars while clinging to the side of his cage, but this is exactly what had happened. Howard's foot had been bloodied, and he tilted his head as if in pain.

He didn't seem badly hurt, but to be on the safe side I took him to Dr. Fuller's office the next day. "His neck is lacerated under the feathers," he said. "He needs to be anesthetized right away and the wound sutured, but that isn't what worries me the most. See the marks on his beak?"

Popping on my glasses and focusing closely, I noticed a couple of indentations halfway between the tip of the beak and his head. "Is that serious?"

"His beak isn't like a parrot's bill, which is made of a hard substance not unlike your fingernails. Howard's beak is composed of soft tissue with blood circulation, and with an injury like this, there is a danger that the beak could actually fall off." Our vet had the gift of making the most extraordinary statements sound so commonplace, it was as if he said them on a daily basis.

As I struggled with this unfortunate snippet of information, Dr. Fuller cupped Howard expertly in his hand in a sort of kung fu grip that I could never duplicate no matter how many times he had demonstrated it. He disappeared to his surgery with the bird, leaving me to baste in worry on my own. It shocked me that in less than five seconds, Stanley Sue had succeeded in slashing Howard's neck, upbraiding his leg, and putting the vise grip on his bill, even with her beak restricted by the bars. Equally amazing was the fact that a defenseless dove would be so bold as to challenge a powerful parrot. I could only explain their ongoing rivalry as the age-old contest of determining supremacy over the flock. I took it as an insult that neither bird viewed me as a contender.

When Dr. Fuller finally returned to the examination room and gently placed the groggy dove into our pet carrier, I noticed that his normally clean-shaven face sported a Vandyke beard. Combined with his wire-rimmed glasses, the facial hair lent him the appearance of a psychoanalyst. I wondered if I might ask him to prescribe some Zoloft to get me through the week. He hadn't been out of the room long enough to grow the whiskers; I'd been so fixated on Howard during my visit, I must have let his new Vandyke fly right by me.

"His neck stitched up very well. I don't think it will be a problem."

"So how will I know when he's out of danger with his beak?"

"You have to get him to eat something," the beard told me. "His beak is probably too tender for seeds. You should try him on something soft. I'm going to send you home with some powdered food that you can mix with water and manually feed him if necessary. Do you know how to do a tube-feeding?"

Seldom would a visit to the vet's office be described as a pleasant experience, but I felt worse about this one by the minute. "Do you mean sticking a tube down his throat into his crop and force-feeding him?" Linda's friend LuAnn needed to do this twice a day with her blind dove Snowdrop, who could not eat on her own. I had watched the tube-feeding once, and it looked miserable for both parties involved.

"I can show you how to do it."

"How about we wait until it's absolutely necessary? I can bring him back tomorrow afternoon if I don't see any evidence that he's eating."

"That's fine," said Dr. Fuller. "But we shouldn't wait longer than that. It's critical that he start receiving nutrition as soon as possible."

I brought Howard home in a mood so bleak, not even a glance at Walter cheered me. Howard and Ollie were the two birds that had been with us the longest, and I couldn't imagine life without him fluttering clumsily around the dining room and hooting with puffed-up dignity at the parakeets, who ignored him.

Recalling that spaghetti was his favorite dinner food, I made a quick trip to the supermarket and brought home a frozen blob of pasta. Dusty, Stanley Sue, and Ollie loved noodles, too, and grudgingly allowed Linda and me to set aside a heated dollop for ourselves. I prepared the spaghetti for Howard in the traditional manner. Donning high-magnification glasses and equipping myself with a precision saw, I pressed several noodles together on my plate and cut them into rice-size pieces. I distributed them on the countertop next to Ollie's cage. Then I let Howard loose.

In a moment of high drama, Linda and I stopped eating and slowed our heartbeats as the newly sutured Howard landed on the Formica. Spying his favorite food, he bobbled toward it, but didn't eat at once.

"Maybe the countertop's too hard," I told Linda. "Maybe we should sprinkle the spaghetti on a wet sponge."

I needn't have worried. Within seconds Howard began wolfing down the noodles, whacking the countertop with greedy strikes of his beak like a woodpecker trying his luck on aluminum siding. Moments later, he assumed his usual spot inside Ollie's cage while Ollie dined on top in the equivalent of a café setting. Raking his beak through the small parrot's dish, Howard scattered a hundred seeds on the floor for every one he popped into his mouth. Usually Linda fussed about the mess, but this time she praised him profusely: "Good boy, Howard."

The next day I revisited my stash of wire-mesh fencing in the barn. Stapling it to strips of wood, I constructed a gawky enclosure that slipped over his hanging cage and, similar to the barrier on the bunny cages, barred Stanley's beak from entry. It was probably the first cage for a cage that I had ever built.

WE SHOULD HAVE run more fencing around the backyard to keep Eileen out, but it would have been like trying to hold water back with a sieve. Kate had given us her okay on the phone for Lulu to move to luxury accommodations with Eileen's newfound friend Henrietta. But I hadn't expected my old schoolmate to simply show up one Saturday morning. For reasons as mysterious as those that had brought her to us in the first place, Eileen had left our orbit to the extent that she didn't care to greet us or ask for our help. Kate had accompanied her and turned to wave enthusiastically in the direction of the dining room, though I doubted she could see me crouched behind Dusty's cage.

Eileen gestured impatiently for Kate to join her inside the duck pen, then stepped back as the realization hit her that she had no idea how to handle anything with feathers. The general stood aside and waved her arms at Lulu's pleasant owner, who lifted and snuggled her beautiful white duck. She paused to make sure that Eileen had latched the pen door, then followed her at a march toward our driveway.

That afternoon I hauled a cage into the backyard, set it on top of the milk house, and gave Roswitha's pigeon her freedom as Linda urged her on. Without a second's hesitation, the bird flew off, circled the yard, and landed on the peak of the barn roof. Throughout the day, she maintained her post like a weather vane that had come to life. As evening began to fall, she still remained, and we worried that her months in captivity might have robbed

her of the instincts to fend for herself. Holding her cage above my
head, I walked toward the barn calling for her.

"Pigeon! Pigeon! You can come back inside if you want."

After a few moments she flapped her wings and left the roof. It
was just dark enough that hawks wouldn't be a problem, and far
too light for tussles with owls as she flew over the remaining flood-
water in the woods, heading home to rejoin her flock—soaring
above and flapping away from the troubles that had found us.

CHAPTER 11

Travels with Stinky

Howard recovered from his life-threatening injuries with his usual nonchalance, and the tumor on Walter's leg didn't seem to have progressed. My mom puttered along without further setbacks, the new geese coexisted swimmingly with their peers, and Eileen hadn't reared her topknotted head in days. Eager to take advantage of this rare interval of tranquillity, Linda said, "Couldn't we get out of town for a weekend?"

Two obstacles prevented us from flinging ourselves into the car and hurling it toward Grindstone City, Michigan; Wawa, Ontario; or another chunk of vacation paradise. The foremost problem was Linda's ailing back. Her creaky lumbar discs went on strike if she stood in one place or sat too long—a condition that would have proved fatal to a sedentary stick like myself. Lying on the back seat of the car during brief jaunts helped keep Linda's spinal contractions at bay, but she couldn't stay supine for a several-hour drive. My cramped Ford Focus didn't exactly offer the comforts of a queen-size bed, let alone a faux-sheepskin rug on the living room floor. She might as well have tried to stretch out inside my mother's bread drawer between a bundle of hoarded paper bags and a hidden purse. But Linda had hatched an idea that might improve her transportability—the inimitable Stinky—and we awaited the chance to test it out.

That left us with the second problem: finding a pet sitter. We'd had a few excellent sitters over the years, but Betty had moved away, Teresa had grown busy with her family, and Sarah had fallen victim to post-traumatic stress syndrome from a relentless series of chores that included singing a night-night song to Ollie. We had no choice but to seek out innocent blood for Victor's beak, and that meant placing an ad in the local weekly newspaper. Plenty of college-age girls always applied. They never failed to impress us with their enthusiasm and imperturbability during the interview process, and seldom failed to disappoint us with their lackluster performance on the job.

A few summers ago, just before we had walked out of the door for a trip to Pennsylvania Dutch country, Linda had told college student Tippi, "Make sure to cover the birds at night, like we talked about before. The covers are in the hall closet, and I wrote down which ones go over which cage."

"I won't forget," she assured Linda. "I even remember what you said about the two black covers for Stanley Sue."

Upon our return a week later, as I attempted to regale Tippi with tales of technology-shunning Amish ringing up quilt sales on state-of-the-art LCD-screen cash registers, Linda glanced in the closet and noticed that the pile of cage covers lay exactly as she had left them. Tippi hadn't so much as unfolded a single cover, when she should have used them to conceal the fact that she hadn't cleaned the cages either. A check of the upstairs answering machine explained her laxness. "I'm on my way over right now," began numerous messages from her boyfriend, alternating with plaintive calls from her parents, asking, "Tippi, why haven't we heard from you?"

Another young pet sitter, Missy, worked as a veterinary assistant and had grown up on a farm with countless indoor and outdoor critters. Her attentiveness when Linda introduced her to the pets encouraged us, as did the questions that she asked about their care. But on the scorching July weekend when we visited the Upper Peninsula, only a propitious visit from Linda's friend LuAnn saved our birds and rabbits from cooking in the giant pressure cooker of our house. "She didn't have enough common sense to switch on the air conditioner," LuAnn said later. "I had to do it for her." These and other incidents involving the justifiably maligned youth of America compelled Linda to target older and presumably more dependable sitters instead. But they proved difficult to find.

As BEFITTED THE zenith of spring, Linda's flowers popped out of the ground in abundance, and her annual crop of classified ads on assorted subjects blossomed in the *Lowell Ledger.* Her solicitation of a pet sitter didn't seem to invite confusion. "Wanted: experienced person to care for our pet birds, rabbits, and cats while we are on vacation. Must be an animal lover." A few folks with the credentials of having once petted though never owned a dog were among the first wave of callers, along with a gruff-voiced man who charmed Linda with the admission that, yes, he guessed he could feed and water a few pets if we paid him enough.

Although we had decided to disregard calls from college students, we repeatedly played back the message from a young woman who assured us that she would love to have the job, provided that we picked her up and drove her back to her dorm each day, because she didn't own a car. "I guess we could lend her mine, since we're apparently vacationing within walking distance of home," I told Linda. We also received the typical call from a doting mom who didn't want her nine-year-old to miss the chance to learn about animals. "Might as well practice on ours," I muttered. "Too bad we don't have an actual guinea pig."

Linda rigorously screened the applicants that made it past the answering machine by subjecting them to a concise series of questions over the course of an hour-long phone call. The first person to survive this trial by endurance seemed ideal when she showed up at our door with a well-behaved scarlet macaw balanced on her wrist. "Ozzie loves everybody," she informed us with an accent that, using my vast knowledge of *The Crocodile Hunter* television show, I immediately placed within the northern Queensland region of Australia.

"Actually, I'm from New Zealand," Doreen said with a toss of her hair.

I had never held a macaw before, and as Ozzie stepped onto my arm and affectionately rubbed a head the size of Tasmania on my sleeve, I wanted to hire her on the spot. Linda seemed reluctant to surrender the keys to our front door, however. After a few minutes of baby-talk with the bright red pterodactyl, I realized that Doreen's avian passion pretty much limited itself to her winged creature. While she politely glanced at our parrots, parakeets, dove, and canary, her attention always boomeranged backed to Ozzie.

"Dusty is a real talker," Linda began.

"Say 'Hello, there,' Ozzie," Doreen told the bird.

"But he's not exactly what you'd call cuddly."

"Watch this," said Doreen, taking Ozzie from me. "Let's play rock-a-bye baby." Flipping him upside down, she cradled his back in her palm while his legs stuck up straight in the air. She sang a short lullaby worthy of Ollie's night-night hat bedtime song. Then, upon announcing, "Upsy daisy," she tossed the macaw in the air, caught the still inverted bird in her opposite hand, and twisted him right side up without ruffling a single feather. None of our birds would ever have tolerated such acrobatics, though Dusty had once dangled headfirst from the top of my boot while trying to fillet my foot.

Once she had returned Ozzie to a spacious cage in her SUV and accompanied us to the barn, Doreen's powers of concentration improved. She commented favorably upon hens Tina and Buffy, recognized the aggressiveness lurking behind Victor's tail wagging. All of this boded well. But there was just one hitch. Shod in a pair of immaculate calf-high Italian leather boots, she planted each foot with obvious misgivings as she navigated the debris-strewn barn floor. When she lifted the water pail to fill it from the hydrant per Linda's instructions, she didn't engage the full length of her fingers in the task, as though she wished to limit her exposure to the phalanges while sparing the far more susceptible metacarpals.

"I think she'd be fine for looking in on the animals while we're visiting my mom for the day," Linda told me after Doreen and Ozzie had taken flight. "But she wouldn't be good if we were gone overnight. She's a little too fastidious for working out in the barn, and she can barely tear herself away from that bird of hers for even a second."

An older man named Harry who had once been a farmer squeaked through Linda's telephone interview on the basis of his charitable works. He liked ducks and rabbits, he told her, and used to keep them. He'd also owned a couple of parrots, though he seemed vague about the details. Although his voice suggested advanced age and thus frailty even greater than mine, he spoke of having recently returned from West Virginia, where he'd been repairing flood-damaged homes with other members of his church.

Linda suggested that he stop by to meet our animals. "He sounds like a nice Christian man," she told me.

Two days later Harry phoned to say that he had just finished visiting a friend at the office of the lumber company two miles up the road from us and was on his way right over. Linda and I stood in the living room, peering out the window for his vehicle. Ten minutes passed. Then twenty. At the half-hour mark, Linda phoned the office.

"Harry?" laughed the woman on the other end. "He's still standing here talking."

A few minutes later we met a grizzled soul sporting a red baseball cap and a glint in his eye that warned of an endless repository of stories. "I'll show you the pen behind the barn," Linda told him. Before we had walked half the distance, his non-Italian leather boots sank roots into the ground as he paused beside our pine tree. "I used to have a bunch of rabbits when I was a kid," he began, and as he licked his lips to prime the pump of reminiscence, I could hear the woody tendrils burrowing deeper. "One day I woke up, and ten of them were dead. I called the vet, and he said that they probably caught some disease from a rat, and a few more might die. I lost eight more of them that day."

"That's terrible," said Linda as she took a step toward the barn that did not earn reciprocation from Harry. "We're crazy about our Walter and Rudy. They live in the dining room if you want to see them later."

"Enough of them survived to butcher," he answered brightly. "They fetched two dollars apiece, dressed, which was pretty good money back then. Last week I went to see a friend, and he charged me twenty dollars for a butchered and dressed rabbit. Twenty dollars! But it sure tasted good."

Having purged himself of this tale of death, he managed to free his feet for a few steps before his inner pedometer activated a set of steel brakes. Linda and I forged on optimistically, but instead of following our lead, he waited patiently in the sunshine until we slunk back to his side. "You got some ducks there," he remarked, though they were barely visible from where he stood.

"Come see Victor," Linda urged. "He's the troublemaker of the flock."

"You know what works best with troublemakers?" He dipped his head, smiling as his chin rested against his neck. "You throw them in the stewpot."

"He's not that bad," exclaimed Linda. "We don't eat meat. We love animals too much."

"My son lives down in Arizona, and a bobcat kept getting his ducks. One night he waited outside with his shotgun and killed it. 'That was one big bobcat,' he told me. 'How big was it?' I asked him. He said, 'Dad, I could barely get it into two garbage bags.'"

The image proved too much for me. "We've lost a few ducks to raccoons, but we don't shoot the raccoons. We don't believe in anything like that. I catch them in a live trap and release them on the other side of the river."

"I'll tell you how to solve your raccoon problem."

"How's that?" I asked, fearing that another garbage bag loomed.

"Get yourself a bottle of fly bait, then mix it together with cherry cola."

"What does that make, some sort of repellent?" I envisioned sprinkling the concoction around the perimeter of our duck pen and a raccoon bounding away after catching a whiff of it.

"You put it in a dish, the raccoons eat it, and it kills them. They can't burp like we can," he told us with a knowing lift of one eyebrow.

Inch by inch, stopping and restarting for one gory anecdote

after another, we lurched toward the duck pen behind the barn—occasioning a market-value assessment of our white Pekin duck Richie, butchered and dressed, of course. Then we reversed course, following the trail of fondly recalled carcasses back to Harry's pickup truck. He never once mentioned the pet-sitting job, acting as if the sole purpose of his visit had been to share treasured moments with us. With the hint of a grin crooking one side of his mouth, he touched the visor of his cap good-bye and rolled off in a haze of memories.

LINDA'S AD FOR a pet sitter also prompted a pair of unexpected calls. The first was sorely welcome. The second made me sore. Our ex-sitter Teresa graciously offered to come out of retirement long enough to give us a weekend away from animal drudgery. Even Linda's full account of the various pets that had come and gone since Teresa's last stint with us—along with the added chores, out-of-cage schedules, and esoteric rituals like the midday pink-cookie treat for the indoor birds—failed to discourage her.

"You guys deserve to take a break," she told us.

"Thank you, thank you," said Linda. "We didn't think we'd ever find anyone."

"It's no problem at all," said Teresa. But she hadn't banked on interference from Eileen, and neither had I.

"I saw your classified ad," reported my old schoolmate, who had defeated our caller ID by harassing us from an unfamiliar cell-phone number.

"You subscribe to the *Lowell Ledger*?" I asked. "Do you read the *Ionia Sentinel-Standard*, too?"

"Marcie Merczenski lives just outside Lowell."

"From Mrs. Edkins's eighth-grade class—"

"She's Marcie Merczenski-Cummiskey now. She has a large and luxurious house in that new development up on the ridge."

"We've already got a pet sitter," I told her as I tilted my head toward the wall clock, whose second hand seemed to be spinning backward. "Thanks so much for offering your services. And give my best to my good friend Marcie."

She treated me to a sputter of exasperation. "I'm calling because I'm just a little concerned that you would entrust my beautiful geese to a stranger."

"Teresa isn't a stranger. She's looked after our animals several times, and I would trust her with any of them."

"When are you going out of town?"

Despite my better judgment, I couldn't resist bragging that on the last Friday of the month Linda and I would be embarking on a dream weekend in the Toledo area.

"I'm marking down those dates in my day planner," she said. "I'll make sure to check up on this sitter, and I'll read her the riot act if she isn't doing right by my geese."

"I forget where you kept your geese when they lived with you."

"I'm just looking out for them. Somebody needs to."

Not for the first time did I puzzle over Eileen's insistence on keeping in contact with us despite her weirdly escalating level of hostility. But I had decided long ago that trying to understand her motives would only increase my own mental turmoil. Though birds, rabbits, and cats weren't exactly what you might term rational beings, their straightforwardness had it all over the convoluted maze of human psychology, and Eileen's psyche seemed to suffer from an excess of dead ends. Even our excessively moody parrot Ollie was a creature of crystalline purity compared to her. Whenever he burbled messages of love on my shoulder only to clamp his beak into my neck muscles a moment later, he wasn't acting out deeply submerged and muddy impulses. He simply enjoyed burbling followed by biting—always had and always would. I never asked, "Why me?" when the vise grip ultimately came, but I invariably posed that question to myself whenever Eileen phoned.

I tried insisting that the date of our trip remained in flux. "We might not actually get away until the coming fall, Eileen. Linda's back is particularly bad this time of the year. It gives her problems during rain and meteor showers." But I didn't get anywhere with the lie.

I did warn Teresa before we left for Ohio that an annoying woman might stop by to offer unwelcome, unwarranted, and wholly inexperienced animal advice. The information didn't faze her. "If she gives me any trouble," Teresa said, "I'll lock her in the pen with her buddies."

IN THE PAST, our trips to exotic locales like Toledo necessitated that we lug along a cooler chocked with ice and cold compresses for Linda's back. But having discovered that heat packs were more effective against inflammation, Linda now shunned motel ice makers for convenience-store microwaves to charge up a hot compress of her own design—the one and only Stinky. Stinky had started life inoffensively enough. Linda's Thomas Edison–style search for a heat-retaining material had progressed through sand, aquarium gravel, and various rare earth elements before she'd ultimately settled on uncooked white rice, which she'd poured into a snake-shaped pillow. Frequent overheating had scorched the organic stuffing, resulting in a charred-popcorn smell each time Stinky left the radar range.

In service station after service station, I'd bide my time fueling the car while Linda recharged her heat pack; then I'd slip into the building to experience the overpowering odor of an electrical fire at a cereal plant. "Fifteen dollars of gas on pump number two," I told a teenager at a truck stop just north of the Michigan-Ohio border. He struggled to connect the seemingly innocuous redheaded woman who'd just left the building clutching a fabric hot dog with a possible industrial chemical spill whose fumes were seeping in from the parking lot. "Coffee smells good," I chirped as I thrust a twenty-dollar bill under his nose. "Must be an exotic Indonesian blend, but you might be brewing it a bit too strong."

My final glance through the car window found the stoop-shouldered attendant shuffling toward the coffeemaker carrying a plastic pail and giant brush. "This is even worse than your meat-colored gel pack," I grumbled to Linda as we tore out of the parking lot. "That looked weird, but it didn't have a smell."

"The rice holds the heat a whole lot longer than the gel."

The important thing was that I had distracted the attendant long enough to forestall a phone call to the EPA or local law enforcement personnel. In fact, by the time it finally dawned on him to investigate the microwave, I figured, we would be safely across the state line. But I was nervous about our heating hit-and-runs anyway. If a cop pulled us over for a traffic infraction, I couldn't imagine what illegal substance he would suppose Linda was smoking while sprawled out in the back seat.

For my part, I tried combating the fumes by cranking open the window and drowning them in fresh air. But Stinky laughed at the inrush of wind and burrowed its odor molecules deep into the pores of the car upholstery. "What do your housecleaning customers say about that thing?"

"Nothing," Linda said defensively. "They might ask me, 'What's that smell?'"

The outgassing addled my senses, turning what should have been a three-hour trip to Toledo into an inexplicable five-hour marathon that brought us to the Toledo Museum of Art a mere forty-five minutes before the stingy four P.M. closing time.

"That doesn't even give us enough time to look at the frames, much less the pictures," I complained to the museum's parking lot attendant, who gave me the shrug that my comment deserved.

Once I managed to blunder back onto the freeway, I hollered at Linda, "Why did we ever come to this stupid city at all?" though it had been my idea. "Why didn't we just take a trip into the country?" I said, though this had been her suggestion from the first.

Bogged down by endless freeway construction and urged on by gleeful orange Department of Transportation signs advising us, "Expect long delays, choose alternate city to visit," we decided to skip the rest of Toledo's attractions and opt for the reliable Cleveland Metroparks Zoo instead. Coveting a stay in a rural America, we took blue highways east and ended up at the Ottawa National Wildlife Refuge on Lake Erie. A great egret waved us past a logjam of birders in minivans who were hoping for a glimpse of a visiting scissor-tailed flycatcher, seldom seen in the Great Lakes. We headed for the woods to walk off our art museum frustration, triumphantly emerging with several pricey morel mushrooms, which had gone unnoticed by birders scanning for warblers.

When Linda accosted a ranger to find out that the ducklike diving birds we'd been seeing were in fact old coots like me, he added that at the Magee Marsh Wildlife Area, a quarter mile down the road, a migrating Kirtland's warbler had been spotted on the beach. I knew this to be one of the rarest birds around, a warbler whose only nesting site in the country was a few tracts of jack pines in northern Michigan, and even then only among young trees that grow in the wake of managed forest fires. But there didn't seem to be any point in us poking around the shoreline for a bird we probably couldn't find and wouldn't know if we did, so we continued east in search of a motel.

Unable to locate the sort of old-fashioned mom-and-pop motel smack in the middle of nowhere that Linda insisted still existed, we settled on a room at the Shorebird Motel in the part marina town, part ConAgra factory city of Huron. Being cooped up in a strange bedroom occasionally triggered a panic attack in Linda. In an attempt to bleed off a trickle of her boundless energy, we took one of our weirder after-dark strolls. Having headed for the beach in hopes of a walk across the sand, we chanced instead upon an eerie Lake Erie fishing pier made of trailer-size blocks of concrete. With only the distant city lights as our guide, we felt our way along the narrow, quarter-mile-long structure. Waves lapping over the cement blocks kept the surface slippery, while gusts of wind encouraged us to press our arms to our sides to stave off spontaneous windsurfing shortcuts back toward shore.

Just as the feeble yellow light of a navigational marker at the end of the pier caught my eye, a huge sailboat rose up out of nowhere to flash its ghostly white sails at us. Except for a rustle of canvas and a slight ripple of water, we didn't hear a sound as the boat skirted dangerously close to the pier before the murk swallowed it up again. I hadn't seen a soul on board, animate or otherwise.

"The Flying Dutchman," I sputtered. "Spirits of the dead." I stubbed my toe against a concrete crevice for the thirtieth time or so as we reversed direction and started retracing our steps. "It's a warning that this is incredibly dangerous." The uneven blocks weren't the worst obstacle, though. Two college students, apparently taking a break from pet-sitting responsibilities, had decided that the middle of a pier in the black of night was the perfect spot for stretching out and embracing one another. I nearly tripped over the lovers and embraced Davy Jones as a result.

The next day, at the Cleveland Metroparks Zoo, I lectured Linda on every animal we saw, explaining how each one reminded me of her. However, my mind was elsewhere. I was preoccupied by a stuffed monkey I'd seen for sale in a gift shop window near the zoo entrance. The toy held the promise of companionship for Ed, the sock monkey my grandmother had sewn for me as a boy and who'd come with us on the trip to keep Stinky company. Crushing disappointment followed, for when I finally had the chance to examine the monkey's pouting molded-vinyl face up close, I realized that the Chinese manufacturer lacked my grandmother's empathy for primates. So I reluctantly left it in the window.

"Don't say anything to *him* about it," I whispered to Linda, inclining my head toward Ed in the back seat as we headed back to Huron for dinner at Denny's and another perilous pier walk. After Ed's failure as Stanley Sue's kitchen-countertop sentinel and his apparent rejection by the diffident Stinky, I didn't want him to suffer another letdown.

Morning got off to a bad start as Linda realized that between the zoo and Denny's she had managed to lose her favorite stocking cap, Sagey, who now joined the ranks of missing hats Greenie and Grapey and misplaced sweater Piney. But her mood brightened when we visited Crane Creek State Park, near the Ottawa National Wildlife Refuge. The state park's Magee Marsh boardwalk proved to be a smorgasbord of songbirds fluttering in the thickets on both sides of the path. Without moving a muscle we had within arm's length a bewildering array of warblers tired and tame from their migration: blackburnian, chestnut-sided, yellow, black-and-white, black-throated blue, common yellowthroat, yellow-rumped, magnolia, and others; plus, we blundered into a green heron hiding in the bulrushes.

Emboldened by our effortless success, Linda asked a birder weighted down with binoculars, cameras, and a spotting scope whether anyone had sighted the Kirtland's warbler that day. He gave us what I considered needlessly precise directions to the bird's last known appearance on the beach.

I envisioned a hushed and tedious wait across from a stand of trees, a flash of feathers in the foliage if we were lucky, another long wait, then the trudge back to the car spent reassuring one another, "We certainly saw *something*." But this was not to be. Instead, at the promised spot on Lake Erie's southern shore, we met a flock of slack-jawed birders who formed a thirty-foot-diameter circle. At the center leisurely pecked and hopped a small grey-and-yellow bird wearing an air of casualness and self-effacement at odds with its exalted status. At one point this elusive Kirtland's warbler—fresh from wintering in the Bahamas and perhaps one of only twelve hundred males in the world—actually skittered between the legs of a dumbstruck observer.

"How many of these are here at the park?" I asked a father birder who was sharing the spectacle with his fledgling son.

"Just him," he told me.

Despite the thrill of a close look at an endangered warbler that was seldom seen during migration, the experience muddied my mind with questions. In a park of several hundred acres, how did anyone manage to locate such a tiny, solitary bird, how did they keep from losing him overnight, and why didn't he simply fly to a spot where he could enjoy his privacy? But what troubled me the most was the irritating coincidence of sharing a beach with a bird associated with controlled forest burns and a wife associated with uncontrolled rice heating. Stinky was obviously more powerful than I ever would have guessed.

EILEEN HAD GOTTEN stinky in our absence. We found a veterinarian's bill on our countertop and a note from Teresa saying that she had taken goose Patty to nearby vet Dr. Leroy for treatment after one of the other geese had bitten her beneath her eye. We galloped to the backyard pen to examine the minor bruise; then I phoned our sitter to thank her for taking prompt action. "Did you have trouble getting the goose into your car?"

"No," she laughed, "I had more trouble with your friend Eileen."

I felt a pinch of dread in my stomach. "She's not my friend, but what happened?"

"She dropped by just as I got Patty back from the vet, and she lit into me with 'How could you let something like this happen to my goose?' and all sorts of nasty things. That girl really got worked up."

"I'm so sorry," I said. "It's bad enough you had to deal with an injured goose, but to suffer through Eileen on top of that."

"I didn't pay any attention to her. I let her get it out of her system, and then I asked her what she would have done differently."

"What did she say?"

"What could she say? She just stomped off. But she called me several times after that to holler at me about Patty. Once she even asked me, 'Did that goose die yet?'"

"I'll cook her goose," I trumpeted, but I didn't get the chance. Eileen's call within the hour threw me off balance. When she began by railing at us for allowing harm to come to Patty, I told her that the goose had received a clean bill of health from Dr. Leroy.

"Well, I wanted to talk to you about your pet sitter," she said.

"What's that?" I replied, ready to lower the boom.

"I was very impressed with her," she told me. "She's a keeper, and I hope you use her again."

CHAPTER 12

....

Elbow Room

Moobie enjoyed watching me peel off my pajamas as I got dressed to visit my mom. It wasn't that she had a predilection for human nudity; it fascinated her that a person could suddenly turn into unfurling flags of cloth. Lying at the end of the bed, she wore an expression of amusement as she tick-tocked her head back and forth between fixating on my discarded garments and focusing on pasty white Bob. She involved herself in the disrobing process by sitting bolt upright and paddling her clawless feet against my hip. Then, as I flung the pajama bottoms toward the laundry basket, she took a chunky swipe at the empty air and began purring luxuriously.

Deciding that Penny deserved her own little slice of Sunday morning pleasure, I trudged upstairs to receive a suspicious glare. Holding me in place at the side of the bed with her stare, she stood up, stretched her legs, and yawned, then flopped down facing the wall in a clear message that she wasn't receiving visitors. I ignored the snub and bent at the waist so that my damp hair just touched the bedspread. Rolling over, she rubbed her head against mine, inhaled the essence of anti-dandruff shampoo, then straightened her body with dilated pupils and extended nails as if she had just eaten a couple of grams of catnip.

Leaving a second cat in the throes of purring, I continued my effort to dole out cheer by picking up the phone and punching in my mom's number to remind her that I would arrive shortly to take her to church. My father's voice on the answering machine startled me. Since his death, I'd been unable to get use to his unintentionally ironic statement "We can't come to the phone right now," and hung up without leaving a message. Figuring that my mom was probably in the shower, I said my good-byes to Linda, Stanley Sue, and Dusty, and hopped into the car with the irrational hope that Father Paul's weekly sermon might be short and that no grade school students knelt in roped-off pews awaiting a lengthy awards ceremony.

I parked in front of Mom's house. I turned and waved cheerily at her neighbor Pat's Chevy across the street as she glided out of her driveway on her way to church, then saluted a movement of the Teanys' living room curtains. My mom met me at the front door while I was struggling to balance my keys in one hand and the log of a morning paper in the other. Still in her robe, she blurted out, "The car is gone," as I slipped into the vestibule.

"Where did it go?" I asked skeptically.

"I left it somewhere."

"When?"

"I was at the foot doctor near Fat Boy just a little while ago," she told me, citing a neighborhood landmark. "I forgot about the car and walked home, and now I can't find it. I walked as far as Three Mile and back, but it's gone."

"In your bathrobe?" I asked. "The car isn't in the driveway?"

"I left it somewhere."

Dropping the Sunday paper onto the nearest sturdy chair, I strode into the kitchen and peered out the window at my mom's empty driveway. The absence of the car struck me as odd until I noticed that the garage door was closed.

A month earlier, while psyching herself up to thread her big Buick through the needle eye of a garage built around 1930 to accommodate a Ford Model A, Mom had accidentally hit the gas pedal instead of the brake. She'd struck the front corner with sufficient force to knock one side of the building off its foundation. Luckily, she hadn't hurt herself, and her next-door neighbor Ted, who was the maintenance manager for an apartment complex, had volunteered to repair the damage. He had just completed the work a couple of days ago, allowing her to park her car inside the garage for the first time in weeks. The sight of the empty driveway this morning had apparently unnerved her—though this didn't explain the confusion with the foot doctor, or why she was still in her pajamas when we were due at church.

I pushed the button that my father had installed in the back room and peered out through the window. The garage door opened like a theatrical curtain, dramatically revealing the red rear end of the Buick. "I'm such a dumbhead," she said. "I was sure that I'd been out with the car today."

"It's nothing to worry about," I said, even though it worried me. "You probably dreamed about the foot doctor just before waking up. I dream about him all the time."

She smiled at the reassurance. "It's nice to know I'm not going crazy." Then she thought for a moment. "Were we going some place?"

"We were supposed to go to Mass, but we'll never make it," I told her without regret. "Though why don't you get dressed, and I'll take you to the Fat Boy for breakfast."

I DIDN'T KNOW what I had expected from Walter's cancer. I must have assumed that it would progress invisibly, like the air sac tumor that had killed our parakeet Rossy a couple of years ago. She had quietly died in her sleep one night. But over the course of the summer, Walter's leg had started to swell, and the tumor eventually erupted. The open wound horrified me, but Linda faithfully dressed and bandaged it each evening while I held him on the kitchen countertop and stared intently at the toaster.

Walter refused to allow the illness to interfere with his routine. After dinner, he would scratch at the plywood board that barricaded the dining room until Linda lifted it and allowed him to gallop into the living room. Grunting, buzzing, and snuffling heartily, he would explore the real estate behind the recliner and the plant stand, add his twenty-five cents to the litter box and another dollar to the plastic floor runner on either side of the box, then mark every object at rabbit head level with the scent gland on his chin. The cancer slowed his pace but in no way diminished his enthusiasm.

The situation grew grim when the wound became infected, and the vet put Walter on an antibiotic. Although the medication encouragingly diminished the size of Walter's tumor, the tumor alarmingly diminished the size of Walter. He stopped eating and became so weak that we would have to carry him into the living room at night to reserve what little strength remained for his scent-marking forays. It seemed time to say good-bye, but as soon as the antibiotic regimen expired, Walter's appetite returned. Within a couple of days, he was back to bounding into the living room, and we held hopes that we had actually starved his tumor into remission, until another one popped up below it.

After so many struggles with so many ill animals over the years — from rabbits to geese to turkeys to ducks and other birds — I could hardly bear to witness another decline. I suggested that it might be best to put him to sleep, but Linda disagreed.

"As long as he's still eating and enjoying life, we should just let him be," she told me. "Wouldn't you rather he died at home?"

"Well, if he could."

"Maybe he'll just pass on like Bertie did. That's how most of the other rabbits went."

We agreed not to interfere unless it became absolutely necessary. Within a month, we reached that unhappy point. One morning, Walter was unable to stand up, so I lifted him, placed him on a towel in a pet carrier, and took him to the vet.

I sat sobbing in the examination room, waiting for the doctor to appear. Then a remarkable thing happened. Walter somehow managed to struggle to his feet. He stood proudly in his carrier, ears pointing straight toward the heavens, a bright light illuminating his eyes. He stared at me as if to say, "I'm okay with this, so you should be okay with it, too."

I wasn't, though. Animal deaths always hit me hard. Despite the fact that the end of Walter's ordeal came as a great relief, I was squashed in the grip of mourning that dredged up all of our other losses over the years.

"You've got to snap out of it, sweetie," Linda told me as I lay on the couch with my arm covering my face for the third day in a row. "Walter wouldn't like you suffering so much."

"I can't help it."

"I worry about what would happen if you lost one of your favorites, like Moobie, Stanley Sue, or Howard."

"Maybe we need to get away for a little while," I mumbled through my arm. "We could visit Colonel Sanders's first kitchen," I told her, as something resembling a snicker rose up inside my throat. "And there's an Australian animal zoo in Kentucky that has lorikeets you can feed."

"Why don't we go do that," said Linda. "Trouble is, we need to find a pet sitter."

"Here we go again."

OUR FALL TURNED into a rerun of early summer. Linda placed a classified in the *Lowell Ledger* for a sitter, and among the applicants who made it through the screening process was a young mother who showed up with her four-year-old son. He impressed us right off the bat by kicking Rudy's cage while Mom politely suggested, "Darling, please don't do that." When I stepped between Darling and Rudy, the youngster decided that he'd retaliate by locking himself in our bathroom.

"Come out, sweetest," she urged him, tapping delicately with her fingertips rather than knocking on the wood. "Mommy has to see the rest of the animals." The cherub made no reply. "Does your husband have a hammer and a screwdriver?" she asked Linda matter-of-factly. "We usually have to take the door off the hinges."

A phone call later in the week didn't seem at all promising. A woman named Dawn advocated her eighteen-year-old granddaughter for the job. Linda described our abysmal track record with most sitters under forty, but Dawn met her protests with an insistence that Jamie showed maturity far beyond her years and had grown up on a farm caring for animals. She offered to oversee the girl, if that would ease Linda's mind.

"Absolutely not," I told Linda. "It isn't worth the bother. Don't even ask them over."

When Dawn and Jamie arrived for their appointment the following day, Jamie easily won us over. While she didn't gush over any of the animals, her quiet regard for each bird, cat, and bunny that we introduced her to was genuine, and she didn't seem fazed by the amount of work involved.

"This is our baby," Linda told her, taking Rudy out of his cage. Jamie held him in a manner that indicated she knew her way around rabbits. "I'll make sure the baby gets extra attention," she assured Linda, thus ensuring herself of the job.

As a test run, we tried Jamie out one Saturday while we visited Linda's mom in Battle Creek. We returned home to a pleasant surprise. Not only had Jamie performed every annoying task that we had requested, including giving the birds their afternoon pink-cookie treat, but she had also left us three notebook pages brimming with her observations. "Stanley Sue took a peanut, but she didn't want to come out of her cage," said one entry. Another note informed us, "One of the brown ducks seems to be limping. I picked her up, and her foot looked okay."

In my exhilaration, I almost picked up the phone to brag to Eileen about Jamie. But as a cheerier alternative, I visited Walter's grave in back of the house.

LINDA'S PARENTS HAD both been born and raised in Tennessee, and our trip to Kentucky tapped into her rural roots. She started speaking fluent hillbilly the second day of our trip as we ate lunch at the Cave Café in the city of Horse Cave.

"Could I maybe get me another one of them delicious biscuits?" she asked the restaurant owner. When the woman returned with a basket of them, Linda said, "You wouldn't know the name of that little prospector guy at the rock shop down the road?"

We'd come to Horse Cave to revisit the clapboard rock shop that had enchanted Linda with chunks of crystal onyx when we had breezed through the area on our honeymoon, more than a decade earlier. We also returned to visit a new attraction called Kentucky

Down Under, where unseasonably cold fall temperatures quashed the Australian outback verisimilitude. Still, we enjoyed the interactive presentation that allowed us to pet a kangaroo, fend off emus bent on devouring our shoelaces, and watch an Australian shepherd dog herd a flock of sheep that had been through the demonstration so many times, they guided themselves into their pen while the dog romped in the grass. Best of all, we entered an outdoor aviary and acted as human feeding stations as rainbow lorikeet parrots landed on us to snatch bits of apple from our hands. Few events in life had ever pleased me so thoroughly.

Linda declined the biscuits in the southern Kentucky town of Corbin, site of Harland Sanders's first restaurant and now commemorated as the Colonel Harland Sanders Cafe and Museum, located on the premises of a modern KFC eatery. During the 1950s, years before a cash-strapped Sanders purportedly parlayed his Social Security check into a coast-to-coast fried chicken franchise, he'd built a motel next to his restaurant. In a visionary piece of marketing, restaurant patrons were confronted with a sample motel unit attached to the dining room as a way of impressing mothers with the cleanliness of Sanders's motel. The Corbin KFC preserved Sanders's original kitchen, cooking implements, model motel room, and memorabilia from the days before he had adopted the honorary title of "Colonel," including posters from an unsuccessful run for the U.S. Senate. But the display case that held his trademark white suit and cane was enigmatically empty.

"Where could they be?" asked Linda.

"They're probably lying on the fishing pier at Huron, hoping I'll trip over them."

Near Lexington we visited the Kentucky Horse Park. "Pastor Larry recommended it," Linda said. "He'll ask me if we went there." The almost complete lack of horses at the 1,032-acre horse park in

general and in the World's Largest Horse Barn in particular saved
the day for me. The park was essentially visitorless, too, apart
from a few presumed acquaintances of Pastor Larry's.

Reality abruptly punctured the airy pastry of our vacation.
Linda had left Stinky at home with sock monkey Ed, citing the
efficacy of a new type of gel pack she had discovered—though
when pressed she admitted that Stinky's smell had finally gotten to her, too. But no compress, hot, cold, aromatic, or odorless,
could have combated the sudden locked-up condition that beset
her vertebrae on our way back from the Horse Park, forcing us to
limp home two days earlier than planned.

"Maybe I shouldn't have encouraged you to pull that hay wagon
on your own," I admitted.

Jamie had performed brilliantly while we'd been gone, and if
Ollie scolded us more caustically than usual at first sight of us,
he undoubtedly preferred our sitter's no-nonsense approach to
the fruitless teeter-tottering between cajoling and hysteria that
we typically plied him with. As Linda drove Jamie back to her
grandmother's trailer, I climbed the stairs and subjected myself to
one uneventful phone message after another. A few responses to
Linda's outdated pet-sitting ad from socially challenged or whis-
key-addled individuals trickled in, along with the usual barrage of
wrong numbers and telemarketer come-ons.

A frantic voice stirred me from my driving-induced stupor.

"Bob, this is Lesley, Ted's wife, your mom's neighbor. Your mom
fell while raking leaves, and I think she needs to go to the emergency room. I'll try your sister Joan if I can't get hold of you."

Her message was dated the preceding Saturday, just hours after
we had left for Kentucky. I couldn't even imagine what had happened in our absence.

• • •

"I JUST GOT THROUGH living with Mom for a week," Joan told me on the phone, and her tone left no doubt that this hadn't been an enviable experience.

"What happened? Lesley said she fell."

According to Joan, she had showed up at Mom's last Sunday morning to take her to church, when Mom hollered from upstairs that she seemed to be having trouble dressing, because her arm hurt. "No kidding," Joan told me. "I was shocked to see how swollen her elbow was. She said that she had been raking leaves into the street and fell on the cement when she misjudged where the curb was. I took her to Saint Mary's Hospital right away."

Linda tried keeping tabs on my phone conversation as she put the birds to bed, refreshing seed and water before covering their cages. Unaccustomed to the telephone being in another person's hands, she would dart toward me like a bee approaching a flower, then hover until I fed her a piece of information.

"Joan says that they X-rayed Mom's arm, and the doctor described her elbow as 'shattered,' though this didn't turn out to be the case. She had to stay overnight at the hospital for surgery the next morning," I told Linda.

"She had surgery?"

"No, no. Joan says they put a heavy cast on her arm, and it really killed her shoulder, because she has no padding between her bones."

"From the arthritis," Joan clarified.

"From the arthritis," I echoed for Linda's benefit. "Hey, why don't you get on the upstairs phone?"

"I can't, I have to take care of the birds," she told me, ducking into the dining room just as Stanley Sue commenced her bell rattling in quest of an undercover peanut.

"I'd spent eleven hours with Mom at the hospital, and I was totally exhausted when I got home," Joan continued. "But as soon as

I walked through the door, the nurse called and told me that Mom was trying to escape. She kept looking for her clothes and her car keys. If a family member didn't come there and spend the night, the nurse said, they'd have to strap her into bed."

"Oh, no." I sank down to sit on the edge of the couch. My arm shot up to cover my face.

"What? What?" asked Linda.

I shook my head and waved her off as Joan described how her husband, Jack, had rushed to the hospital in Joan's place and slept on a cot in Mom's room. The next morning, the doctor decided that her elbow was fractured rather than shattered and that she could probably get by with physical therapy instead of surgery. "So, they scrapped the surgery, Bob, but they'd given Mom morphine for the pain, and she was really out of it. Mom had no idea that she had spent the night at the hospital. She was positive that we were at church selling raffle tickets."

"Raffle tickets!" I exploded.

"What about raffle tickets?" Linda asked.

"She kept saying, 'If we've collected all the money for the tickets, can't we go home?' Finally, I looked at Mom and said, 'Repeat after me: I have a broken elbow, and I am in the hospital.' And she said it, word for word."

"Good!" I told her, then hastily recapped the story for Linda. "So did that do the trick?"

"After looking me right in the eye and saying, 'I have a broken elbow, and I am in the hospital,' she proceeded to ask if we had sold the raffle tickets, and could we go home?"

LINDA AND I caught up with Joan, Bett, and my mom at an assisted-care facility with the vaguely biblical, remotely Mediterranean name of Testament Terrace. Using telephone skills that rivaled Linda's, Bett had discovered via long distance from

Fort Wayne that the Terrace made a few apartments available on a short-term basis for respite care. Acting with her usual super-human efficiency, she had breezed into town from Indiana and immediately installed our mom in a spacious three-room unit with walk-in closet and a bathroom the size of a small Aegean isle.

"Why do I have to stay here?" Mom asked as we sat sipping tea in front of her picture window.

"Remember how you've been saying you wonder if you'd like living in an apartment? Well, this gives you the opportunity to find out," Bett said.

"Why can't I just go home?"

"Because of your arm."

"What's wrong with my arm?"

"You broke your elbow."

"I can still take care of myself."

Joan and I exchanged the look. During the week that she had stayed with Mom, Joan had told me, Mom had tried to walk down-stairs one morning with her left arm immobilized in a cast, her right hand clutching a cup of coffee, and her entire body wobbling with every step she took, like a bowling pin that had just been clipped by the ball. "I made her sit and go down the stairs the rest of the way on her butt," Joan had said.

"You might like some of the other ladies who live here," Linda suggested as she stood up to peer at a squirrel in the courtyard. The rest of us had gotten used to her hopping to her feet at fre-quent intervals due to her sore back, but Mom shot her a quizzical glance.

"What other ladies?" she wondered as Linda headed into the kitchen to heat her odorless gel pack in the microwave.

"The ladies who live on either side of your apartment," said Bett. "You met Bernice."

"What happened to Ted and Lesley?"

"Ted and Lesley are in their house, and you're in Testament Terrace. Did you want them to move into an apartment here, too?" she teased, coaxing a grin from Mom.

Over the last few months, my mother's sense of place had begun disintegrating. The previous April, Bett and I had taken Mom on a trip to Albuquerque, since she had mentioned missing the vacations she used to go on with my dad. One afternoon as we had returned from gawking at petroglyphs and headed back toward our hotel, Bett had pointed out the rosy shadows dappling the Sandia Mountains in the distance. This had prompted a surprising comment from Mom: "Fort Wayne sure has a lot to offer."

"Bob and Joan will take you to your physical therapy sessions," Bett continued. "Once your elbow is back to normal, you can go home. Unless you decide they pamper you so much here, you don't want to leave."

Bett enjoyed an amazing rapport with Mom. She could easily slide across suggestions that would have met with stony silence had Joan or I delivered them. I doubted that we could have convinced her to try out an assisted-living situation at all. While Mom wasn't exactly thrilled about her separation from home, Bett had engineered events to make it seem as if moving to Testament Terrace had been her decision as much as Bett's. But beyond Mom's mere disgruntlement over her new accommodations lurked something far more serious. The shock of falling and breaking her elbow, along with the resulting disorientation of moving to unfamiliar quarters, had deepened the hold of the Alzheimer's disease. It wasn't just that her memory had slipped. The present moment retreated from her, too.

"What time is it?" she asked Bett.

"What does the clock say?"

"What clock?"

"The clock on the wall."

"What wall?" she asked without sarcasm or irony. Bett pointed. "Oh, *that* wall."

Changing the subject, Bett joked about Mom's neighbor Bernice, who enjoyed playing cribbage. "I'd better warn her that there's a cardsharp on the premises," Bett joked, informing the rest of us, "Mom beat me at three games of cribbage in a row last night."

As we were chuckling over this, a confused expression crossed Mom's face. "I know this is an awful thing to ask," she said. "But did Dad die?"

WHEN I CAME HOME from work, I stuck my head inside the mailbox, grabbed the mail between my jaws, and raced inside the house on all fours. Or at least the end result was the same as I plopped down on the couch with a fistful of envelopes, which I sorted into four piles: Bob's mail, Linda's mail, junk mail, and mail from worthy causes that might contain self-adhesive return-address stickers that could find their way into the top drawer of my dresser.

Among the mail for me was an envelope from Eileen Kucek, betrayed by a return-address sticker from a charity she had probably never contributed to. My intentions were always good regarding the stickers in my dresser drawer, even if I hadn't yet gotten around to making a donation to the Save the Dodo Fund. But I still had plenty of time. I carefully worked my finger underneath the envelope flap and with a single deft movement managed to tear the entire envelope in half while preserving the integrity of the letter. It took some work to decipher the florid handwriting, which deviated significantly from the Palmer method penmanship we had learned at Blessed Sacrament Elementary School.

"I cannot continue the friendship due to your inhumane mistreatment of companion animals," Eileen wrote on creamy yellow notepaper with a pink-and-violet floral border. "Your negligent abuse of my two geese while you were on vacation was unconscionable. I would prosecute you if I could. I don't know what you think you're doing. It's obvious you learned nothing about God's creatures from your Catholic education."

I certainly couldn't argue with that last statement, since concern for ducks, geese, hens, parrots, doves, cats, rabbits, European starlings, and Baltimore orioles had never breached the Baltimore catechism of my youth. Nevertheless, the letter enraged me, even though it spelled the end of the annoyance named Eileen. When a person who hadn't taken leave of his or senses criticized me on some trumped-up charge—say, that I was meek and cowardly—at least I could argue my position if I wanted to, though I didn't want to, because arguing made me cry. Being criticized by Eileen was an entirely different story. That woman had gone so far around the bend she could see her own rear end ahead of her, and disputing her surreal outlook would be a waste of breath.

Part impressionable sponge, part protean masochistic stick, I stuck to the couch, reading her letter over and over again, reluctant to resist her baseless accusations. The inevitable ring of the telephone interrupted my wallow in pain.

"Hi, it's me," Mom told me. "I've done a stupid thing."

"What's that?" I croaked.

"I went to the hospital guild luncheon, and another of the gals must have driven. I'm here at the restaurant without my car, and I need a ride back home."

"You're not at the restaurant," I said. "Remember? You're staying at Testament Terrace until your elbow gets better."

"Oh, that's right," she said. "No wonder it looks like somebody's apartment."

"It's just for a few weeks," I told her. "You'll be back in your house in no time."

"Thanks, honey," she said. "You always make me feel better."

Within the hour, the phone rang again. "Bob, I'm downtown in Dad's office, and I need a ride home." I explained the situation to her one more time and braced myself for the calls still to come that day. It could be worse, I told myself. She could be blaming me for the loss of her electric trimmer or the package of something that somebody left for her somewhere. But from the severity of her confusion, it was beginning to look as if Mom's stay at the assisted-living facility might turn out to be more permanent than any of us had intended.

WALTER'S LUMBERING SPIRIT trapped us. Each time one of our rabbits had died over the years, I had tried to view the situation as an opportunity for phasing out of keeping these charming but short-lived home-demolition experts. The surviving rabbit of the pair always had another idea, though. Rudy's apparent ambivalence toward Walter during their months together—in separate cages, of course—plus his vivid independent spark made me hope that he wouldn't suffer from the loss of his big buddy. But Rudy showed signs of neediness right away. Linda got little peace on her faux-sheepskin rug whenever the little brown bunny roamed loose. He would butt her with his head, scuff her legs with his forepaws, and treat her supine body as a steeplechase jump—on one occasion scratching her cheek with his claws in the course of a low-altitude leap—all in an uncharacteristic quest for attention.

Not simply to placate Rudy but also to preserve her own well-being, Linda decided that we needed to find Rudy a companion. This time she made up her mind to choose a rabbit that could actually be with Rudy in the same room at the same time without a wire barrier between them.

"Impossible," I insisted.

"Other people have rabbits that get along."

"Other people lead normal lives."

"We'll take Rudy with us and let him pick out a friend."

Instead of buying a rabbit from a breeder, Linda wanted us to adopt a homeless bunny, so she phoned our wildlife rehabber friend Marge Chedrick, who said, "You're not interested in a duck that will play catch, are you?"

"A duck that plays catch?"

"She's a spoiled white Pekin that had been attacked by a dog. While she was at Dr. Hedley's office after her surgery, the staff taught her to roll a ball back that they rolled to her. But she isn't very good with other ducks." Marge told Linda that she didn't have any orphan domesticated rabbits at the moment, because she had just given a batch to her helper, Chris. "But she'd be happy to see one of them get a good home."

Chris's setup was about as good as it got for a bunny. Inside her spotless house a huge shaggy Angora rabbit had wrapped the young woman and her diesel mechanic husband around her little toe. In the backyard, a group of rabbits coexisted harmoniously in a heated shed with an attached exercise pen.

"I want him," said Chris, when she laid eyes on Rudy. "Are you sure he isn't a wild rabbit?"

"He's part Netherland Dwarf, part Polish," Linda told her.

"Polish people are pretty wild," I commented, and my comment justifiably hung in the breeze.

In order to find a suitable pal for Rudy, Linda first placed him inside the rabbit shed. Within seconds, a grey-and-white female twice his size vigorously chased him out to the pen, where a second bunny took up the pursuit and drove him back inside to face the intolerant female again. After the pair of rabbits had sent him scurrying in and out of the shed a few hundred times, Chris managed to grab him and return him to Linda's arms.

"Figures," I said.

"These are pretty territorial," Chris told us. "I've got a couple of newcomers in that hutch over there. He may do better with one of them."

Linda picked out a large, silly-looking New Zealand White that she described as resembling "the Cadbury rabbit," after a television commercial for chocolate eggs that ran around Easter. She set the bunny on the trampoline that dominated the backyard, scooped up Rudy, and placed him next to the New Zealand female.

"Who's going to spot for them?" I asked nobody in particular.

The two rabbits began nuzzling and continued to nuzzle in their carrier throughout the ride back to our house. They were lovey-dovey best buddies until Linda turned them loose in our dining room. Taking her cue from the rabbit in Chris's shed, the newly named Frieda hectored Rudy beneath the table, harassed him under the bird cages, and goaded him into leaping over the plywood board barrier and skedaddling into a far corner of the living room.

"Here we go again," I said.

"Don't worry about it," Chris told Linda over the phone. "She'll settle down once she's comfortable in your house."

Comfortable wasn't the word. Frieda was elated. True to Chris's prediction, within a day she had made up with Rudy, the better to direct her energy toward exploring every nook and cranny of the downstairs. Having spent her first months of existence inside a hutch, Frieda luxuriated in the vast open prairie of our living room. Her blobby method of uncontrolled bursts of high-speed hopping promised to surpass Walter in the ridiculousness department. And in contrast to our late, great Checker Giant, she showed instant affection for her people.

On Frieda's second evening with us, I was sitting on the floor with Linda watching, quite appropriately, *Monster House* on TV, when Frieda galloped out from behind the recliner, crashed into my leg at full throttle, and instantly stretched out on the rug as if a lie-down had been her intention all along. When I reached out to pet her, she lovingly licked my hand.

"Did we get a dog by mistake?" I asked Linda.

Petting our new bunny and watching her romp and play with Rudy delighted me so much, I kept an ear cocked toward the phone, certain that a call from my mom or a verbal footnote from Fileen would spoil the idyll. But any invasions had apparently been postponed until another day.

CHAPTER 13

. . . .

Aquarium

I should have known that something bad was coming when the K-A-U-F-M-A-N coincidence struck. If that didn't do it, then the two sightings of a ghost cat in the basement should have tipped me off.

The miserable post-Thanksgiving wintry weather had arrived, and the grey icicle of another birthday hung over my head. After what we'd been through the past twelve months with my mom—along with the long weeks tending Walter—adding another candle to my cake didn't seem like much of an achievement. In a more celebratory mood, Linda asked if I wanted any particular book as a birthday present.

"Another bird field guide wouldn't hurt," I answered, since I owned less than a dozen. I lived in hopes that the more field guides I accumulated, the greater would be my chances of merely glancing out the window and spotting a rarity like an ivory-billed woodpecker. "There's a series of books called Kaufman Focus Guides," I told her, referring to a memo to myself that I'd written on a sticky-note before folding it and tucking it inside my wallet.

Unwrapping the gluey wedge and interpreting the smeared pencil scrawls tested my manual dexterity and ocular perspicacity. "The title is *Birds of North America,* which isn't a lot of help." A snappier name, such as, *Enslaved by Birds,* would have made the book easier to remember. "Just remember the name Kaufman Focus Guides."

Bounding upstairs, I returned with another field guide. "Here's *Butterflies of North America.* It's one of the Kaufman Focus Guides," I told her. "The book I want will look a lot like this, but it's a field guide to birds, and the author's name is Kenn Kaufman."

"Let me write that name down."

"Kenn—with two *n*'s—Kaufman. And don't use a sticky-note," I suggested.

When the magical natal day finally rolled around and threatened to flatten me, I stopped moaning over the toll of years long enough to open a few packages. After thanking Linda for three pairs of socks and a pound of Kenyan coffee, I tore apart the balloon-themed wrapping paper to reveal a coffee-table tome entitled *Lives of North American Birds* by Kenn Kaufman, in place of the tote-friendly field guide. "Oh, this looks nice," I remarked with a lack of enthusiasm.

"Isn't that the book you wanted? I asked the little guy at the bookstore for a bird book by Kenn Kaufman, and this is what he gave me."

I muttered something unintelligible then assured her that it would be fine.

As an added birthday perk, Linda announced she was treating me to the $4.99 buffet at the Peking Happiness restaurant in Ionia. I drove while Linda lay in the back seat with her pillow and gel pack. As I followed a dump truck hauling a load of gravel up and down the winding, hilly two-lane road and ran the wipers to keep the windshield more or less free of pebbles, I sunk into a deeper than usual mire of self-pity. *I only asked for one present,* I whined to myself. *You'd think she could have gotten it right.*

At the restaurant, as I picked at my dill-pickle sushi roll, Linda went back to the buffet to heap another plate with such Cantonese delights as squash, corn on the cob, and macaroni and cheese. I was silently lamenting the demise of the Weigh and Pay, which had gone bust within a month of my meal with Bill Holm the previous winter, when a man at the table directly behind Linda's empty chair caught my attention.

"It's Kaufman," he told the frowning boy sitting next to him. "Kaufman, spelled K-A-U-F-M-A-N."

I had no idea what the two were talking about. I suspected that Bobo the cosmic clown had decided to make me feel foolish about sulking over a birthday gift from Linda.

WHISKERS CURLED UP on the basement rug, then flopped around as I petted him. The shyer cat named Baby watched the scene with skepticism before finally deciding that her back required stroking, too. The two cats belonged to Linda's housecleaning client, Nancy Ann, a strong-willed young woman with cerebral palsy. Upon moving from a relative's house to a group home for the disabled, she had discovered that she needed to petition a board of directors to allow her cats to stay with her. In the meantime, the pair had nowhere to go, and we'd ended up boarding them.

Normally we wouldn't confine cats to our basement. But with a room full of birds just upstairs plus a trio of cat-intolerant cats of our own, we didn't have a lot of choice. Happily, Whiskers and Baby loved it down there. While Whiskers hunted for the hordes of mice that streamed inside each day—we had installed a tiny service door for their convenience—Baby would spend hours stretched out on the windowsill regarding the barren winter wastes.

Chickadees flitting around the leafless spirea bush hypnotized her
with their activity, and as an added perk, indoor-outdoor explorer
Agnes occasionally hissed her disapproval from the opposite side
of the glass.

Whiskers, a big male rag-doll mix, tended toward irrational
exuberance, so I couldn't fall into my usual feline-petting reverie
with him without risking a nip on the hand. Realigning my arm
a few inches, I scratched calico cat Baby behind the ears, then
turned my attention to a medium-size black cat that had hopped
from the side of our unfinished stairway onto the basement floor,
passing through the unoccupied fledgling flight cage like a breeze
through the branches of a tree. Agnes, our small black cat, was at
the moment asleep on the arm of the couch in the living room upstairs, and this solid-appearing yet shadowy form definitely didn't
belong to her. It disappeared as soon as it hit or didn't hit the ce
ment. The ghost cat had returned.

A week earlier, shortly after Nancy Ann's friend Al had first
dropped off the skittish Whiskers and Baby, I had seen the not-really-
there black feline for the first time. As the two flesh-and-blood visitors tentatively investigated the new space, the apparition popped
into our basement long enough to take a few steps, vanishing as
soon as I gave it a second glance. Why it had accompanied the
pair, I couldn't imagine, but it clearly possessed the tenuous and
intermittent toehold in reality that people popularly associate with
ghosts, unless ethereal apparitions have nothing to do with spir
its. Perhaps at the moment of death a kind of turning inside out
of the pockets of the physical form occurs. Unimportant traces of
bodily existence show up like pennies that materialize under the
cushion of a favorite chair, only to be misplaced again.

Or maybe more like paper clips. Shortly after Joan and Bett
moved my mom to the furnished apartment at Testament Terrace,

Bett phoned me to ask, "Remember the rubber bands and paper clips Mom claimed Dad was leaving around the house? I guess he approves of what we're doing. Before we had even started unpacking Mom's things, I found a green rubber band and a paper clip on the floor of her new bathroom. I have no idea how they could have gotten there."

Perhaps, I thought, if paper-fastening products rained down from heaven, then the K-A-U-F-M-A-N coincidence might be another form of precipitation. Clouds filled with apparent meaningfulness grew heavy over time, dumping symbolic snowflakes onto our heads. The problem was, I never knew how to interpret the fallout. Trying to glean content from apparent absurdity tugged my underpowered brain in conflicting directions as I wondered whether propitious or ill events hung before me. If I had taken a mental step back in time, I might have recalled the coincidence involving another field guide—the *National Audubon Society Field Guide to North American Weather* which had nettled me in the wake of my father's death.

AFTER I ARRIVED home from my morning job, I opened Stanley Sue's cage door to allow her to wreak her usual mild havoc on the dining room. The descent from her cage and clamber up Rudy's cage were sluggish. Once on the summit, instead of taking a few token beak swipes at the rabbit snoozing safely far below the wire top, she sat on the edge of the cage huffing and puffing.

"Something's wrong with Stanley Sue," I called to Linda, who hurried in from the tiny back room, where she had been working on the month's bookkeeping for her tiny church. "She's having trouble breathing."

Of all the critters in the house, Stanley Sue received my closest attention. I hadn't noticed the slightest sign of any problem earlier, except that the previous night she hadn't squawked and rung her bell with her usual annoyance.

"She doesn't look very good," Linda said, as Stanley's Sue chest rose and fell alarmingly with each breath. "We'd better get her to the vet today."

Dr. Fuller, the gifted avian vet who usually treated her, couldn't squeeze her into his afternoon schedule at such short notice. Dr. Hedley, who consulted for several zoos in the Great Lakes area and had saved the lives of a number of our pets, managed to clear space for her immediately.

I brought Stanley Sue into the examination room in a shoe-box-size pet carrier. Prickling my conscience with a plaintive series of peeps, she inveigled me into opening the carrier door and letting her hop to the top to wait for the doctor. But the door started to ease shut beneath her. When I extended my hand to prevent it from pinching her scaly grey toes, I startled her. She flew heavily around the room in two slow spirals before sinking to the floor in the corner. As soon as she landed, she toppled over onto her side and didn't get up.

I rushed to her, lifting her body in both hands and placing her on the towel in the carrier. She lay breathing heavily for a half a minute and managed to make it back to her feet just before Dr. Hedley came in. With a shaky voice, I described what had happened.

"Ran out of gas, huh?" he asked with a look of concern.

"I thought she was dead," I said.

The parrot chittered in protest as he held her on her back and listened to her chest with a stethoscope. "She's got pneumonia."

The diagnosis shocked me almost as much as Stanley Sue's collapse. I fought a falling-in-the-elevator sensation as a prickling of heat throughout my body announced the leading edge of a panic attack. It was one thing to hear bad news about an animal that had suffered a lengthy illness. But Stanley had appeared perfectly healthy just twenty-four hours earlier, and I couldn't accept the idea that she was gravely ill.

"I'm sorry," I said. "This is very upsetting."

He peered at me over his glasses. "Of course it is. She's your buddy." His voice projected strength and confidence, two qualities that had never taken root in me.

"Do you think she'll be okay?"

"There's a good chance, as long we caught this soon enough," he answered as he slipped her back inside the carrier. I pushed my finger through the grate and wiggled it genially near her beak in a halfhearted gesture of reassurance. "We'll try her on an antibiotic and see if she starts to show improvement in a couple of days. In the meantime, it is vitally important to keep her very warm."

When I came home, I found Linda in the kitchen squatting in front of the refrigerator, eating banana cream pie from a spatula. "How is Stanley?" Straightening up, she stopped chewing when I told her what had happened.

Following Dr. Hedley's instructions, we turned Stanley Sue's cage into a tent that would keep in the heat, covering all sides but the front with blankets. Then I carried in a space heater and proceeded to install a tropical climate in the dining room.

WE STARTED GETTING late-evening calls from the staff at Testament Terrace that my mom was wandering the halls, waiting for Joan or me to pick her up. "We send her back to her room, and she's okay for a while. Then just when we think she's settled down, she's out wandering again." A few nights after I had taken Stanley Sue to the vet and was watching a home improvement show with Linda, the night manager phoned. "Mrs. Kelsey just walked into her room and found your mom going through her dresser drawers, pulling out clothes. She said she needed to pack for a trip to Port Huron to visit her sister. It might calm her down if you talked to her."

When I gave my mom a call, she didn't mention anything about leaving town. But she did claim that she had the front-door key to her former neighbors Ted and Lesley's house. "I've got to get it back to them, or they'll be locked out." I suggested that the errand could probably wait until morning, and she surprised me by agreeing and deciding to go to bed. Just before hanging up, she said, "Have you seen Dad recently?"

I was speechless for a moment. The question somehow reminded me of hearing his dislocated voice on the answering machine. "He's been dead a few years now. Remember?"

"That's odd," she replied. The news didn't seem to upset her. "I could have sworn I saw him this morning when I was walking to the dime store."

Since she couldn't recall Dad's passing, I didn't see the value in pointing out that the Jolly Store had gone belly-up at least twenty years ago and was miles away from Testament Terrace. "I think about Dad a lot, too," I told her, and I could imagine worse delusions than passing his smiling figure on the sidewalk.

I GOT OFF THE phone with Mom just as Linda brought out the last two slices of banana cream pie. It proved to be as much of a hit with our twelve-pound rabbit Frieda as it had been with the pair of humans in the house. She interrupted our snack by hopping up onto the couch and thrusting her feet and face onto Linda's plate.

"Frieda," Linda complained, "you're going to make me drop it."

"She shouldn't be having sweets anyway. She already weighs a ton."

After being unceremoniously shooed onto the floor, Frieda demonstrated her displeasure by running behind the recliner and glaring at us. Eventually, her love of being pampered trumped her disgruntlement. She loped back to plop down beside the couch so that I could pet her. Recognizing an opportunity when he saw it, brown bunny Rudy snuggled up beside her, pressing his small body against her massive bloat so tightly, I couldn't stroke her head without petting his as well.

"It's like a dinghy beside an ocean liner," I told Linda.

My mood had eased since dinner, when Stanley Sue had shown improvement by digging into her veggies, potatoes, and gelatin dessert after days of poor appetite. She had even treated me to an angry whistle when I had thrown the black cover over her cage.

I definitely needed a break from worry. Stanley Sue's sickness had become my sickness. Ever since her collapse at Dr. Hedley's, a steady drip, drip, drip of dread had distracted me from concentrating on anything but her. *Stanley Sue,* my feet tapped out as I walked down the basement stairs. I'd see people chuckling together in the grocery store aisle and think, *They don't know what I know.* If I relaxed my guard or tensed—I wasn't sure which—the dread increased its grip and leaped into the foreground. My locomotive gears would freeze as I stared dully into space until some stimulus jarred me loose. If by an uncharacteristically optimistic surge I managed to banish the worry, I'd pay for my relief moments later when the fear resurfaced with vengeful vigor.

It didn't help matters that Stanley Sue hated being handled, and medicating her twice a day added to our distress. In full bloom of health, she could be timid about stepping onto my finger, and I couldn't risk her flying in a panic around the room and passing out again. So each morning and evening I would open the cage door, toss a hand towel over her, and carry her to the kitchen countertop. Linda would hold her as I wriggled the tip of a syringe between her jaws. The trick was squirting the antibiotic slowly enough that she would swallow rather than spit it out; but if I took too long, she would chomp down on the syringe and destroy it. By the time I returned her to the cage, her pupils were wide with anxiety, her chest was heaving, and my stomach hurt.

Although Stanley Sue's appetite was better, her breathing remained labored. Linda phoned Dr. Hedley, who suggested that we try a different antibiotic. For a couple of days, I fooled myself into thinking it had helped, but that weekend she plummeted downhill. Dr. Hedley had left Michigan to sit with his sick father out west. Late Sunday afternoon, Dr. Fuller returned Linda's call from a bed-and-breakfast in northern Michigan. He instructed us to completely cover Stanley Sue's cage and move her to a room that we could heat to eighty-five degrees. He would see her the next morning.

Joan drove Stanley Sue and me to the vet. Linda couldn't drive me, because of her back problems. I could have driven myself, but I welcomed the moral support and well-heated SUV. As Dr. Fuller examined the whimpering bird, I sat on a chair in the room and erupted in a torrent of tears.

"He's been under a lot of stress lately," Joan said to Dr. Fuller. "This isn't just about Stanley Sue." She was thinking of my father's death and my mother's Alzheimer's disease.

I was too ashamed to glance up at Dr. Fuller, who had treated our turkeys, rabbits, ducks, geese, and indoor birds over the years but had never seen me in lunatic mode before. I couldn't explain the psychological sickness that I was suffering over my parrot, because I didn't understand it myself. A hand had reached inside me and flicked on a switch labeled "Despair," and I couldn't find it in the dark to turn it off. I decided it was red, like the button on my mother's furnace.

Without holding out any hope, Dr. Fuller offered to keep Stanley Sue overnight. "We'll give her a few nebulization treatments," he told me, which meant placing her in an empty aquarium and pumping it full of oxygenated air mixed with an aerosol antibiotic. "That's the most effective way of getting the medicine deep into her lungs."

"Do what you can," I sobbed as I floated past him on a flood of tears. "I'll understand if she doesn't make it."

Out in the parking lot in the passenger's seat of Joan's SUV, I slumped forward like an accident victim, with Joan clutching my arm. A wintry mix of rain and sleet ticked against the glass. Her wipers cut two arcs across the windshield. "She's going to be all right, " she assured me, taking my hand. "She's going to be all right."

I STARTED SEARCHING for signs that she would be okay.

I tried divining meaning behind license plates, newspaper articles, snippets of overheard conversation, items appraised on *Antiques Roadshow,* song lyrics, bank statements, *TV Guide* summaries, cereal boxes, spam e-mail, crossword puzzles, fortune cookies, billboards, dreams, *New Yorker* magazine cartoons, weather reports, gastric upset, and whatever else crossed my path. I blamed this grasping at supernatural straws on my Blessed Sacrament Elementary School years steeped in saints, miracles, heavenly portents, and, of course, incessant guilt—though the truth may have simply been that I was mentally ill. Nevertheless, I kept searching. But nothing transcendental emerged. The ghost cat and K-A-U-F-M-A-N had already spoken their piece.

AT LEAST STANLEY SUE had returned home. Dr. Fuller had phoned to tell me, with a smile in his voice, that I could pick her up. But he obviously hadn't approved of my breakdown in his office.

"These birds are extremely perceptive," he warned me as I hovered near the examination table, "so it is important that you maintain a positive attitude around her. If you're upset, she'll read that. Her recovery depends on getting plenty of encouragement." It also depended on medication, the proper temperature, and nutrition. For the foreseeable future, Stanley Sue had to live in an aquarium in our back room to keep her warm and out of drafts— and to prevent her from straining herself by climbing the bars of a cage. To supplement the small amount of food that she ate on her own, I had to tube-feed her a special high-protein, high-vitamin mixture twice a day.

Tube-feeding represented a particular horror that made dosing her with antibiotic seem as easy as flinging table scraps to a hen. Holding the towel-wrapped parrot firmly against my chest, I learned to work an angled metal nozzle down her throat and into her crop, being careful not to take the wrong passage by mistake and cut off her air. Once I had situated the end of the tube in her crop, it would make a telltale bulge an inch below her beak. Then I needed to keep her absolutely still as I depressed the plunger of a fat syringe and trickled in the liquid food. The procedure never went smoothly, thanks to my fear of hurting her. I often had to give up following a botched attempt and try again a few minutes later, once bird and Bob had calmed down. Although I exhibited cowardice over most aspects of my life, I probably couldn't be faulted for squeamishness when it came to the tube-feeding. It was a delicate, nerve-racking, cringe-inducing procedure that reduced each day to a ticking off of hours before I had to do it all over again.

Less unnerving but still fussy was keeping the back room at eighty-five degrees in the middle of December, since it required continual adjustment of a space heater that hadn't been built for precision. The first two nights that Stanley Sue had spent back home, I slept on the couch in the living room. Every two hours I

woke up and, with the aid of a flashlight, checked the thermometer inside the aquarium, then nudged the heater thermostat up
or down. It took me a few days to figure out how to keep the room
temperature from bouncing around. Once I finally moved back
into the bedroom, I still got up once or twice a night to peek at
her. If I wielded the flashlight too intrusively, she would nod her
head in disapproval and tap her beak against the glass.

She took the abuse remarkably well. I had no idea what an intelligent creature thought of being confined to a glass box. I hated
subjecting her to the discomfort and indignity. I removed her bell
from her cage and taped it to the lip of the aquarium so that it
hung down inside. She couldn't exactly ring it, but she could rattle
it in greeting or displeasure, and this seemed to please her. Considering that she was so shy that even introducing a new perch
to her cage sent her into nervous throes, she coped courageously
with the fish-bowl existence.

Some days, she seemed to show progress. Her breathing dif-
ficulties lessened, her eyes grew brighter, her appetite increased.
Other days her poor lung function necessitated a hurried trip to
Dr. Fuller's office and another nebulization treatment. Because the
antibiotics hadn't cured her, he drew blood to check for a fungal
disease or virus, but the tests came back negative. "We really need
to take an X-ray to find out what's going on inside of her," he said,
"but in her present state, that much handling might be risky."

The ups and downs drove me crazy. I tried to compensate for
the absence of a medical diagnosis by seeking omens in the usual
detritus of my life, from clues on *Jeopardy!* to graphics on candy
bar wrappers. Nothing pointed toward a cure. My anxiety level
shot up when Linda arrived home from grocery shopping one afternoon to announce that she had run into a friend of Henry Murphy's, who'd informed her that our master gardener had dropped
dead from a heart attack.

"He sure was a character," Linda told me. "A couple of days before he passed on, he was over at the cemetery standing on a tombstone, trying to get his kite to fly."

Cemetery? Flying? I thought. *This doesn't sound good.*

STANLEY SUE'S SICKNESS didn't exactly put me in a holiday frame of mind as symbols of Christmas sprung up throughout the house. Santa Clauses invaded our bookshelves. The coffee table sprouted scented candles, ceramic snowmen, and a radioactive red candy dish. Strings festooned with greeting cards traversed the dining room, presenting a navigation hazard to the birds, while the Christmas tree in the living room gave the rabbits a fortified hiding place. Rousting them meant risking a poke in the eye with a branch or, worse, dislodging an ornament and earning a reprimand from Linda.

Most years, I'd joke, "It's my turn to have a 'Bob Christmas.'"

"What would that consist of?" Linda would ask, playing along.

I'd answer, "Not one thing," with a wistful sigh.

But holiday cheer was serious business to my wife, and any holiday applied. I rarely escaped the Fourth of July without slapping mosquitoes off my neck while fireworks popped overhead, and even the amorphous Labor Day necessitated a stroll through some park simply to distinguish the occasion from plain vanilla calendar dates. If worry prevented me from being dragged into Christmas festivities with my usual glumness, the least I could do was try to avoid completely ruining the season for her. And she wouldn't let me cancel the celebration anyway. Due to the precariousness of Stanley Sue's condition, we hired Jamie to sit with Stanley Sue and the tricky thermostat while we spent the afternoon of December 24 making merry with Linda's son Ben; his wife, Ann; their kids; and Linda's mom. I watched my watch and barely paid attention to anything else.

Christmas Day at Joan and Jack's proved even bumpier, despite a meat-optional breakfast buffet and the cheery disorder supplied by five cats, two ferrets, a wolf-dog, and a sparrow. Holidays had lacked their center since the death of my father, who had apparently played neutron to the uncharged lesser particles of our family. This year my mother had slipped out of orbit, too. She had forgotten the whole concept of opening presents.

"Just tear the wrapping," Joan urged her. But even after I ran a finger under the pieces of tape to pop them and unfurled the paper to the first fold, she hesitated. Then she placed the present on the floor beside her chair and examined the wrapping-paper shell instead.

"Whose house is this?" she asked Joan as we nibbled on Bett's molasses cookies.

"It's my house."

She waved a hand dismissively. "Oh, go on!" She had come to think of Joan and me as college-age kids still living at home.

"How's your bird?" Bett's husband, Dave, asked.

"I'm guardedly optimistic," I managed to answer.

Just as I was mentally patting myself on the back for putting on a vaguely cheery face, Joan gave Linda a sculpted necklace of an African grey parrot. With its bright red tail, it resembled Dusty but inevitably reminded me of my maroon-tailed Stanley Sue. I ducked into the bathroom and stared at the soap dish for a while.

"We need to get going," I told Linda mere seconds after we had opened the last present.

"Thanks for coming to see me," Mom said.

"You're in my house," Joan reminded her.

When I got back home, Stanley Sue dipped her head, grabbed a beakful of the shredded paper that lined the bottom of the aquarium, and gave it a short toss. "Are you throwing confetti?" I asked her. But her pleasure at seeing me was short-lived, as I proceeded to tube-feed her. Happy holiday.

I DECIDED TO GET Stanley Sue out of the fish tank. If she had to die, she would at least die inside her cage and not in a glass house designed for guppies. I shoved aside the stacks of newspapers that had so far escaped the recycling bin, then nestled two extra dining room chairs together to create a hole in the clutter for her cage. The relocation boosted her morale. She took two helpings of dinner veggies from my spoon, crawled up to her hanging rubber ring at bedtime, and reached out to jangle her bell in protest when I snapped off the light.

Barely had I settled into the shallow indentation of an optimistic groove when Linda received a phone call saying that her mother had been rushed to the hospital with, of all things, pneumonia. I didn't burn my brain cells metaphorically linking her respiratory sickness with the bird's, except to note the evil correspondence as I drove Linda to Battle Creek. Then I headed seventy-five miles back home to begin caring for thirty-some animals on my own.

I slept poorly, worrying about Linda, her mom, and Stanley Sue, and cursed the alarm clock when it hollered in my ear. Getting the duck and goose chores finished before leaving for work meant straggling out of bed under black-of-night conditions to clear snow, chip ice, fill wading pools, replenish drinking water, top off food, bump into things, and make sure that high-strung ganders Matthew and Angel didn't bolt out the doors. Back inside the house I uncovered the birds, fed our three cats—Whiskers and Baby had long since rejoined Nancy Ann—overcooked instant oatmeal on the stove, let the rabbits hop around the dining room as I bolted down my gruel, clipped rectangles of toast to the parakeet and dove cages, coddled a squawking Ollie, filled seed

cups and water bowls, and, taking a deep breath, tube-fed Stanley
Sue before slip-sliding to my workplace.

Back from work shortly after noon, I trudged out to the waterfowl pens, tugging open the doors to allow the ducks and geese
a chance to turn up their nostrils at a snow-covered yard. I re-
filled their pools and water dishes and did the same in the barn
enclosures. Indoors I let Howard, the parakeets, and the canary
out of their cages. The blustering dove chased the smaller birds,
who easily outmaneuvered him. I checked the rabbits' food and
water, then retreated to the back room for an attempt at a nap
disguised as quality time with Stanley Sue while I waited to hear
from Linda.

I opened her door and let her clamber to the top of her cage.
She watched me as I snaked my legs beneath Linda's desk, threw
a pillow onto the floor, and did my best to achieve some comfort
in the little room. Troubled by the lack of news from Battle Creek,
I fell short of my normal afternoon descent into merciful oblivion.
After a few minutes of supine anxiety, I sat up and faced six weeks'
worth of unpaid bills. As I assuaged our power company, telephone carrier, and trash service, Stanley Sue navigated her bars
to pluck a grape from the tea cart. "That's an awfully good girl," I
said. She chewed it, adding the skin to the peanut shells littering
a strip of chain-store advertisements at the foot of her cage. "Keep
it up, and we might be able to skip the you-know-what-feeding
tonight," I promised. I had just belatedly paid the fall leaf-raking
bill when my hand leaped to the ringing phone.

Linda described a long night at the hospital sitting with her
mom, who had drifted in and out of consciousness. "The nurse
down the hall took me aside and said, 'I thought you should know,
your mother is dying.' Then, about an hour later, Dr. Lee finally
showed up, and he said that he didn't expect her to last until

morning. He said, 'She's old. That's what happens,' as if he couldn't be bothered taking any trouble with her."

That matched up with what we had heard about Dr. Lee's bedside manner from her mom. I couldn't bring myself to ask straight out if she had died. "Is she?" I stammered. "Is she still with us?"

"She's about the same as last night," said Linda, taking no notice of my clumsiness. "She isn't in good shape. She had a heart attack while they were giving her albuterol to help her breathing."

"Oh, no." I glanced at Stanley Sue, who had keyed in on the concern in my voice. I carried the cordless phone into the living room, where the bird wouldn't hear me. "How bad was the heart attack?"

"They described it as 'minor.' They're mainly worried about the pneumonia right now."

After Linda hung up, I was grateful that I had endless animal chores ahead of me to dull what passed for mental activity. These were tasks that the two of us usually split, if you defined "split" as ninety percent Linda, five percent Bob, and five percent that Bob didn't get to as promised. But excuses cut no ice with demanding pets, beginning with barn ducks and hens that expected their table scraps, greens, and chunks of bread before I scraped dinner together for the parrots and me. Once we had all squawked and eaten, I put Ollie to bed, wiped the dining and kitchen linoleum, vacuumed, let Dusty out of the cage, and retreated to the living room with the rabbits lest he bite my toes. After roaming the floor and calling out, "Hello," he refused to go back, forcing me to tease him into attacking and clinging to a towel. The trick was getting parrot and towel through the door of his cage before he managed to climb up to my hand. Then I covered the birds, checked food and water dishes, read from an old Perry Mason mystery, and at just about nine-thirty gave the rabbits their nightly oatmeal treat before covering them, too.

The following night, I wrapped up the chores earlier and made it to bed before nine. Each successive night, my bed moved closer to the dinner table, until soon I was hitting the hay and trying not to dream about it by eight-thirty. Still, I realized that I had the easy part of the deal. Linda stayed at the hospital all day, making sure that whenever her mom awoke, she was on hand to ply her with water, urge her to eat, and maintain the kind of positive spin that I barely even knew existed.

A week after I had driven Linda to Battle Creek, I met her at the hospital. Her mom wore an oxygen mask, spoke nearly inaudibly, and seemed frighteningly frail. I could hardly believe that she had been worse than this, but Linda assured me that she was on the mend. I wished I could have made the same claim about Stanley Sue. Her breathing hadn't improved, and we'd finally reached a point where her best chance was an X-ray that could provide a diagnosis. It was the least intrusive of the tests she might need.

I dropped her off at Dr. Fuller's office that Friday and spent an anxious morning at my workplace fretting over the possible results. Shortly before I wrapped up my work, my phone rang. As a high-voltage shot of dread washed over a feeble undercurrent of hope sparked by the turnaround of Linda's mom, I heard Dr. Fuller tell me, "I'm afraid I have bad news. Stanley Sue passed away during the X-ray procedure."

CHAPTER 14

....

Muskegon Wastewater

The thump in the middle of the night woke me up. It sounded as if something had crashed into the top of the house. I had just fallen asleep, after hours spent kneading my pillow, bending and unbending my legs, and flopping my head into different positions while I fretted over Stanley Sue. Several weeks after her death, I still couldn't get out from under the grief. Toxins bubbled through my brain, while my body was encased in enough layers of lethargy to fill a municipal waste-disposal site.

As I lay listening in the upstairs bedroom, where I snoozed when plagued by restlessness so as not to disturb Linda, I tried to explain away the thump as a raccoon plopping onto the roof from an overhanging branch or a brick detaching itself from our chimney, until a rustling in the corner of the room overpowered the hammering of my heart. An intruder seemed to be nosing aside a plastic bag containing secondhand mystery novels at the foot of the bed. I figured it must be a cat in search of a mouse, but when I flung myself off the mattress and flipped on the light, I found Penny asleep at the top of the stairs, while Moobie sprawled her huge self across the living room rug. I discovered Agnes lurking in the basement as I beamed the flashlight into the corner to make sure that none of Linda's rickety storage shelves had toppled beneath the weight of orphaned appliances, stacks of old magazines, and cartons of knickknacks.

Linda, of course, continued sleeping soundly. She hadn't heard the wall-jarring thud, just as she had snoozed through the blood-curdling primate howls a few winters ago. She also hadn't suffered the ghost-cat visitations, a phone call from the space people, a fairy intrusion from the garden, Ouija board *Star Trek* episode predictions, psychic messages from Kenn Kaufman, or Bobo's possibly malevolent clowning, though she had shared the brunt of Eileen's meddling.

Back in bed on the second floor, I tried reading a Calvin and Hobbes "best of" comic-strip compilation to calm myself, but mainly stared off the page at the carpet. Instead of blaming paranormal forces for the unexplained noises, I clasped and unclasped my hands in a hot-cold pang of worry, wondering if I wasn't truly losing my mind.

My mental train had jumped the rails the night after Stanley Sue had died of what Dr. Fuller suggested might have been cancer, based on the evidence of her fatal X-ray. I insisted on sleeping on the living room couch to be near the room where she had spent her final weeks. Part of me immediately stepped back with arms folded and warned, *Uh-uh. Nope. Don't even think of doing that.* But my larger, spongier self decided that taking an emotional nosedive down an elevator shaft was a fine idea. Three nights later, Linda urged me to return to our bed, citing the psychic misery my davenport bivouac was causing me, not to mention the strain it put on her back.

"I can't keep bending over and consoling you," she said.

"I'm trying to cry myself to death," I explained.

"If you keep acting like this, you're going to have to see a doctor."

Little did I realize that the prolonged spate of depression was threatening my health. It didn't help matters when I realized that Stanley Sue had died five years to the day of my father's death, and almost to the hour. As the days wore on, a cold developed into a particularly virulent case of bronchitis. I sat with a heating pad strapped to my chest and my faithful box of tissues at my feet. Bacteria and despair were bad enough, but soon I developed heart palpitations that put me in fear of sharing a heavenly perch with Stanley Sue.

A student nurse instantly picked up on my collapsed state of mind as I huddled in an eggshell-colored office awaiting the family doctor. In the presence of her supervisor, she gently asked if perhaps somebody in the family had died.

"A pet," I blurted out and began to sob.

Once the nurses had left the room and shut the door behind them, I heard the supervisor tell the younger woman, "That served you right."

An EKG indicated normal heart activity, a chest X-ray revealed that my bronchitis hadn't turned into pneumonia, and my doctor diagnosed anxiety as the reason for my occasional arrhythmia. He put me back on the Zoloft that I had weaned myself from a few years earlier. The medication took the burr off the edge of the rim of the lip of my psychological sinkhole, but it didn't touch the obsessive concerns that Stanley Sue's death had illuminated inside my head in high-wattage, life-interfering glory.

The fact that I was more upset at the passing of a bird than I had been at the passing of my father popped the lid off a cauldron of burbling guilt. But while my dad's death hadn't been my fault,

I had been responsible for Stanley Sue's welfare. I had failed her. I had missed the early signs of illness, and she had died under my care.

Memories of her final days poisoned me. I couldn't think of her without endlessly replaying mental loops of her crash-landing in Dr. Hedley's office, her confinement in the aquarium, and, worst of all, my having to force-feed her. This was particularly painful, because I had always felt a kind of telepathic link with her. Our bond had grown especially tight in her last days, when it had seemed as if she was as concerned about me as I was about her. She'd made brave attempts to eat fruits and vegetables she didn't want simply to please me. I'd even speculated that she understood the seriousness of her sickness. Realizing that I couldn't bear to see her die, she'd chosen a moment to let go on a rare occasion when she'd found herself away from home. This wasn't easy to accept or even to think about.

Funeral rituals had helped mitigate the pain of my father's death. I'd had little time to dwell in misery while participating in the planning of the visitation, service, burial, and reception. This distraction had comforted me, as had the support of family and friends. But no such mechanism existed to ease the blow of an animal's death. Despite the best intentions of people close to me, I missed the catharsis and onset of healing that a public ceremony provided. With no socially acceptable channel into which to ladle my grief, I felt lonely and foolish for allowing myself to become devastated by the loss of a bird.

Often the thoughts that kept me up at night weren't even quasirational. In the full light of day, or what passed as such during a Michigan winter, I couldn't figure out why so fragile and misguided a concern had robbed me of my sleep. So as I pulled the covers up, bracing myself for another puzzling thud on the roof of the house, I tormented myself with the weirdest dollop of self-pity to stream down the mental pike to date.

I'm nothing now, the voice said. *I'm just some idiot without his parrot.*

MY FIRST VISIT to the Alzheimer's Unit at Testament Terrace didn't exactly wash away my grief. I stepped off the third-floor elevator and into a David Lynch movie, as stabbing piano music pulled me toward the residents' lounge. A lavender-haired woman with faraway eyes at odds with the determined thrust of her jaw tore through a heated performance of "White Christmas," followed by a nerve-jangling "Jingle Bells."

"She's a little out of sync with the season," I told Bett as we stood on the perimeter of an arc of elderly folks who sat blinking at the piano.

"Jennifer told me she plays Christmas songs all year."

I nodded at the Testament Terrace nurse, who had perked up at the mention of her name.

Joan lowered and shook her head, sharing my glumness at consigning our mom to the company of people who were as in the dark about the when and what of Yule as she had been. But she couldn't remain on the assisted-living floor due to her nocturnal wanderings, packing for nonexistent trips, and escalating forgetfulness.

As we toted her belongings from the old apartment to slightly less fashionable new quarters just out of earshot of the piano bar, a staff member from the assisted-living section took me aside and told me how much she would miss my mom.

"I wish you could have met her ten years ago," I said.

"She's very sweet just the way she is," she replied. "I'll be serving her a meal, and she'll lean over and ask, 'Now, is there anything I can do for you, dear?'"

I could list many adjectives to describe the mom who had raised me: even-tempered, tough-minded, hardworking; critical but caring. "Sweet" better described my dad, however, and I wondered if my mom's disease hadn't allowed a submerged quality to shine through.

A few days later, I joined my mom as she ate lunch. Across the table, Francine asked the server, "What do you call this?" when a slice of pizza hit her plate. "I've never seen anything like this before." I found myself thinking that even Stanley Sue would have recognized one of her favorite foods. My mood began to sink, until a resident named Emily buoyed me by responding to my idle comment that the flowers on the serving cart looked nice.

"Park Side Floral donates them," she said. "The flowers are used in funeral homes. Then, if the families don't want them, they go to hospitals and places like this."

I hadn't expected such clarity from a person with Alzheimer's disease. Before I left Testament Terrace, I watched two of my mom's neighbors amble down the corridor and locate the doors to their rooms without a stick of difficulty. My mom couldn't do that, and it pleased me that these women might help her along.

I made my own way to the front door of my mother's house. I had an appointment to meet an antiques dealer who wanted to buy the remaining contents of the house. I'd tagged my father's decades-old hand tools as off-limits with a NOT FOR SALE sticky-note, along with two antique rocking chairs, four ceramic figurines, and, just to be amusing, the living room wall.

"You didn't leave me anything of value," glowered a markedly unpleasant man who reminded me of a hectoring galoot you might meet behind the baseball-pitching booth at a carnival.

"Three balls for a buck," I wanted to tell him. Instead, I said, "You've got the china cabinet, two bedroom sets, the dining room table . . ." My voice trailed off as he abandoned me to race from room to room like a cartoon cop in search of a fizzy stick of dynamite.

"Hardly worth what it will cost me to haul it all away," he said. The pittance he offered was so low, I considered asking if I could exchange my prize for the stuffed dog. But the fact was, he had us over a barrel. My sister had sold the house a few weeks ago, and we had run out of time as far as clearing it out. I acted angry, because he was alive and Stanley Sue was not, so I told him we'd have to get back to him on his offer. He slammed the front door, slammed the door of his car, and almost slammed into Mr. Teany's Oldsmobile when he jerked out into the road.

I stomped upstairs in a stinky state of mind. *I'm nothing*, the voice told me. *I'm just some idiot without his old bedroom.*

I lay down on the wooden floor and tried to mentally tune in to soft lapping waves of my boyhood days as my parents bustled about downstairs after I had gone to bed, perhaps watching *I've Got a Secret* on TV or *I've Got a Secretly Depressed Son.* I decided that if I had somehow been able to remain a mere lad and stay here over the years, Stanley Sue could have stayed with me, Stanley Sue could have stayed alive, and so what if none of this made sense. Certainly if my mom and dad's old phone number were still in service, the space people could call me up, they would call this very instant, and when they asked to talk to Richard, I'd tell them, "Speaking." Then, behind Linda's pumpkin patch in that spooky spot beside the barn, they'd pick me up in their peanut-shaped craft, and things could be a whole lot worse.

IF I HAD BEEN down in the dumps before, things got worse when the power died.

Heralding the electrical disruption was a crow-size pileated woodpecker that grabbed my eye while we were eating Sunday breakfast. "Good grief," I told Linda, "There's a hatchet attacking a tree just down the hill." At least that's what it looked like until I picked up the binoculars. Occasionally we would hear the madcap laugh of a pileated in its early June mating fervor, but the extravagantly topknotted avian cousin of Eileen usually concealed itself from view.

That night, a friend of the woodpecker pelted our house with handful after handful of hard peas. At least that's what it sounded like until I picked up on the fact that an ice storm had decided to usher in the first week of April. Just before we turned off the lights for bed, they turned themselves off. Power failures in our wooded non-neighborhood were almost as infrequent as pileated woodpecker sightings and about the same duration, but this one ground on and on.

Had it been a normal April, the lack of electricity would have been a minor irritant at most. But winter refused to pack its bags and leave, despite a kick in the slats from the calendar. The outdoor thermometer registered a measly eight degrees the following morning, so I decided to save the lives of our indoor birds by firing up the generator, which I'd never actually used before. Linda's Pastor Larry had convinced me to buy it years earlier to prepare for the prophesied Y2K technological collapse. As it turned out, only my pocketbook suffered from the millennial turnover.

A contractor had outfitted our outside power entry with a hefty power cord that allowed us to plug in the whole house as if it were an enormous toaster. But first I needed to fetch the generator from its home among the hay bales, which meant crossing the ice pack that lay between the back door and the barn via my Frankenstein's-monster-as-an-infant walk. In the gloomy barn interior I tried thinking up an alternative to moving a mechanism that had seemingly doubled in size and weight since I had bought it, not unlike most of our pets. Then, for an audience of frightened chickadees, I performed the pratfall-filled comedy of pushing the monstrosity toward the house.

Our lack of power was my lack of power. Starting a string trimmer with a pull-cord typically tore my arm out of its socket. The generator required a two-handed tug that pitched me backward into the pine tree, renewing my by now intimate acquaintance with the frozen ground. The engine expelled so much smoke when it finally turned over, that for one brief moment I thought I was back in San Francisco, attempting to find my dorm room in the fog.

Getting the machine up and running was only half the battle. It lacked the juice and disposition to simultaneously power all the circuits in our electrically overloaded home. Having switched off every breaker before starting the generator, I gently coaxed them on again one by one until a sputter of complaint from the other side of the cinder block wall informed me that I had insulted the engine with excessive demands. It took me the bulk of the morning to learn that we could use the stove as long as we didn't run a faucet and start the water pump, and if we wanted to heat water in the microwave, we had better not plan on also refrigerating juice.

Realizing that I ought to have a supply of gasoline to fuel a gasoline generator, I chopped the ice off the windshield, spun a few doughnuts in the driveway, and set out in search of gas cans to fill with gas. A quick jaunt down the unexpectedly salted and otherwise nicely seasoned road revealed that the power failure extended beyond our house and poultry pens. Most local businesses had shut down at the urging of cash registers that refused to register, not to mention the absence of lights. Fortunately, the local Meijer store not only blazed brightly on generator power, but the Meijer gas station was also only too happy to queue up the multitudes in the same predicament as me.

"Power's out as far as Lansing," a stout fellow in an orange hunter's jacket called across the lane to a woman at a pump as I dribbled gas into jugs.

"My sister in Ionia has power," she called back, her breath puffing out steam in the cold. "Everyone else in her neighborhood is out, but not her."

It always seemed to go that way. People who owned electrical-utility stock got all the breaks, and I made a mental note to call my broker just as soon as I found a broker.

Gassing up the generator required shutting it down, clicking off the circuit breakers, filling the tank, restarting the engine via the pull-cord, picking myself up from the pine tree, reattaching my arms, letting the motor idle a bit, then slowly switching on the breakers again, all the while alert for any change in pitch that indicated that the generator might decide to die. The thing would run for about six hours after fueling. Because the instruction manual advised against letting it run dry, I set my alarm for the wee hours of the morning to enjoy the entire gassing-up exercise shivering in the dark. Not that I slept well anyway. As soon as my head hit the pillow, I could hear nothing but the not-so-distant chug and drone of the generator. Whenever it sputtered for a second or sang a couple of notes slightly flat, I jerked awake as surely as if someone had yanked a pull-cord attached to my brain.

At least fixating on the generator gave me a subject to obsess upon other than Stanley Sue. Although smart enough to understand the folly of allowing my thoughts to drag me from one misguided worry to the other, I hadn't mastered or even apprenticed at the knack of switching off the mental blather. I had read books about "not thinking," practiced meditation and self-hypnosis, and hypnotized myself into practicing meditation on reading books about "not thinking"—but all to no avail. The incessant thoughts kept popping open valves that leeched noxious neurochemicals into my system. Where was the power failure that I needed for a jolt of mental health?

THE ELECTRICAL OUTAGE lasted four days, just fifteen minutes short of the predicted Bob outage as sleep deprivation and gas-fume inhalation took their toll. Once I recovered from the shock of being able to flush the toilet while simultaneously toasting a waffle—and it took a long reach to accomplish that feat—I realized that our pileated woodpecker had been a bona fide harbinger. As the temperature suddenly shot up, an impressive array of songbirds popped into the open in search of food.

Although we'd often heard a male indigo bunting singing ecstatic couplets from dawn until dusk in late spring through midsummer, we'd seldom succeeded in visually separating the shy bird from the treetops. But one Saturday afternoon while Bett spooned away at a generator-size slab of Linda's strawberry shortcake, I gasped to note three brilliant blue males pecking at the ground beneath the bird feeder while two brown females perched in the very pine tree that still contained shards of my flesh.

"Oh, my gosh, look at that," I croaked, passing the binoculars to my sister and wildly gesticulating at the garden.

"You go ahead," she insisted, gamely passing them back to me. Another often heard but rarely seen tree-topper, the great crested flycatcher, sat nonchalantly on the wire fence flashing a yellow belly at me without the slightest trace of embarrassment. Two male scarlet tanagers lit up the carnivorous pine tree later, while a migrating eastern towhee—"Just passing through, folks"—serenaded us for a few days with its bell-like song.

Good birding in our yard tantalized me with the prospect of adding new species to my sighting list at one of the best spots for viewing winged wildlife in western Michigan. I called my friend Bill Holm and scheduled a visit to drink in the unspoiled natural beauty of that teeming cup of naturalist's ambrosia, the Muskegon County Wastewater Management System. Being around animals always helped my state of mind, and I knew this outing was exactly what I needed.

Muskegon Wastewater was actually a far cry from the sludge-engorged ecological quagmire its name suggested. Thousands of acres of primarily pleasant woods, fields, and wetlands attracted otherwise finicky owls, waterfowl, shorebirds, songbirds, and the occasional golden eagle. The focal point for binoculars was a nearly four-square-mile wedge of treatment ponds frequented by countless ducks, geese, and gulls. The rubble-strewn shores concealed sandpipers, plovers, godwits, willets, knots, whimbrels, and their improbably named long-billed ilk.

While the water seemed clean enough in the larger ponds, a copper-green stain on the surrounding rocks caused me to wonder if the birds couldn't locate healthier quarters elsewhere. In fact, a year earlier one caustic-smelling mechanically agitated "bubbler" cell had given me my first ever sighting of a greater yellowlegs, a foraging wader that apparently enjoyed a more robust and irritation-resistant breathing apparatus than had Stanley Sue. A few minutes of peering into that pond one summer was about all my lungs could take.

Bill and I rendezvoused in the parking lot of a Target store in northern Grand Rapids, and he targeted his new Volvo toward the waste facility. To waste my time during the ride while deepening my depression, he played the CD *Buddy Ebsen Says "Howdy."* "Is the whole thing this bad?" I asked as a simpering female chorus shored up Ebsen's atonality.

"The whole thing is this *good*," Bill declared. "It's his finest album."

But I couldn't really complain, since I had given him the disc for Christmas.

A yard sign reading USED HUNTING PANTS FOR SALE indicated that we were approaching the entrance, providing me an opportunity to ponder what type of person would buy used hunting pants before Bill whipped through the front gate. I positioned our entry permit on the dash as Bill slowed to a tire-groaning crawl in response to the insect buzz of what we eventually identified as a grasshopper sparrow. Frantic thumbing through three field guides confirmed a second and more gifted striped singer as a savannah sparrow.

"Those are both life birds for me," I gloated. I had started keeping a list of any species that I spotted for the first time in my life. "Now if we could only see the bobolink."

"Bobo's bird," suggested Bill. "Perhaps it's the link to the great unimaginable, the missing link in all theology and philosophy, the—"

"Bobo's gone," I interrupted. "I haven't had a single coincidence for months."

"He's probably off planning some grand coincidence, but he's never gone. And besides, what about Linda's mother's deed?"

He had me there. After her recovery and discharge from the hospital, Linda's mom had decided to arrange what she called her "final affairs" by prepaying for her funeral and updating her will. On our most recent visit to Battle Creek, she had shown us where she kept her important papers: in the garage freezer, underneath a carton of generic vanilla ice cream. It was a hiding place worthy of my mom. Glancing at the deed to the house, Linda noticed that the original property owner had been a man named Parrott.

"Sometimes I think you *are* Bobo," I said. "That would explain why you lack normal appealing human attributes."

"I don't deny that I am Bobo's chosen one. I told you what happened when I was born."

"You probably did, but I repressed it."

To my dismay, Bill unfolded a small birth-certificate packet that he carried in his wallet and produced a card made fifty-two years ago by his sister Barb. It was adorned with drawings of clowns. "Read it if you dare," he said. "Out loud, so Bobo can hear you."

Reluctantly, I complied: "'Boooo!!! Hi there. How are you today? says Mr. BoBo Clown. Hope you're OK on this merry, merry day.'"

"How about that?" asked Bill.

"No wonder I blocked it from my memory. Now I'm really depressed."

"You should be watching *Judge Judy*. She's the funniest person on TV. No one can be depressed while watching *Judge Judy*." Bill did much of the copywriting for his clients while parked in front of the television. "She revels in being mean, and she's naturally mean, but at the same time, it's an act."

"Watch where you're going," I interjected, hoping to derail a rant. In fact, the car was standing still.

"She's very complex," he continued. "You should see her when she's on *Larry King* trying to act human. It's a disaster, because she tries to be pleasant, and— What's that? Aren't those bobolinks?" A half dozen birds with black wings and underparts, white rumps, and straw-colored napes rose up from the field with the tinkling song of a broken music box.

"Another new one for the life list." I made an entry in my notebook.

"At this rate, Bobo will never let us get past the entrance road." That statement broke the spell. The fields fell silent except for a crow that criticized the boxy silhouette of Bill's vehicle from the stub of a steel post. Taking advantage of the lull, Bill eased us forward in the direction of the service drive, snaked past the administration building, waved innocuously at a wastewater-plant employee, overshot the service drive, then doubled back to climb the perimeter dike. In the back seat I noticed a six-pack of bottled water, an outdated field guide, plastic tubs of snacks that Bill's innumerable and possibly psychosomatic food allergies could tolerate, a teeny-weeny pair of binoculars, and a strap-on pouch for carrying these items in case he ventured outside the Volvo. I coveted a bottle of water, but I was too lazy to reach for it and Bill was too oblivious to offer it.

"Northern shovelers," Bill said as we eased along the center dike. "Nothing but damn northern shovelers." A cloud of green-headed, white-breasted, chestnut-flanked, shovel-beaked, pencil-necked ducks lifted off from the largest pond. They often numbered in the thousands at the facility. "That's right, you cowards, scatter," Bill said. The sunlight glinted off a green van across the pond moving slowly in our direction. A moment before it would have been too late, Bill yanked the steering wheel and diverted us down the row of smelly bubbler treatment cells.

"Pew," I remarked.

"I thought I saw something. Okay, I'm avoiding those shoveler lovers over there in the van."

The bubbler cells were frothing, cement-walled pools, and the acrid chemical smell competed with the roar of machinery to render the entire area unfit for man or beast. But three birds stood on a concrete abutment as if the setting were as natural as their favorite forked branch. "Stop!" I said. "Horned larks. No, right in front of us."

"I told you I saw something."

"That's four new species today," I said, ticking off the larks—and adding them to my list as they winged away in irritation.

Slowly we started to circumnavigate the ponds. I searched for shorebirds among the rocks while Bill scanned the water for non-shoveler ducks and kept a suspicious eye on the green van. "I think it's those nuts we saw last year with the SHOVELER WATCHER jackets," he said. Bill didn't care for birders—much less bikers, boaters, bowlers, beekeepers, other avid hobbyists, or, for that matter, anyone who had an interest in anything—though he enjoyed watching birds as much as I did.

"Whoa, what's this?" He lowered his window and leaned out. A pair of birds paddled in a circle not thirty feet from the car. They resembled sandpipers, but with their red throats and reddish-striped grey backs, they were nothing I remembered from hours spent dreamily paging through my field guides. Bill located the bird in his Calvin Coolidge–era guide, which I believe still included the dodo. "They're, uh, red-necked palindromes. Or phallic symbols. Or something."

"Phalaropes," I said. "But they can't be." I scrambled to confirm it in my Kaufman Focus Guide. Unless the tectonic plates had shifted during the night, Muskegon still lay far south of the birds' Canadian Arctic range. Yet the phalaropes were unmistakable.

"Migration," concluded Bill. "Or global cooling."

"Well, that's the catch of the day."

And it used up the rest of our luck. After a fruitless, shoveler-filled drive alongside the landfill area, Bill announced, "I've got to pee bad," descended the dike, and disappeared among the weeds.

I unfolded myself and stretched my legs just as the green van appeared from a side road in a curtain of dust. It slowed and pulled up past Bill's car.

"Bob?" A man got out of the van and walked toward me. "Bob Tarte?"

He hadn't changed much since junior college, or at least his field markings had remained distinctive enough that I could identify Nick Farley without looking him up in Kaufman—squarish, vaguely Volvo-shaped head, stooped shoulders, and a gravelly voice that sounded as if he had swallowed a handful of sunflower seed. We exchanged pleasantries, and as Bill climbed up the hill to fetch a swig of bottled water, I introduced them to each other. "I didn't know Nick was a birder," I said.

"I'm really not," he replied, which appealed to Bill. "It just gives me something to do."

He told me he had read about my father's death a few years earlier and expressed his belated sympathies. "Now, this is going to seem really off the wall," he said, "but by any chance did Eileen Kucek show up at the funeral home?"

Bill nearly spit out his water in classic Danny Thomas *Make Room for Daddy* fashion.

"Yes, she did," I said. "Why do you ask?"

"Remember Tim Crosley from Catholic Central? His mom died in December, and Eileen was at the funeral. Tim hadn't seen her since—I don't know—madras shorts were in style. Anyway, she drops in on him all the time, and he can't get rid of her."

"Tell him to tough it out," Bill suggested. "He'll be off the hook when someone else's parent kicks off."

"Does Tim Crosley have pet ducks?" I asked.

"I don't think so. Why?"

"Eileen has a thing about ducks."

"Stuffed ducks, maybe."

"What do you mean, 'stuffed ducks'?"

"She's got a stuffed duck in her vestibule. No, I guess it's a woodcock. She's got a stuffed woodcock in her vestibule." Noticing my puzzled expression, Nick explained, "She and her husband are hunters. They just got back from a goose hunt up near Tawas Point. They were gone the whole weekend, and let me tell you, Tim was happy for the vacation."

I COULD HARDLY avoid the irony that a trip to the wastewater-treatment system had significantly lifted my spirits. Little did I know that the cheering appearance of birds in that unhealthy environment foreshadowed a brightening avian presence that would flutter above the stagnant stew of my own internal ecological disaster. Something like that happened.

Our telephone brought us so much trouble over the years, the beast deserved its own cage in the dining room right beside Ollie's. It disguised a squawk as a ring as I poured myself a cup of coffee. When I recognized the name on the caller ID as one of Linda's duck-pen cleaner-uppers, I should have let our answering machine earn its keep. But in the wake of Nick's revelation about Eileen and her pathological interference in people's lives, generosity seized me. I hadn't been singled out and cursed by fate after all. An entire Catholic grade school class had fallen under the same topknotted cloud of ill luck as me.

Tossing my better judgment to the floor to mingle with Howard's seed husks, I picked up the phone and bid Bruno a pleasant hello, figuring that he was angling for odd jobs. "Linda's out shopping, but I'll have her call you back."

"I'm calling because my friend's got this bird, and he's going to let it go."

I'd been twirling the phone cord, but I stopped abruptly. "What kind of bird?" I asked, wondering how the answering machine would have handled the situation. "Is this a wild bird or a pet bird?"

"I don't know what it is, but my friend's tired of it going to the bathroom all the time, and he wants to just open the cage and let it go. I told him I knew these people with birds and not to let it go until I called Linda."

"Well, I guess you'd better bring it over," I said, and he agreed. "Thanks for calling," I added, suppressing the urge to beep.

I expected that Bruno's buddy might have chased down a flightless robin fledgling in his backyard or scooped up a sparrow that had stunned itself flying into a window. I never imagined he would consider sending a caged bird with no street smarts out into the world. But I realized that this had been the plan when a NASCAR-jacketed Bruno walked into the living room with a gorgeous cockatiel inside a battered cage.

"He doesn't want this bird?" I asked. The teenager shook his head. "Where did he come from?"

"His dad gave it to him. Me and John are moving into an apartment, and we don't have room for a lot of stuff, so he wanted to get rid of the bird. He eats too much seed."

"Well, you've done a good deed," I told him in my best Ward Cleaver fashion. Although Beaver's father wouldn't have approved, I fished around in my wallet and handed him a twenty for his trouble. Linda had told me that he hadn't been able to find a job so far.

"What's the bird's name?" I shouted as the NASCAR logo headed out the door toward John's muffler-challenged wreck.

"He didn't name it anything. He said you can keep the cage."

Keep it? I hardly dared pick it up. It had a taped-on section of a plastic bag in place of the missing cage top, two taped-together food dishes, and even a broken perch splinted with a piece of tape. I hoped that the cockatiel didn't have a tapeworm. Since I couldn't envision using the abused cage in our dining room, I needed to find an alternative. In the basement, I surveyed the few cages we had: they were scaled to fit parakeet-size birds, but not a long-tailed cockatiel. Only one would fit the newcomer. Swallowing, I walked over to the corner where I had stashed Stanley Sue's cage. Once I had lugged it up the stairs, the cage all but skittered across the room on its metal legs and settled into its familiar spot beside the telephone.

Over a decade ago, Ollie had taught me that the smallest hook-billed bird could inflict a bite painful enough to make your eyeballs roll back into your head. With great trepidation I unlatched the cockatiel's door and ventured my hand inside, wondering if I'd be warned before losing a chunk of flesh. The bird raised the spidery crest on its head as if in provocation, then nimbly hopped onto my finger, crawled up my wrist, and parked itself on my shoulder. I had difficulty prying its toes loose from my shirt to convince it to check out its spacious new quarters. I let it linger on my finger, the better to luxuriate in its impressive coloration. Each feather on the bird's back, nape, and wings started with a center blob of grey, reconsidered that as too bland, then kept the grey at bay by lassoing it inside a fat yellow border. This combination gave the feathers a slight suggestion of opalescence, which explained why that particular plumage pattern was commonly called "pearl."

But it was the face that immediately endeared the bird to me. The buggy, active eyes, the wispy grey crest that shot up like a feathered fountain, and an overall amused demeanor reminded me of one of those Galápagos Islands lizards that had learned to tolerate human company. Scientists debating the link between dinosaurs and modern birds needed to look no further than our cockatiel. And I already considered the bird ours. In other words, I'd been Moobied. But I didn't know how Linda would react.

While I was herding the hens and ducks inside the barn, I heard the cannonball slam of Linda's car door and felt the ground tremble as she clomped toward the house. I lobbed bits of bread toward Muscovy duck Victor—he caught five consecutive pieces in midair—and scattered a container of table scraps on the cement floor, expecting my wife to barge in at any moment and startle the hens. I finished the feeding without incident, snapped off the lights, and bade a hissing chorus of Victor and Ramone good night. Peering up through the dining room picture window before toddling back into the basement, I saw Linda on the phone making her nightly call to her mom. Just as my foot hit the stairs, I heard the explosion from above.

"What in the world is this?" she asked her mom, who must have wondered what in the world was going on. "Who are you? What are you doing here? Why are you in Stanley Sue's old cage?" She shot her final question at me as I came up from the basement. "Who does he belong to?"

"You," I told her on the spur of the moment. In the long run, and for many reasons, it seemed like the easiest thing to do. As soon as Linda hung up the phone and I had explained the cockatiel's presence, I called Bill to brag about having added another life bird, more or less.

CHAPTER 15

....

Bella

L inda named the cockatiel Lulu. The name stuck until the morning Lulu froze my feet to the linoleum by hanging upside down in Stanley Sue's cage while fanning her wings and tail feathers in a display so extravagant that it would have embarrassed a peacock. The spectacle impressed the heck out of me. Partly it was like seeing an exotic headdress worthy of Carmen Miranda come to life, and partly it made me feel as if I'd caught a keyhole peek at some secret ceremony.

Our how-to book on keeping cockatiels trumpeted the alleged fact that only male birds engaged in these flirtatious displays. On the basis of that authority, we changed Lulu's name to Louie. The name stuck until an unpleasant surprise unglued it. As I ate my breakfast bowl of oatmeal in preparation for a grueling half-day at the office, I flicked my eyes at our cockatiel and blurted out the unappetizing statement "There's some kind of bloody mass hanging out of Louie's rear end."

By the time I had rushed the bird to Dr. Hedley's office, the blood had rubbed off in the carrier, revealing not the tumor I had feared but an egg trapped mid-transit.

"She's egg-bound," our veterinarian told me, referring to a condition in which a bird's reproductive ductwork doesn't work. "It's not all that uncommon, especially if this is her first egg. But it can be quite serious if you don't attend to it."

Dr. Hedley treated our supposed male bird in the back room for a few minutes, the egg slid out, and that was that. Except for another perceived gender change and a touch of postpartum soreness, Louie suffered no ill effects.

"Egg-binding is often caused by a calcium deficiency," Dr. Hedley explained. "The easiest remedy is to grind up an antacid tablet and sprinkle it in her food. That will give her something to 'grab on to' the next time she lays an egg."

Over the next week, Louie squeezed out three more eggs without impediment, then tired of the novelty and quit. We tired of the name changing and continued to refer to her as Louie, which I decided possessed a latent feminine aspect if I said it in a high-pitched voice. Considering that Stanley Sue had come to us as a male named Stanley and later turned out to be a female, whereupon I dubbed her Stanley Sue, gender blurring by the bird that lived in her cage seemed entirely appropriate.

Our cockatiel had another trick up her sleeveless leg to show us. Every morning, Linda slapped together a toy for Dusty by stringing wooden shapes on knotted leather shoelaces and hanging them in his cage. Naturally, he destroyed each toy within an hour. Otherwise, the brotherhood of African grey parrots would have yanked his membership. Although he gnawed off the points of his wooden stars and split his wooden beads in half as if they were pistachios, he did nothing as crass as biting through the laces.

Instead, he amazed us by untying the knots via a Houdiniesque manipulation of toes and beak. My loud praises of this feat went a long way toward improving our rather rocky relationship.

But newcomer Louie nearly knocked Dusty off his leather throne. When I made a version of the shoelace-and-bauble toy for Louie, she bested the big parrot by untying each knot in under fifteen seconds, using just her beak. Thus, a toy with four wooden pieces amused Louie for about a minute, which was less time than it took for me to string the thing together.

Unlike Dusty, who refused to loosen the laces if I fixed my eye upon him, Louie wasn't the least bit shy about performing her stunt for an audience. That made her the only one of our birds who faithfully fulfilled our brags in front of company. Dusty balked at talking, Howard hovered but rarely landed on my head, and Ollie neither bit us into oblivion nor unleashed his usual torrent of hideous squawks for the amazement of strangers. But Louie proved utterly dependable with the shoelace trick. All I had to do was tie a knot and she immediately undid it, to the oohs and ahhs of onlookers.

This did not please Dusty, who was loath to lose the knot-loosening concession, so he came up with a dazzling topper of his own. His modus operandi had always been to drop the leather laces to the floor of his cage when he had finished untying them. But one afternoon as I was about to change his water, I noticed that he had looped a shoelace through the metal bracket that held his dish in place. My exaggerated acclaim for this latest stunt turned genuine when I realized that he had decorated the end with a fancy knot that neither Eagle Scout nor New England fisherman would be apt to duplicate.

"Oh, my gosh," I asked him, "did you do that?" He stretched his neck and bit his rope toy in response, in a sure sign of his delight.

His handiwork became an almost daily ritual. Before leaving for work in the morning, I'd put in my request: "Are you going to tie me a knot today?" If Dusty found himself in a generous mood, by midafternoon he'd leave me another of his creations. More often than not, he'd dunk the knot in his water dish, and I'd have to hang out his little piece of artistry to dry.

"Two of those would make a nice pair of earrings," Linda observed.

"Let's give him some gold wire and a few diamonds and see what he comes up with," I suggested.

Instead of filling the gap left by Stanley Sue, my interactions with Louie and Dusty made me miss her all the more. I started thinking that the only way to get over her death would be to get another Timneh.

Bill Holm oh so helpfully advised me in the matter while we tramped through the woods near the river, making too much noise to find any migrating spring warblers.

"If Turbo were to be, say, crushed by a boulder, I'd grieve."

"Turbo? Who's Turbo?"

"But I would probably buy another Volvo and love it," he rattled on. "I couldn't bring myself to call it Turbo, because nothing could replace him. Volvos are not interchangeable."

"Only the parts and pieces," I said.

I didn't see this as an issue of interchangeability. But I had to admit that should anything happen to Bill, I would certainly want another self-obsessed Swede for a pal.

The simple fact was that I seemed to need a Timneh the same way a schizophrenic needed voices in the head. But I wouldn't expect another parrot to take Stanley Sue's place—not unless it miraculously developed a penchant for clipping off rabbit tails, slitting open dove necks, and eviscerating the woodwork. Stanley Sue would eternally remain my sweetie no matter what other Timneh brought its complicated disposition into my life.

OVER THE YEARS, Linda and I had taken in orphaned birds — from starlings to geese — as well as the occasional wayfaring cat. Few folks offered us mammals, which had resulted in a glaring deficiency in the skunk department. As I poked my head down the stairwell in response to voices just inside the living room, I knew without a doubt not only that Linda was discussing an animal but also what kind of animal was involved.

"I didn't know if you'd take it," a man said, "so I didn't bring it with me." Even from the top of the stairs, I begged to disagree. He might have left the skunk at home, but he carried its essence with him.

"Sweetie," Linda called. I followed my nose downstairs, and she introduced me to Lou Parrish, our neighbor from a mile down the road. "A poor mother skunk got run over in front of Meijer, and one of the babies sat next to her body for six hours." I shook Lou's hand, wondering if this act transferred Pepé Le Pew's calling card to me. "The baby hadn't had any food all day, and Lou's kids felt so sorry for it that he finally picked up the baby and took it home, and gave it food and water. His daughter held it in her lap and petted it, and she didn't get sprayed."

I nodded at our neighbor. He seemed fatigued by the rescue process and apparently ignorant of the fact that the miasma of skunk clung to his clothes. The baby must have picked up the smell from its flattened mom. I hoped that Lou wouldn't offer me a ride in his assuredly odoriferous van to pick up the foundling. I had no grudge against skunks, since they infrequently visited us. Yet I felt slightly disturbed that we were evidently the go-to people in the area when it came to them.

Linda didn't even need to open her mouth. I knew what she was going to ask. "Can we take the baby and keep it in the barn? Lou's got to go out of state this afternoon. He has to visit his son in Oklahoma, so he can't take care of it."

I couldn't come up with an excuse to head out of state myself. "I guess it's okay. As long as it stays in the barn," I added with my usual naïveté. Fate, aided by Linda, would soon decide otherwise. I failed to take another important fact into consideration, too: one of us would have to transfer the skunk from Lou's pet carrier to a rabbit cage in the barn. That task automatically fell to me.

After Lou dropped off the baby, I suited up for the transfer. I didn't expect to get sprayed, but I decided to play it safe by swaddling myself in multiple layers of clothing. If I did get blasted, whatever the nylon ski parka failed to deflect wouldn't get past the sweater underneath. If it did, I relied on a flannel shirt to keep the scent from getting to my skin. Shielding my hands, eyes, and face—while providing exquisite accessorizing touches—were gloves, a stocking cap, and a surgical mask. Making my way toward the front yard, I kept behind the pine trees as much as possible lest I cause a vehicular accident among those unprepared for the sight of an Arctic physician out for a stroll on a spring day.

I could easily have found the carrier on the front sidewalk with my eyes shut—and they essentially were, thanks to stocking-cap slippage. Without stopping to examine the carrier contents, I hurried my pungent cargo to the back door of the barn. Recognizing me despite the padding, mask, and headwear, Barred Rock hen Brenda blocked my path by whining for treats as soon as I got inside. Her plaintive voice attracted fellow flock members, and they crowded my feet for first dibs on whatever tantalizing morsels might emerge from my hand luggage. I didn't need an audience for what could easily turn into my moment of ignominy. The chickens failed to shoo, forcing me to rattle their pans of scratch feed to draw them to a less populated part of the barn. Myrna, the small beige cross between a Buff Orpington hen and a tea cozy, never walked when an opportunity to be carried presented itself, so I manually transported her a safe distance away.

Setting the carrier on top of the stanchion rails, I popped open the front grate and pulled out the half-grown baby, which took not the slightest offense to being held as I fiddled with the door of the rabbit cage and deposited the orphan inside. Continuing to ignore me, it stuck its snout into a metal dish containing canned cat food and diced grapes. Overwhelmed by the animal's charm, I stripped off my gloves and petted its back through the bars with my index finger, enjoying the bristly texture of its fur. With its jet-black eyes, wide white stripes, and trusting nature, the baby was impossible to dislike—although its carrier wouldn't win any friends until it experienced a close encounter with a hose.

I CONDUCTED SO many Internet searches over the next two days that I nearly made Google gag. My first goal was locating breeders in Michigan who raised African grey Timneh parrots, in case I made up my mind that I wanted one. Based on the evidence of their Web sites, some of these breeders had a chirp on their shoulder when it came to the people who might be buying their birds. The worst was a fellow located just north of the border between Michigan and Mars whose sales philosophy boiled down to this: *If you buy an ill-tempered parrot from me that screams, bites, plucks its feathers, and refuses to talk or eat, it's your fault, so don't bother me about it.*

Naturally, I was eager to buy from him. Then I found a breeder in nearby Lansing whose Web site emphasized the health and happiness of her birds and entirely omitted demonizing them.

(Note: she didn't raise any orange-chinned pocket parrots like Ollie.) I exchanged a few e-mails with Julie, who told me that her Timneh hen had recently laid an egg, which indicated a potential visit from the stork. But she cautioned me that even if the egg turned out to be fertile and hatched, it would be months before I could take the youngster home. The bird needed to develop oodles of socialization skills, such as no screaming, no biting, and no plucking feathers. Just as important, it also had to undergo health exams, inoculations, DNA testing, and finish in the top third of its class in the SATs. So we decided to keep in touch and see what developed.

I also scoured the Web for the skinny on raising skunks. I wanted to reassure myself that a skunk wouldn't spray a non-threatening nonentity like myself who supplied it with its daily vittles. I also didn't relish getting stink-bombed if I offended it by offering the wrong kind of food. I didn't even know what I didn't know about skunks. I nearly got blinded skimming the massive amount of information posted by aficionados of the pungent family Mustelidae, whose members include weasels, ferrets, otters, and that guy wearing bad cologne who gets in the elevator with you. One Web site featured a photo of a woman being used by numerous fully scented rehabbed skunks as a jungle gym, which went a long way toward easing my fears. Another site stressed the need to provide a vegetarian diet, which meant that our orphan could sit at the dining room table and eat right off my plate.

Eager to share my skunkological scholarship, I ambled out to the barn to find Linda peering beneath an old storage cabinet, calling, "Skunky! Skunky!" This didn't bode well.

"Don't tell me the skunk is loose," I said.

"Last night I put food in his dish and I was just about to try and pet him, like you did, when he sort of started at me, or I thought he did, and I was afraid I was going to get sprayed, so I jumped back," Linda told me. "And I think that maybe I forgot to latch his cage door."

It smelled as if the skunk had stayed in the barn, though a determined creature with any climbing ability could have found a nook to navigate or a cranny to convey it to freedom, and the barn had plenty of both. Hoping to convince it to stick around and enjoy a pampered lifestyle until it grew up a bit, I grabbed a nearly empty can of cat food from the refrigerator, added diced vegetables, and set it on the cement floor near the skunk's abandoned cage.

By the next morning, every speck of food had disappeared. "The skunk is still around," I assured Linda.

"One of the hens could have eaten it."

I scoffed at the suggestion. "First of all," I lectured her, "chickens don't like canned cat food, and there was enough of that in there to discourage them. Second, if the hens had pecked at the can, they would have knocked it across the barn. They're not exactly gentle with those beaks." More than once we had offered a piece of lettuce to Eloise or Rosie and nearly lost a finger in the process.

Adding another mix of cat food, fruit, and veggies to the can, I replaced it and told Linda to anticipate a visit from our skunk later in the day.

When late afternoon lugged itself across the land, I opened the barn door to find our fat hen Buffy attacking the can with the precision of a neurosurgeon as she whisked up the last few microscopic morsels of cat food. The peas, corn, and diced grape had already journeyed down her gullet.

"I guess the skunk got away," I said. We both hoped that the youngster had the necessary survival skills to make it out in the world.

AT THE SAME TIME, we had another wily customer to deal with in the barn. Beset with spring fever, our white Embden gander, Matthew, had started pressing his romantic perspective upon the female geese with excessive gusto, resulting in rows of feathers plucked from their usually graceful necks. Temporarily housing him with fellow gander Angel proved disastrous. Matthew beat the tar out of the larger goose, forcing us to move him to the barn until his hormone levels ebbed.

Our expert carpenter, handyman, and dead-mouse-in-the-stove extractor Gary had built the pen attached to the barn with a dividing fence down the middle, which gave us the option of keeping Matthew by himself. I exercised that option after witnessing the tail end of a fight between the usually invincible Victor and the lovesick gander, which ended up costing Victor a toenail. As a testament to Victor's intelligence, or at least his trust, he tolerated my handling his foot and applying a dab of antibiotic to his wound. I couldn't even imagine attempting such familiarity with Matthew.

The Embden expended his energies pacing back and forth along the fence and honking at the females far across the yard. "We miss you," they honked back, though I assumed they enjoyed the break from his denuding *amour*. After a few days, his restless fire subsided to a simmer and the pacing stopped.

Whenever I did my chores on his side of the pen, I gave him a wide berth not out of concern that he would go after me, but because I didn't want to add to his stress. I spoke softly to him, informing him in advance, "Now I'm going to change the water in your bucket," or calmly herding him inside each evening with a rippling of my fingers prompting, "Let's go get our treats."

He tolerated my presence; then his tolerance turned to interest. While I cleaned the floor of the barn with water and a push broom, he would step inside and, with his bright blue eyes, supervise. One evening, on a whim, instead of shooing him into the barn I called his name, and he trundled in. To make sure that this wasn't a coincidence or his reaction to the mere sound of my voice, the next evening I called, "Buffy! Victor!" Matthew didn't stir from the outdoor pen. But when I wailed, "Matthew!" he waddled in and fixed me with his glittering eye, shaming me into tossing an extra treat in his direction.

Matthew was the last bird I'd consider hand-feeding. A small strip of fencing indoors separated Matthew's side of the barn from the middle section where the ducks and hens meandered, and I noticed him standing next to it in anticipation. Carefully I poked a piece of kale through the wire, keeping my digits on my side. He took it without drama. In an uncharacteristic fit of boldness, I leaned over the fence and offered him the kale from my un-protected fingers. With a gentleness that equaled his earlier un-checked ardor for his girls, he delicately plucked the greens from me, pausing once to tenderly nibble my hand as if to exercise his curiosity.

This soon became a nightly ritual. He'd come inside to watch me clean, or stay out until I called. After I was on the other side of the fence, he'd pad over and accept his bread and greens from my bare hands. I enjoyed these encounters so much that when the mating frenzy had died down throughout the flock, I carried him back to the goose pen with a heavy heart. I knew that his reunion with the girls would close the door on our close rapport. But I had Linda. I had my other birds. I had rabbits. I had cats. So I let Matthew have his harem and forget about me.

He surprised me the following week. While the geese foraged in the yard, I pulled up a few acres of dandelion leaves, which our tamer geese Liza and Hailey loved. They took the leaves from my hand as Angel, Patty, Matthew, and the ducks muttered to themselves in the background. But after a moment Matthew joined the two African geese and snatched the greens from my fingers. He did this with a degree of reluctance, not wishing to compromise his top slot in the pecking order, but that he did it at all was the supreme compliment.

On my drive home from work, I spotted a coyote. Though I'd never seen one in situ before, I recognized it instantly. With its head hung low, mouth open, lolling tongue, and outstretched tail, it trotted across a field about a mile from our house.

A ripple of concern passed through me, but I knew that our ducks, geese, and hens were in no danger as they puttered around in their pens. Then I started thinking that if a coyote roamed this close to us, five years ago it could have stood in the woods in the moonlit shadow of our bedroom, raised its head toward the starry sky, and blasted me awake with a bloodcurdling howl. At the time, I'd sworn that there was nothing canine about that howl—but in retrospect, I wondered.

My mother dealt with misperception in her own unique fashion. After Linda and I had taken her out for ice cream one Saturday afternoon, we returned from watching the geese at a neighborhood park to stroll the carpeted corridors of Testament Terrace. "That sure is an attractive bouquet," Linda remarked as we approached an artificial floral arrangement topping a round table. "They keep everything looking so nice around here."

Mom beamed. "Bob helps me with the housekeeping," she said, referring to my departed dad.

I told Bett about this on the phone, and mentioned that it must console Mom to occasionally think that Dad was still alive. "I miss hearing her talk about the old days, but that's pretty much gone. I wanted to hear that story about Dad being arrested."

"Dad was arrested?" Bett asked. "When was he arrested?"

"You've never heard that story?"

I didn't have the details, which made me sorry that Mom couldn't fill them in. But I did remember Dad telling me that—years before my presence glorified the world—he had gone out on the porch in his pajamas one Sunday morning to get the newspaper just as a police car made a U-turn and pulled over across the street. Dad walked up to the parked cruiser and informed the officer that his driving maneuver had violated the law. In response, the cop hauled my dad off to jail, and he sat there in his pajamas until my mother bailed him out.

"Dad must have told me that story three or four times," I said to Bett. "But I haven't heard it since high school."

"I've never heard it before."

"Well, how about the time he bought a 78 record called 'Remember Pearl Harbor' and broke it in half at the front counter of Dodd's Record Shop?"

"No," she chuckled, "I don't know that one either."

This came as something of a revelation. While I'd expected the three of us to remember our father in different ways, I'd never considered the possibility that he might have told each of us different stories about his life. The next time we got together, I decided, I would ask Bett and Joan for their favorite anecdotes from and about him. I might actually learn something.

I had definitely learned something from Matthew the goose, and from the other animals, too. The mixture of wildness and comfort they brought to my life was life itself in miniature. There was no arguing with a gander—or with a parrot that bit off a bunny's tail, mice that nested inside the dining room chair, creatures that shrieked in the middle of the night, or a crazy former classmate. There was no reasoning with death or Alzheimer's disease. I could resist them, ignore them, or gnash my teeth over them, but I couldn't prevent them from occurring. My likes and dislikes all rolled together didn't add up to a golden orb weaver's egg when it came to stopping the spinning, seasonal procession of events. Weather fair and foul ruled. The ice storm didn't care if I objected. Floodwaters chuckled at resistance. Snow made sport of rain-forest dreams. The saucer people faded in and out, but occasionally they used the telephone. So I might as well accept the call.

JULIE PHONED ME with the bad news that her Timneh egg had turned out to be a dud. But she told me about a friend of hers, Susan, who had bought back a female Timneh from the people she had sold her to, because their children kept bothering the bird. Julie assured me that Susan was so conscientious that when Julie's husband had been in the hospital, they had trusted their Quaker parakeet Koko to Susan's care. Julie e-mailed me a photo of the Timneh gnawing a pad of sticky-notes that was eerily reminiscent of the photo of Stanley Sue chewing a raisin box that had originally convinced us to buy her.

I phoned Susan and, through the shrieks of macaws in the foreground, managed to decipher the directions to her house in Belleville and learn that the Timneh's name was Bella. *Bella from Belleville, said Bobo.* I repeated this to myself around ten thousand times through the course of my three-hour drive across the state. It sounded sort of propitious—and obnoxious enough to bore it-self deep into my brain, not unlike the chorus of the Little River Band's "Reminiscing," which tormented me from an oldies radio station for a full nanosecond before I managed to wallop the off button.

I discovered that Susan had surrendered her sunroom to her parrots. Sidling toward a wicker chair for an introduction to Bella meant attempting to avoid a pair of pterodactyl-size macaws leaning out from a couple of birdie play stations. Cayenne and Hannah may have only been teasing, but most birds can't resist bullying less courageous creatures—and they revel in giving cowards such as myself an extra tweak. Squawking fiendishly, they brandished their gargantuan beaks as I ducked and dodged my way through the feathered gauntlet. Cayenne's pincers flashed uncomfortably close to my shirtsleeve, and I braced myself for the groan of tearing fabric.

I learned that gaining a seat didn't mean that I had achieved sanctuary. "These wicker chairs belong to the birds," Susan informed me as her Congo African grey parrot Gracie strutted across the floor and began scaling the front of the chair in which I had parked myself.

"Is she friendly?" I asked as I hopped to my feet, taking care not to step within reach of the macaws. I didn't trust the mischievous glint in Gracie's eyes, though I was pleased when she stood on the armrest and told me, "Nice shoes."

"She'll trick you into picking her up," cautioned Susan. "But I'm not sure if I'd try it." I took the warning to heart as Gracie proceeded to excavate the well-gnawed front of the chair's arm. "Bella's different. I had a houseguest from South America last summer, and she told me, 'You have to watch these other birds, but I never have any trouble with Bella.'"

I still felt timorous about taking the Timneh from her. "Does she bite?" I asked, expecting an immediate denial as I extended my hand toward the bird.

Her thoughtful pause halted my forward momentum. "Bella has a mind of her own. She might pinch your finger if you're holding her and she wants to go somewhere else, but she won't hurt you. She's a very sweet bird."

While I'd been excited for hours about the prospect of meeting Bella, I still wasn't prepared for the jolt I received when she stepped onto my hand—thanks to her sharp toenails digging into my flesh. "I meant to trim those," Susan said as I winced.

While most Timnehs look like other Timnehs, Bella had an expression all her own. A fold of skin above each eye made it seem as if she were slightly lowering her lids in a laid-back but decidedly playful attitude. When I brought a finger near her head to see if she might let me stroke her back, she opened her beak and clicked a friendly admonishment that sent my hand scurrying to the safety of my pocket.

"What do you think?" I asked Susan. The purpose of the visit was for her to appraise me as a prospective owner while I appraised Bella, who considered me with a soft look quite unlike the usual steely stare of a grey.

Susan shot a photo of me holding her bird, then packed Bella into the pet carrier I had brought, along with wedges of orange and apple for fortification on the road. I daydreamed about snitching some fruit for myself as a prelude to ransacking the rest of the house, but I was too excited by Bella to revert to crime.

"SWEETIE, COME HERE, come here quick!" Linda called from the dining room. "Come here and look outside."

In an attempt to expand my intellectual scope, I'd been reading John A. Keel's book on strange phenomena *The Mothman Prophecies*—but for only the fourth time—as the home-redecorating show *While You Were Out* tootled in the background. Grumbling, I set down my learned tome on the coffee table, stepped over Moobie, who had already started her evening shift of begging for countless cat treats, and shuffled toward Linda's voice.

"You'll never guess who's out there!"

"The aliens?" I asked just a bit hopefully.

"Skunky."

"She'd better not be back."

"Why not?" Linda asked as I joined her at the window to watch a skunk root beneath our bird feeder.

"I thought you meant Eileen."

"Isn't that Skunky down there?"

"Looks like it," I said.

On the evidence of my nose, I knew that skunks visited us after dark once in a while, but in the fifteen years that I'd been living in our farmhouse, I had never actually laid eyes on one. As far as seeing skunks, I'd been skunked. Thus, it seemed reasonable to assume that Skunky had indeed stuck around to raid the spilled-sunflower-seed spoils since escaping our barn. Hoping to capitalize on our brief but successful relationship, I braved a spraying by tiptoeing out the basement door clutching a bag of grapes to my cadaverous chest. But the skunk took umbrage at having small pieces of fruit tossed in its direction and skittered away into the evening gloom.

Just before we went to bed, Linda checked for the visitor again by shining a flashlight through the dining room window. A quavering oval spotlighted an obese possum ill-advisedly squaring off against the skunk. "You shouldn't be doing that," Linda muttered. The first time old pointy nose snapped at the polecat, the skunk simply backed off and continued foraging under the feeder for seeds and bugs. But when the possum exhibited its bad buffet etiquette again, the bombardier spun around, reared up its back, and raised its tail to high heavens.

"Did Skunky just spray Possy?"

"It sort of looked that way, but I don't smell anything."

I had spoken a moment too soon. A wall of skunk scent slammed into the house like a stinky eighteen-wheeler. The skunk stomped off but, with barely a wrinkle of its nose, the possum continued consuming every seed within reach. Either he lacked a sense of smell or personal hygiene ranked at the bottom of his priorities.

I had never been at ground zero of a skunk blast before. The effect was, to put it mildly, impressive. The gas attack stripped the finish off our furniture. The living room carpet curled up and ran out the front door. "It's not so bad," I coughed as I groped my way toward the bedroom through the low-hanging cloud, only to find myself in the back seat of the car talking to the transmission hump. Back inside and safely under the sheet, which kept floating to the ceiling, I writhed and tried to sleep. Finally, with a T-shirt knotted across my nose and mouth, I either succumbed to the fumes or passed out from lack of oxygen.

A merciful wind outdoors and a battery of electric fans in the house dissipated the smell by the following evening. We had just settled down for an odor-free night on the living room couch and floor, reading our respective books, when Linda sniffed loudly and announced, "Guess who's back."

"I'll try the grapes again," I told her. But when I stuck my face against the dining room window, I didn't see Skunky beneath the bird feeder. It was Possy, wearing Skunky's cologne.

"Oh, great," Linda said. "Now we've got two smelly animals."

"I'd better call Agnes inside. We don't want to make it three."

THE PHONE RANG. What a surprise.

I had just started cleaning the birdcages after holding a bowl of water three-eighths of an inch off the bathroom floor for Moobie, squirting a syringe of antibiotics between our goose Squawk's jaws in the backyard waterfowl pen, and tossing a soft rubber ball for Penny. Our grey cat would crouch on the top landing while I stood at the bottom landing and flung the ball. She would either leap up and catch it in midair or let it bounce off the upstairs wall and charge down the steps after it. At least that was how the game was originally played. Advanced age and typical feline perversity had changed the rules. Now she would lie at the top of the stairs and occasionally make the slightest halfhearted feint toward the ball, delighting instead in watching me scramble out of breath up and down the stairs to retrieve it whenever it didn't putter all the way to the bottom. She could play this game of watching *me* play with the ball for hours, but would reluctantly call it quits once I'd collapsed in a wheezing heap.

As I tidied up after the birds, Bella stood on the countertop, indulging in her second-favorite out-of-cage pastime of hurling an empty Zoloft pill bottle to the floor as quickly as I could put it within range of her beak. She had apparently consulted with Penny about this, because she seemed to enjoy seeing me fish the bottle from beneath the dining room table as much as she reveled in tossing it into a hard-to-reach spot. But her favorite activity was flying across the room and landing on my shoulder just as I had delicately balanced the parakeets' water and food dishes upon the plastic tray that I had extracted from the bottom of their cage. If she didn't succeed in making me spill the whole caboodle to the floor, the wind power generated by her wings scattered a snow-storm of seed husks throughout the room.

I had, however, temporarily curtailed her mischief by laying out food items on the countertop for her to chew and throw, including a couple of grapes. So I felt safe answering the phone, especially when the caller ID informed me that Joan, and not some heretofore forgotten former grade school classmate, waited on the other end of the line.

"I've got two pieces of good news, Bob," she told me. "The first is that Beethoven is doing fine. He's acting like a brand-new ferret again."

"That's amazing." I hadn't expected him to pull through last week's surgery for a pancreatic tumor, but Dr. Hedley had performed with his usual excellence.

"He's all bright and chipper and just raring to go each day as soon as he wakes up. But that's not the only thing. I just visited Mom."

"Uh-oh."

"No, she was in a really good mood. She was the best that I had seen her in years. She was all smiles when I had lunch with her at Testament Terrace, and would you believe that when the food took a while to come, she called over one of the nurses and said, 'Waitress, is our lunch almost ready?' I could hardly keep from laughing. So even if she isn't exactly sure where she is much of the time, she isn't asking to go home."

I began to tell her the saga of Skunky when suddenly a clatter of wings arose behind me, and toenails in need of trimming clamped onto my shoulder. "Bella, stop it," I complained. "She's pecking at the phone," I told Joan. "I'll change ears."

"I'll let you go."

"That's probably best. When she's out of her cage, she hates being ignored."

For a while Bella behaved politely on my shoulder as I pulled the tray from Ollie's cage and washed it in the sink. But as I fell into a shallow reverie, I apparently lingered too long in a single spot, failing to provide the constant change of scenery that the exuberant parrot required. I had been thinking about how quickly the two of us had bonded, and how happy she seemed in her massive green cage, swinging from an impressive array of toys—any one of which would have terrified Stanley Sue. I had to admit that she was more amiable than her predecessor, never launched into a bell-ringing fuss at night insisting upon yet another peanut, and hadn't shown a proclivity for attacking our other birds. She clearly had advantages over Stanley Sue, and just as this thought began prickling my conscience, she rewarded me with a perfectly timed nip to my ear.

"Ouch, stop it! That's very bad," I told her, scooping her onto my hand and carrying her back to her cage. I had to bribe her into stepping off my finger and latching onto her perch by wiggling a peanut in front of her. She shot me a mischievous look before deciding to take the treat.

"Bella certainly has a naughty streak," I said to Linda as I walked into the living room, but Linda wasn't there. A cacophony of goose honks indicated that she had gone outdoors to change the water in the pens, hose down the gravel, and replenish their food.

I plopped down on the couch, uncertain whether to grab the mystery novel from the coffee table, a birding field guide, or a CD from Bill Holm. I thought about Perry Mason, Kenn Kaufman, and Harry Nilsson, but I couldn't think clearly. My ear was throbbing. I thought about Bella. And I thought, *Well, this is love.*

CHAPTER 16

....

The Creature in the Woods

Took, took, took, took, took."

I was busy battling the fair-weather version of the hose demon. As I pulled the hose to drag it from the girl ducks' pen into Angel's, the demon pulled back, snagging it on the tiniest and most self-effacing pebble in the entire yard. Yet no matter how hard I yanked, I couldn't tear the hose loose, forcing me to trudge up the muddy bank, miss my footing, catch myself from falling with one hand, and further denigrate myself by having to lift the hose off and around the merest speck of gravel that had somehow ensnared it.

I was stomping back down the hill, scattering female ducks Clara, Gwendolyn, and Marybelle, when I heard the sound from the woods again. "Took, took, took, took, took." I had heard it a few years earlier while slaving over my duck chores, followed it to a tree near the river, and come up empty. When I'd described the call to members of a birding newsgroup, suggestions for its source had included a black-billed cuckoo, northern saw-whet owl, and green heron. But when I'd listened to my well-worn birdsong CD, none of the bird vocalizations filled the bill.

"Took, took, took, took, took."

Shutting off the spigot, I eased myself down the slippery slope and found myself unexpectedly bathed in sunshine as soon as I stepped over the backyard fence. I maneuvered around three piles of scratch feed that Linda had arranged for visiting turkeys and the fat woodchuck whose burrow had collapsed the cement floor at the entrance to our barn. Just before I reached the bone-dry swamp and the beginning of the path that I had cut through the weeds, a flash of movement in a hackberry tree caught my attention.

Through the branches I could just make out the grey breast of a pigeon-size bird, but the bird was climbing toward me. Pigeons and doves don't climb. I cursed myself for failing to run into the house for my binoculars. How did I expect to find the *took-took* bird without them? Fortunately, the grey bird didn't seem bothered by my presence, and it was close enough that, with a bit of luck, I might be able to identify the species.

I did better than that. I called the bird by name.

"Stanley Sue," I said as she clambered down to within an arm's length away. "What in the world do you think you're doing?"

I didn't expect death to have given her powers of speech that she hadn't enjoyed in life, but if anything her eyes were more expressive than I had remembered. She cocked her head for comic effect, then opened and closed her beak in a parody of my question. She swiped her beak on a twig, hung upside down as if to step onto my extended hand, thought better of it, and retreated to the broken stub of a branch near the tree trunk.

"Took, took, took, took, took."

She looked toward the river and the source of the call. When she whistled sharply in annoyance, I imagined that I also heard the clatter of her bell. She fluffed her feathers as if to relax. Then, shooting me a sly glance, she hopped off the branch, pumped her wings a few times, and soared off toward the sound with the confidence of a hawk.

"Wait," I told her. In my typical nonathletic fashion, I raced after her. But in a confused tangle of limbs that barely approximated a run, I found myself trotting back up the hill instead. Against the blue-grey background of our house, goose Liza glanced up from excavating the lawn to honk as she caught sight of me. The other geese followed suit, accompanied by the ducks, erupting in a cacophony of brass and woodwinds in expectation of the lettuce snack that I didn't have.

From the pen behind the barn, first one hen and then another wailed a lament at missing out on the entirely phantom treat as I began reeling in the hose. Chickadees spun their wings, battling for a prime spot at the sunflower-seed feeder, while a white-breasted nuthatch landed upside down on the suet holder. From the woods came the drumming of a woodpecker and a cardinal's inevitable trill.

All this excitement proved too much for the indoor birds. Bella and Dusty competed to outwhistle one another. A disturbed Howard cooed. The perpetually crabby Ollie squawked. I started to close the basement door behind me, raising an arm toward the river to wave good-bye to Stanley Sue, when black cat Agnes shot inside, then immediately rubbed against my leg, begging for a dollop of canned cat food.

"What's going on out there?" Linda called to no one in particular from upstairs.

Scuffing the mud off my feet, I called back to no one in particular, "Hold your horses, I'll be right there."

Acknowledgments and Culpability

Thanking everyone who helped in some way with *Fowl Weather* would involve more vowels than my publisher has allotted me, but I do need to mention a few hundred of the noteworthy—including my extremely supportive wife, Linda, who bears the blame of first bringing animals into our lives. Her love, strength, and good humor dazzle me.

My two sisters, Joan and Bett, reviewed each chapter and contributed suggestions on passages about our mom. I also owe them a significant debt for their care of her, especially in situations where I'm useless. And that means most of the time.

Bill Holm not only read and pontificated on *Fowl Weather* as it progressed, but he also helped reconstruct and confabulate dialogue for scenes in which he appears. "Anything to make me even less likable," he told me.

Others who have read and commented on portions of the book include Mike Bombyk, Donna Munro, Brian O'Malley, Dave Hucker, Pamela Brown, Dennis Keller, and Christina Websell.

Special thanks to my agent, Jeff Kleinman; my editor, Kathy Pories; the superb publicity department at Algonquin: Michael Taeckens, Aimee Rodriguez, and Katherine Ward. Maureen Mackey at *Reader's Digest*, Shelley Irwin at WGVU radio; Paul Ingram at Prairie Lights Bookstore; my dramatic rights agent, Howard Sanders; and Patricia Heaton, who bought the dramatic rights to *Enslaved by Ducks*.

Finally, for their friendship and support, I would like to thank Wayne Schuurman, president of Audio Advisor, Inc.; pet sitters Jamie Beean, Linda Coppard, April Anderson, Ben Carson, and Kelly Carson; birders Dirk Richardson, Dan Minnock, Bruce Bowman, Su Clift, and Susan Falcone; handyman extraordinaire Gary Dietzel; Peg and Roger Markle of Wildlife Rehab Center Ltd.; rehabbers Sjana Gordon, Dawn Koning, and Shannon Lentz; veterinarians Richard Bennett, Edward Farnum, Roberta Zech, and Bruce Langlois; Scott and Barbara Carpenter of Blue Ribbon Feed Company; Greg VanStrien of VanStrien Heating and Plumbing; Philip Hemstreet; and all of my readers.